The Christmases We Used to Know

EVERGREEN MEMORIES. These Plainfield, New Jersey "lumberjacks" had a jolly Christmas in 1959. Nancy Castles, now of Coral Springs, Florida, shared this photo memory of her father, brother and her with their homegrown prize.

Ewing Galloway

JUST WHAT I WANTED! **Kids and Christmas go together like Santa and sleigh bells. A joyful expression on the face of a tyke like this one rekindles memories and makes grown-ups feel young again. Remember sitting on Santa's knee? You'll recall this and plenty more from holidays past in this book. Here's wishing you a very Merry Christmas!**

Contents

Reminisce Books
International Standard Book Number: 0-89821-160-3; Library of Congress Catalog Number: 96-67060

For additional copies of this book or information on other books, write: Reminisce Books, P.O. Box 990, Greendale WI 53129. Credit card orders call toll-free 1-800/558-1013.

Cover photos: front, SuperStock; back, Robert Cushman Hayes

SuperStock

Prologue

By Clancy Strock, Contributing Editor, Reminisce Magazine

CLANCY STROCK

Many months ago, we editors at *Reminisce* asked our readers to help us assemble an unforgettable book of memories about old-time Christmases.

"Tell us about the Christmases you used to know," we asked in an issue of the magazine. Soon the stories and pictures came pouring in—quite a few more than we could pack into one volume.

There were stories about festive foods, school pageants, unforgettable gifts, memorable Yule trees, the sweet agony of the endless night before Christmas, holiday decorations both at home and "downtown", family gatherings and all the other things that commonly come to mind when we hear the word "Christmas".

But after reading them all, I discovered that this book isn't about Christmas at all. It's about something even more miraculous. It's about love in its purest form.

It's about giving...not presents, but *love.* It's about parents sacrificing for children, and children sacrificing for parents. It's about sharing with strangers who aren't as well off as we are. Sometimes it's about families who had very, very little but shared even that with others who had nothing at all.

Why Only at Christmas?

I sat in my chair and the inevitable question came to me: Why does this outpouring of love and kindness seem to come so easily for a few weeks at the end of each year, but seems so rare the other 11 months?

Why do the grumpiest people suddenly show you their decent, likable side during the holidays?

What would cause an uncle to trudge 7 miles each way through a Christmas Eve snowstorm to bring back a puppy that his nephew so desperately wanted?

You'll read about that uncle's love in Chapter Eight, by the way, but back to the question at hand: Were people just naturally more generous years ago? Were they more likely to practice the true spirit of Christmas?

I guess we'll each have to search our memories and make up our own minds about that. My hunch is, human nature hasn't changed all that much in a half century.

Gail Denham

GREETINGS OVER THE YEARS. **Colorful cards are just one traditional way we express fond feelings at Christmas.**

Probably this outpouring of goodwill in December has a lot to do with the fact that we spend much of the month thinking about other people instead of ourselves. How can we spread some happiness around? Making others happy is what will make us happy.

What will bring joy to our spouse? Our parents? Our children?

So we do the best we can as best we are able.

And it doesn't stop with our immediate family. The holiday that celebrates the birth of Christ turns our thoughts toward Christian charity.

FAMILY TREE. **Christmas past recalled in Strock family photo.**

We drop our loose coins and even folding money into the red iron kettles where the Salvation Army Santa rings his or her bell. We volunteer to staff kitchens at shelters for the homeless, helping to prepare and serve traditional Christmas dinners to the unfortunate. We help put together and deliver brimming food baskets to homes of the needy.

Firefighters and policemen gather up old toys and work long hours turning them into like-new gifts for children.

Those and hundreds of other kindnesses are so common today that I refuse to believe we've become a heartless and greedy society.

Just as it always has, something magical happens during the Christmas season. Have you ever noticed how friends and even strangers really seem to mean it when they wish you a Merry Christmas? It's a nice change compared with the automatic, mindless "Have a nice day" you hear the rest of the year.

Walk down any city street during the other 11 months of the year and watch the faces of those coming toward you. You

watch the faces of those coming toward you. You won't see many smiles. But the smile-to-scowl ratio changes dramatically during December. Most people seem quite a bit jollier.

Music in the Air

I also believe that the music of the season has a lot to do with our good spirits. Who can be grumpy when the air is filled with *Jingle Bells, Santa Claus Is Coming to Town, Rudolph the Red-Nosed Reindeer* and *Frosty the Snowman*?

Over the centuries, songwriters have captured all the many meanings of Christmas in words we can never forget:

"Oh, there's no place like home for the holidays..."

"Faithful friends who are dear to us, gather near to us, once more..."

"Joy to the world, the Lord is come..."

"A thrill of hope, the weary world rejoices..."

If words like those don't raise your spirits and brighten your days, you really do deserve a lump of coal in your stocking.

During the late '30s, when I was in high school, I was part of a brass quartet that went to the local hospitals and homes of shut-ins to play Christmas carols.

Usually we stood outside in the snow. Sometimes people came to the windows, sometimes not. I hope the music we made brightened their lives as much as ours were brightened by just being there.

But the music I remember most of all was the annual Christmas songfest at my grade school in Sterling, Illinois. A wide staircase went from the basement up to the second floor at Central School. Every student would gather on the stairs the last day before Christmas vacation and sing carols. Three hundred young voices filled the building with joyous music. With every carol, the feeling soared.

Just as emotion-charged is the singing in those old film clips of soldiers, sailors or marines far from home. There the boys stand on the deck of a ship or are crowded into an airplane hangar or sitting on some hillside in Korea singing Christmas carols. Only the truly hard-hearted could watch them without shedding a tear.

Whether it's a school Christmas pageant or neighborhood carolers outside the door or shipboard in the stormy Atlantic or the televised midnight Mass from St. Patrick's Cathedral, Christmas is a holiday that's defined by music.

Who can be untouched by it? No wonder total strangers smile and wish you a Merry Christmas!

Families Together Again

Another thing about Christmas is there's nothing else like it for bringing families together. Over the years, people have taken sleighs through blizzards, bucked drifts with the old Essex and driven sleepless 400 miles through the night on two-lane roads in Alabama or Nebraska or New England.

Others endured jam-packed railroad depots and slept on air terminal floors waiting for the weather to clear... they did whatever it took to be *home for Christmas.*

Christmas is the all-powerful magnet that draws families

CLANCY'S CLAN. **It's been quite a while since the whole Strock family has been able to gather together for Christmas. But when they did, they had a good time. A granddaughter, Dana (above), loved her stuffed monkey, then helped her mom, Dianna (right), take care of nephew Andy. Another daughter, Cathy (upper right), joined Clancy's mother, Gladys, in enjoying the opening of a present. Gathering the family together at Christmas is what makes for some great memories.**

SuperStock

HOME FOR CHRISTMAS. **Be it a frame house in a small town, a log cabin on the family farm or a brick apartment house in the city, there's no place like home when Christmas rolls around. The Christmases of our memories are always like this scene—fresh snow, the church steeple bells pealing out carols, smoke from the chimneys and smiles on the faces of everyone you meet.**

back together. We're home again! We exchange hugs and handshakes all around, add our gifts to the pile under the tree, marvel at how much little Courtney has grown and pay our respects to Great-Aunt Grace. Oh, yes, it's good to be home!

Little Money, Lots of Love

Often, those homes were pretty humble. In this book, you'll find many stories about the lean years of the 1930s. There generally wasn't much under the Christmas tree during the Depression. But what everyone seems to remember most of all is the love that went with even the most meager gift. Pocketbooks may have been thin, but hearts were large indeed.

Cruel as this sounds, I'm sorry my grandchildren have not experienced at least one lean Christmas. To them, a great Christmas is measured by whether or not all their wishes were fulfilled, and never mind how pricey some of them were.

I wish that 50 years from now they could recall a Christmas—as I do—when the few gifts we shared were tediously handmade out of desperation, but came wrapped in layers of love. Anyone can *buy* gifts, but love has no price tag.

My gifts to Mom that she saved were not the fancy store-bought ones I was able to buy in later years. The ones she cherished most were the crudely made presents fashioned by young, awkward hands. I guess they reminded her of the times when love was about the only reward she received for her hard life during the '30s.

That's at the heart of what I discovered when I finished reading the stories in this book and sat back to think about it. We started out to put together a book about early-day Christmases. But we ended up with what you have in your hands now. It's a book about caring for and about each other, which is what Christmas is really supposed to be about, isn't it?

If you enjoy these stories nearly as much as we did when we assembled them, then we will have succeeded…in helping you feel the old-fashioned love and joy in this magical holiday.

No matter what time of year you may be reading this book…*Merry Christmas.* ▲

ALL TOGETHER NOW...**Those little hearts were beating like hummingbirds as everyone hoped they wouldn't be the one to forget their lines at the all-important Christmas pageant. The annual program was the big event of the year at school or church, and the kids wanted to do their best.**

H. Armstrong Roberts

Chapter One

Plays, Pageants and Proud Parents

No community event loomed larger years ago than the annual Christmas pageant at your school or church. Like it or not, *everyone* had a part in the production, from the little tykes right up to the eighth graders. Rehearsals went on for weeks.

When the big day finally arrived, the cast played to a standing-room-only crowd of parents, aunts, uncles and grandparents. The air was filled with excitement. Even a raging blizzard couldn't keep people away.

Behind the scenes were the teachers and mothers who then—as now—worked long and hard to put the whole thing together.

To begin with, there were the usual casting problems. Who would be the wise men? Who would be Mary? Who would be the innkeeper? All it took was the diplomacy and negotiating skills of a world-class diplomat.

I'll never forget a *New Yorker* cartoon from years ago. The Christmas pageant was in progress at an obviously up-scale suburban school. An angry executive-type in his Brooks Brothers suit was protesting to his mink-draped wife, "But why does he *always* have to be a humble shepherd?"

Stardom in Silence

Me, I was lucky. I stammered. A speaking part was out of the question, so there were no lines to memorize. I usually stood silently in the background, dressed as a palm tree.

My wife, Peg, was less fortunate. She was supposed to sip from a cup of wine (actually milk) at the inn and then deliver some joyous words. But the milk had soured! It's hard to be joyous when you're 9 years old and have a mouthful of sour milk.

Then there was the matter of costumes. Angels were no problem. An old bed sheet did nicely with minimal tailoring by Mom. Halos and wings, although a necessity, had a tendency to slip, slide and fall off, adding a nice touch of anticipation to things. But everyone tried hard not to laugh when accidents happened.

It used to be easy to costume the shepherds and wise men. Everyone had a raggedy, heavy, patterned flannel bathrobe around the house that had seen better days. And old towels made good turbans. Anyhow, who among us had ever seen a genuine wise man?

Only the overly ambitious and extremely foolhardy added camels to the cast. Two giggling, wriggling boys inside a camel outfit are guaranteed to wreak dramatic disaster. A Christmas pageant is not the proper setting for low comedy.

Reluctant Stars

As a rough guess, I'd say 90 percent of any school or church Christmas pageant cast would rather be anywhere else on earth than up on that stage. The cast is assembled much the way sailing ships of yore were crewed—bribed, threatened and pressed into service.

They aren't waiting for their moment of glory in the spotlight. Instead, they're consumed with the fearful certainty that they'll forget their one big line. What they want is not stardom and applause, but a chance to escape at the earliest possible moment, as several of the stories on the following pages recall.

I can never forget the evening when I was walking with my eldest, then 8 years old, to the church where the pageant was to be held. She suddenly blurted out that she had been given a line to recite but had lost it.

We located the harassed teacher, who checked her script and wrote out the Bible verse for us. Then, 10 minutes until curtain time, my daughter and I had an intense crash rehearsal in the hallway.

"I usually stood silently in the background, dressed as a palm tree..."

When Dianna's turn came, she stood onstage looking a lot like a terrified deer in the headlights of an oncoming semi. It was obvious her brain was running on empty. After a few seconds of dead silence, the teacher prompted her in a loud whisper: *"For God so loved..."*

Hesitantly, the pride of the family mumbled the four words and again froze.

"*...that He gave...*" hissed the teacher.

And so on. I turned to a stranger sitting next to me. "Poor kid," I said. "I'll bet her parents are embarrassed if they are here."

—Clancy Strock

Bright Christmas Ensured by Santa's Visit

By Helen Moyer, Lake City, Minnesota

ELECTRICITY came to rural Minnesota in the 1940s, but the schools were last to get it—after all, classes were held during daylight hours.

In the fall of 1947, District 99 in Wabasha County was finally going to become electrified. Our little school was wired, and all that remained was the hookup of the private line to the main supply line going past school. Our Christmas program was nearing, and our parents and teachers hoped with us that we'd get electricity in time for this important event.

Neighbors Came Together

For those unfamiliar, these variety programs of Christmas carols, skits and recitations were commonly put on by students years ago. Our program was a real coming-together of everyone in our rural neighborhood. We students made and delivered invitations to all the neighbors, names were drawn for a gift exchange and Santa always paid a visit.

To encourage the utility to make the final connection before the program, a school board member suggested we children each write a "letter to Santa". Our letters would be sent to the power company, and we were to state why we needed to have electricity in our schoolhouse. We kids had plenty of reasons!

Not long after we sent our letters, there came a knock on the schoolhouse door. It was Santa himself! *He* was going to do the final electrical hookup and wondered if we wanted to come outside and watch! Santa had cleats on his boots and climbed the pole like a pro.

We made the front page of the *Graphic*, our local weekly newspaper. But best of all, we had electricity for the Christmas program, including stage lights. ▲

Santa Climbs Pole

Children of the Geppert school (District 99) five miles south of Lake City, are watching intently as Jolly Santa Claus himself connects their school with the REA power lines of the Peoples Co-op. Power company. The connection was made after a written plea to Santa, in care of the power company, that lights be provided for the Christmas party at the school tonight.

NORTH (ELECTRIC) POLE. **It wasn't quite the North Pole, but it was the pole Santa climbed that winter in 1947 to hook up Helen Moyer's school. That's Helen (third from left) watching Santa work.**

Uncle Charlie Won a Footrace with Santa

By Bernice Anderson, Prosperity, Pennsylvania

AFTER CAROLS had been sung, a play presented and speeches given at our church program, it was time for Santa to hand out presents.

Since this was the Depression, a dollar was hard to come by. Yet the community collected what it could and had enough to buy candy, oranges and Cracker Jacks for all the kids. As I recall, Mt. Zion Baptist Church in Castile, Pennsylvania had a standing-room-only crowd that night.

Santa began calling names and we each went up to claim our treat. My Uncle Charlie, my dad's twin brother, was there, but his wife and three children were home sick.

When Uncle Charlie made a third trip to see Santa, the jolly old elf had had enough. He thought my uncle had been there one too many times. Santa started moving around the church away from Uncle Charlie. Naturally, this ended up in a race around the inside of the church. After about three or four rounds, Uncle Charlie picked up an empty box and tossed it over Santa's head.

Never have I heard such laughter! To be sure, Uncle Charlie won that race, with treats for himself and his absent family.

I still have the tiny china Santa that I found in my box of Cracker Jacks that evening. Every year when the decorations come out, my little Santa brings me back to that memorable night. ▲

SuperStock

BUSY ELF. **Santa had a memorable night with Bernice Anderson's persistent Uncle Charlie.**

Blizzard Couldn't Stop This Caring Father

By Maxine George, Hobbs, New Mexico

IN THE 1930s, I attended a one-room school in Missouri. When I was in second grade, our whole school practiced for weeks to put on a Christmas program. I volunteered the use of my baby doll and her bed to appear in the play as Baby Jesus in his crib.

There was a big snowstorm the night before our program, and though it was hard to ride our ponies to school in the morning, we kids were excited. All the parents and neighbors planned to come to the 2 p.m. program in horse-drawn sleds, and Dad was to bring my crib and doll.

The roads were drifting shut as the program was about to begin, and Dad hadn't yet arrived. I kept an anxious vigil with my nose pressed to the cold windowpane. The whole world was white, and tears streamed down my cheeks.

It seemed like I'd stood there for hours when I suddenly spotted a dark figure struggling through a neighbor's field. I recognized Dad as he crawled through the fence at the edge of the school yard. He was carrying my doll and bed! Mom had bundled them in a blanket to keep them dry.

I rushed out through the snow to meet him, sobbing with happiness. I was so glad to see him! My parents' sled had become stuck in the drifts, and other men were digging it out. Dad, meanwhile, struck out through the blizzard on foot to ensure that Baby Jesus would be there for the program. He knew how important it was to me.

Hardly a Christmas goes by that I don't close my eyes and see Dad trudging through the snow to bring me something I cared about. It was a wonderful gift for a little girl to know she was so loved.

Julie Habel

BLIZZARD-PROOF. **Even a storm like this one didn't stop Maxine George's dad from saving the day.**

Would Her Christmas Wish Come True?

I HAD JUST turned 4 in 1909 and was to be in my first Christmas program at our little church in Dickens, Iowa. I had a little poem to recite all by myself:

Christmas was made for babies
all their own to keep.
For Christmas is the birthday
of the Baby cradled with the
sheep.

When we arrived at the church, I saw a tree taller than any I'd ever seen before. The candles burned brightly, with men standing near with wet rags tied to fishing poles to extinguish any candle that might cause a problem.

Many unwrapped presents were also in the branches, one of which was a big beautiful doll. I had never wanted anything so much in my young life as that dolly!

When the program started, my dad stood in the rear of the church. He wanted me to speak up so he could hear me way back there.

When my time came, I climbed the three high steps to stand in front of the tree. I never took my eyes off that doll, so someone had to turn me around to the audience so I could say my poem. My father was smiling when I finished, so I knew he had heard me. I turned for another look at the doll before I climbed down off the stage.

At long last, it was time to put out the candles on the tree and to give out the presents. Starting at the bottom of the tree, name after name was called. Then I heard my name and received some new clothes for my old doll.

I wanted to cry because I knew that new doll was not mine. The last gift to be given out was that longed-for doll.

As I hung my head, I heard my uncle say, "Is there anyone here tonight by the name of Ina Jones?" I couldn't believe it! But my father was carrying me to the front to claim the most precious gift I had ever received. I still have that beautiful doll, and she remains my most precious memory of Christmas.

—Ina Tow, Burnsville, Minnesota

Betts Anderson/Unicorn Stock Photos

CHRISTMAS DOLL, **like the one above, was the only thing little Ina Tow wanted.**

Phone Call Wished a Merry Christmas to All

OVER 80 years ago, I recited this poem at the Christmas program held at Holy Family Catholic School in Saginaw, Michigan. I was only 7 then, but I've never forgotten this holiday verse:

I wish I had a telephone,
With golden cords unfurled.
Long enough, and strong enough,
To reach around the world.
I'd call up everybody
Along the line and say,
"A very Merry Christmas
To you this Christmas Day."

—James Mortimore
Huntington Beach, California

Glowing Girl "Felt the Part"

IN the early '40s, the Christmas pageant was *the* event of the year at Irving Grade School in El Reno, Oklahoma.

Our music, art and drama departments used students from all six grades for the production, ranging from little first-grade angels on up to sixth-grade boys as the wise men.

The starring roles of Mary and Joseph were prized, and the announcement was eagerly awaited by all the sixth graders. To my surprise and delight, I was chosen as Mary.

I certainly was not the most popular girl in class, nor the prettiest. But when I was dressed in the beautiful robes and blue silk headpiece and said my lines onstage in the spotlight, I really felt the part.

Everyone said I had a beautiful glow and peacefulness about me, and I'll never forget how good I felt.

—Shirley Stephenson, Abilene, Texas

Everyone Polished Up for Christmas Pageant

THE CHRISTMAS PROGRAM was a mighty big production at our country school during the early 1930s. How we all worked, planned and shared in this special occasion!

Our teacher's Christmas tree was always the center of attention, reaching from floor to ceiling. Large red paper bells were hung, and red and green crepe-paper swags crisscrossed the ceiling. Below those colorful decorations, we set our stage by hanging bed sheets on a wire.

The night before the program, we were bathed and polished by our proud parents, and the next morning, we dressed in our Sunday best.

The program included many favorite songs such as *Up on the Housetop* and *Santa Claus Is Coming to Town.* After the program, we looked forward to gifts from Santa. Sometimes we received little cardboard boxes filled with hard candy, nuts and colorful ribbon candy.

I remember one year when my teacher gave out large oranges wrapped in gaily colored hankies. Mine was imprinted with bluebirds. After the gift exchange, we had popcorn balls and bright red apples. To this day, red Delicious apples remind me of those wonderful Christmas programs. *—Shirley Jipp*
Blair, Nebraska

This Christmas Stocking Came in Patriotic Colors

MY EARLIEST memory of Christmas goes back to 1910, when I was 4 years old. Our church in Moores Hill, Indiana had a children's program for Christmas, and my teacher asked Mother to teach me this little poem:

Robin Rudd/Unicorn Stock Photos

PAGEANT MAGIC. At Christmas, even the humble one-room schoolhouse could be a magical place.

In Holland, a shoe is waiting,
In Germany, always a tree.
But this good old American stocking
Is best for you and me!

When I said that last line, Mother instructed, I was to hold up an old knee-length stocking she'd found in our attic. It was red, white and blue.

I excitedly got bundled up to walk to church but forgot the stocking. Poor Father had to run back home through the snow to retrieve it. He saved the day by making it back to church in the nick of time.

I'm nearly 90 now, but I'll never forget that little poem and how proudly I held up the red, white and blue stocking.

—Beulah Drake, Salem, Oregon

***CHOIR OF ANGELS,* at least at Christmastime. The Junior Choir was in fine form in 1948, according to this photo from Lois Hudspeth of Eldora, Iowa. Her son Alan is second from left in the back row, and daughter Elaine is fifth from left in the front row.**

City Bus 'Carried a Tune'

By Jim Thorley, Munster, Indiana

ANYONE who hasn't gone through the great bus-riding era in America has missed a real adventure. Those days left me with many fond recollections, especially one indelible memory of Christmastime.

During the 1930s, we in the Calumet region of northern Indiana were dubiously blessed with a local bus line called the Shore Line Motor Coach Company.

Great clouds of navy-blue exhaust accompanied these ancient vehicles along their routes, and hisses and clanging noises from underneath the coaches went along with the ride at no extra cost.

Modern safety rules about passenger numbers were certainly not in effect or were ignored completely. During rush hours, there were more people standing than sitting, clinging to rods overhead. The aisles were so jammed that you couldn't fall over if you wanted to.

"All of the bus riders were singing at the tops of their voices..."

This solidly packed condition prompted the historical phrase "Step to the rear of the bus, please", and if the driver said it once, it seemed like he said it a thousand times.

Crowded as those buses were, chivalry wasn't dead. Many a tired steel worker would stand gallantly in the aisle after relinquishing his seat to some lady who had just spent the day galloping through Goldblatt's Department Store.

Friendly Riders

People riding together often rehashed the day's events. I saw my father on numerous occasions talking and laughing with a man sharing a bus seat.

When we got off at our corner, I'd ask Dad who the man was. "I don't know," he'd answer. "He sure was a nice fella, though."

One ride I'll never forget happened a few days before Christmas vacation. The members of my high school choral club, including me, had stayed after school to rehearse some carols for the upcoming holiday program.

We scrambled aboard the waiting bus and took our seats. A couple of the girls glanced over their sheet music and started to hum one of the songs we were rehearsing. Some of us picked it up and hummed along in harmony. Soon we were softly singing.

Urged on by the rest of the people on the bus to sing aloud, we students cheerfully complied. Soon everyone in the bus, from students to workmen, shoppers and even the bus driver, were singing carols at the tops of our voices, rolling merrily down the street.

Happiest Bus in Indiana

When we pulled up at corners to let someone off, the singing never stopped. The ones getting off kept singing and waved as the bus rolled away. Those getting on the bus were caught up in the holiday spirit and joined in. It was the happiest bus in Indiana.

When I jumped off at my corner, I waved to the carolers and they all waved back. The bus rolled away down the street, and as it grew smaller in the distance, I heard faint strains of *Silent Night*. I shuffled home through the snow and wished every bus ride could be like that one. ▲

BUSLOAD OF MELODIES. **There's something about the Christmas season that sets folks to singing, even when they're on a bus. Jim Thorley recalls a time in the 1930s when a local Shore Line bus (above) became a mobile melody machine, thanks to the high school choral club members who continued their rehearsal on the way home.**

Violin Virtuoso Made the Grade

WHEN I WAS in sixth grade many years ago in Chicago, I began taking violin lessons. After about 3 months of lessons, I had progressed to the point where I felt I could play *Silent Night* in our school Christmas pageant. I was scared yet excited.

As I stepped onto the stage, I looked at the music teacher. Her eyes were on mine, and she was ready to cover whatever mistakes I made.

The introduction came and the audience of 350 fell quiet. I was sure no one had ever before played the violin on that school stage. I felt like I was at Carnegie Hall.

As my bow met the string and the first tone came out, I heard a sigh of relief as if the people were wondering what kind of sound the instrument would make.

The strains of *Silent Night* filled the auditorium. As I played, the principal motioned the audience to join in. They did. I felt so relieved and so honored as the song ended, and the applause never seemed to stop.

Today, I'm a retired orchestra director of 31 years, but I still teach budding young musicians at a private studio. They all learn to play *Silent Night*.

—Carl Kokes, Peru, New York

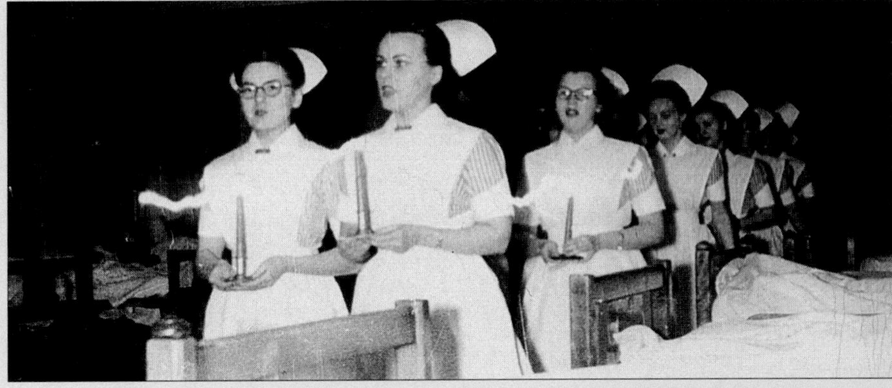

***CAROLING CURE.* The tradition of student nurses caroling through the hospital wards was one Marjorie Schlei still fondly recalls. The joy the patients showed was a real Christmas gift.**

Student Nurses' Carried on British Tradition

AS A first-year student nurse in 1947, I took part in a Christmas Eve tradition that began in the hospitals of wartime England.

We dressed crisply in pin-striped dresses, white aprons and caps, and black shoes and stockings. Then we carried lighted candles and slowly walked through all the halls and wards while singing Christmas carols.

The evening was sad for many of us, because we hadn't been away from home on Christmas Eve before. But that was forgotten as we walked slowly along, raising our voices for the year's greatest holiday, and watching so many wan and lonely faces brighten.

Almost 50 years later, a more meaningful memory would be difficult for me to recall.

—Marjorie Schlei
Sussex, Wisconsin

Peace on Earth Would Be Assured

CHURCH SERVICES were especially beautiful on Christmas Eve in 1941. It wasn't a happy time, because war had been recently declared and rationing was in effect. But our church was filled to capacity that evening, and my sisters and I climbed the steps to the loft and joined the other choir members.

Below us, the church had been decorated with cedars and holly heavy with berries. The scent of the boughs mingled with the aroma of burning candles as the Christmas story unfolded. Shepherds kept watch over their flocks, and angels heralded the Savior's birth.

As we sang *Silent Night,* the congregation rose and proceeded down the aisle. Scattered among the communicants were relatives, schoolmates, friends and neighbors wearing the service uniforms of our country.

I was so proud of these brave young people who were home for the holidays and who would soon return to their duty stations across the country or in far-off lands.

In my heart I knew that as long as we had such brave young men serving our country, "peace on earth" would be assured.

—Jean Raby
Indian Head, Maryland

***CHRISTMAS ANGEL.* Decked out in her wings and robe for the school play, Lore Warren of Hayward, California was really an angel on this Christmas in the 1930s. Lore says her father made the dollhouse, which had lights, and her mother made the doll clothes.**

How Old Is Santa Claus?

IN THE EARLY 1940s, I was 7 years old when I recited this poem for our Christmas play at church:

How old is Santa Claus,
and where does he keep?
And why does he come
when I am asleep?

It seems like his hair
would get covered with black.
And if he goes headfirst,
how does he get back?

I'd just like to see him once
stand on his head,
And dive down the chimney
like Grandma has said.

It seems like his hair
would get covered with black.
And if he goes headfirst,
how does he get back?

Mama knows about him
but she won't tell me.
I'll stay awake Christmas Eve
and then I'll see.

I've teased her to tell me,
but Mama, she won't.
So I'll find out myself.
Now see if I don't!

—Imogene Frye, Killen, Alabama

Was Joseph's Visit a Coincidence?

By Gladys Gottschalk, Champaign, Illinois

WHEN I WAS 7 years old, my Christmas Eve was really going to be special—I'd get to read the Nativity story at our church Christmas program!

It was during the 1930s, and we lived on a farm near the little village of Anchor, Illinois. Mom, Dad and my older brother had been an attentive audience as I practiced reading from my Bible each day. Mom made me a new dress for my big night, and I had a practically new red sweater passed down from my cousin.

On Christmas Eve, I was dressed and ready to go when my brother announced he couldn't make it to the program. Our cow was expecting her calf that night, and he had to stay home to see that all went well. I was disappointed but was looking forward to that little calf!

Ready to Perform

Mom, Dad and I made our way to the little church in town. Fluffy snowflakes were gently falling, and I could hardly contain my excitement!

The church was filled with parents and friends, and Miss Edna was playing *Joy to the World* on the old piano. All of us children marched in and took our places in front. After the recitations and some carols, it was my turn to read. I stood by the little cradle with my own doll filling in as the Baby Jesus.

When I finished, I looked up and saw a man standing at the church door. He was wearing very old clothes, and the usher took him to a seat next to Dad. As the service ended and everyone filed out, Dad talked with the man for a bit, then invited him to come home with us.

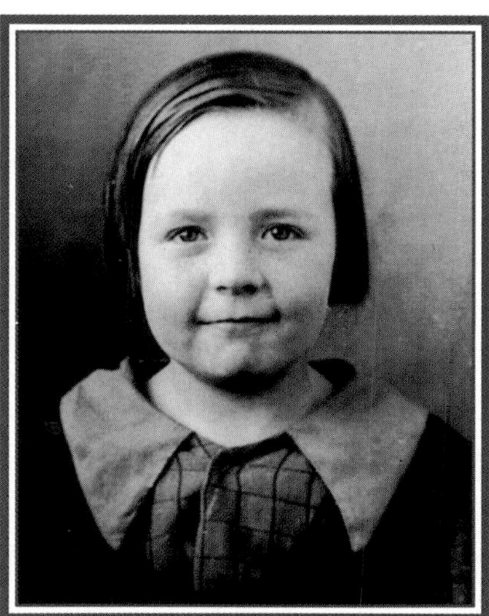

***CHRISTMAS MIRACLE?* A visitor helped the family of Gladys Gottschalk (above).**

His name was Joseph, and he said he'd been riding the evening train, as transients so often did in those Depression days. A trainman discovered him in a boxcar and told him to get off. Hearing our Christmas music, Joseph was drawn to the church.

He accompanied us home, and after some time, my brother hurried from the barn into the house. The cow was having a hard time delivering her calf, he said. To make matters worse, the wind was closing the snow-filled roads, so no vet could get to our place.

> "Hearing our music, he was drawn to the church..."

Joseph said he might be able to help, so he and Dad went to the barn.

Mom added fuel to the dining room heater and to the cookstove in the kitchen. Soon, the teakettle was steaming and she made hot cocoa.

I didn't care much about that, though, and I kept looking out the window, watching for the men to return. Soon I saw the lantern light and then heard foot stomping on the porch. In came Dad, my brother and our new friend, Joseph. Everyone was smiling and I knew it was going to be okay.

Visitor Was a Hero

The cow and calf were fine, Dad said, thanks to Joseph's gentle handling. Our friendly visitor stayed the night, sleeping on a couch in our dining room. The next day, he told us he was trying to get home to his family but had no money.

We didn't have much either, so Dad got in touch with some friends at church. Between them, they bought him a train ticket.

Before he left, we all went to the barn to see the new cow family. It was so cozy! There, in the hay, was the cute little newborn calf. I promptly named him "Joey", after Joseph, who had helped with the delivery.

Today, whenever I read the Christmas story in my Bible, I recall the friend who came to us on Christmas Eve. It was such a coincidence that I read about a man by the same name at our church program that very night...or was it?

Bloopers Added Ho-Ho-Ho's To Holiday Shows

Eyes Had It...and That Was More Than Enough for Her!

OUR SCHOOL Christmas programs were such nice affairs in which every pupil recited, acted or sang.

The teacher and older boys strung a wire clear across the room and hung up white sheets with safety pins. This "stage curtain" slid open and closed for each performance.

There were many mistakes and lots of telltale coaching from backstage before the programs were finally over. Then Santa would come bounding in the door with a loud "Ho! Ho! Ho!" and pass out our presents.

In 1932, when I was 5, I was supposed to recite a poem at the program. For weeks, my older brother and sister made me practice so I wouldn't embarrass them.

On the big night, I stood behind the curtain in my brand-new home-sewn dress. I peeked through a slit in the curtains and all I saw were eyes—*millions* of big round eyes, and they were waiting for me!

I turned and ran for the basement! When the time came for me to recite my little poem, there was nothing anyone could say that would coax me onstage to recite:

Roses on my shoulders,
slippers on my feet.
I am Papa's darling,
don't you think I'm sweet?

I never did recite my rhyme that night. But I've certainly never forgotten it.

—Dorothy Behringer
North Branch, Minnesota

Song Tripped Him Up

DURING the early '40s, I attended a rural one-room schoolhouse near Kalispell, Montana. In the weeks before Christmas, our school really began to bustle, as each child from grades one through eight practiced their parts for the big holiday pageant.

I was 9 years old and was going to sing *White Christmas*. After practicing with my teacher, mother and grandmother, I had that song down cold! I half expected to see ol' Bing himself show up just to see how it should be done.

When the big night arrived, we kids stood backstage, our excitement level soaring! Parents and relatives jammed the room, and the fragrances of shaving lotion, perfume, fir bows, coal oil and cow barn were in the air.

The curtains opened, announcements and introductions were made, then, one by one, the participants went nervously onstage and did their stuff. Suddenly, it was *my* turn.

The teacher whispered, "Do it right, Jerry!"

I waved as I stepped to the stage ...well, almost to the stage.

My toe caught on the edge and I tripped. I landed in a heap on the stage and a little curl of dust rose up around me. There was total silence, but everyone was sure paying attention. I was the hit of the show when I hit the stage!

I got up and moved to center stage. The teacher gave me the key and I began to sing. I must have left my nervousness on the boards, because I sang great. With the empathy of everyone in the building, I had nowhere but up to go with my performance.

—Jerry Robocker
Port Orchard, Washington

Marc A. Auth/New England Stock Photo

"I NOSE MY PART." **Even the most "experienced" performer gets a little nervous before the big pageant. Better to scratch that itch backstage than in front of the family.**

Pre-Program Catastrophe Didn't Dampen Enthusiasm

CHRISTMAS EVE when I was 6 years old will always remain in my memory. The annual Christmas program was soon to begin at our little country church, and my brother and I had parts to recite.

We had each taken a bath in the kitchen, and Vernon was practicing his verses one final time. When it was my turn to practice, Vernon stopped me and

said that I'd never be loud enough for the people in the back of the church to hear.

He instructed me to back up and try my part again. This continued a couple of times and I kept backing up into the kitchen. By now, you've likely gotten the picture—yes, I did tumble over backward into that standing tub of dirty bathwater. Over I fell with a great big splash!

My new red plaid skirt was wet. I burst into tears and thought my world had come to an end.

But Mother wiped off the skirt and pressed it, and I wore it for the pageant, though it was a little damp. Our family made it to church on time, we children took part in the program and no one ever suspected the calamity we had just experienced. *—Sandra Munyon Watertown, Wisconsin*

No One Thought This Performance Stunk

BACK when I was in first grade, during the 1950s, you might say I was "a little stinker".

Our Idaho grade school's Christmas program featured a skit with wildlife in the forest. I played a skunk, one of three in the program, and wore a costume my grandma made. During the skit, the three of us skunks were to crawl across the forest floor.

As the smallest skunk, I scurried after the others but got too close to the edge of the gymnasium stage. I rolled off the stage, a good 4 feet onto the gym floor below, nearly landing in the front row of parents and grandparents.

Luckily, I was unhurt and everyone got a big laugh out of it.

—Paula Farris, Nezperce, Idaho

Wrong Verse, Right Night

ONE YEAR, both my sisters practiced so long and hard for our school Christmas program that eventually they knew each other's recitations as well as their own.

On the evening of the program, my younger sister was called on first. She got up and recited, then said, "Oh, that was the wrong one!"

She then proceeded to give the correct verse as well. Big sister was not very happy with her! *—Marion Weekly Fresno, California*

Santa Provided Extra Spark for Program

ALL WAS going well at our school Christmas program in 1915, and my twin sister and I were a pair of excited 7-year-olds.

A large pinyon tree stood in the center of the room, decorated with paper chains, strings of popcorn and cranberries and small candles in clip-on holders. When the candles were lit and the gas lamps turned down low, that tree would be a sight to behold.

After all the stories and Christmas carols, we heard a hearty "Ho! Ho! Ho!", and Santa arrived to pass out the gifts. The presents were hung on the tree, with the children's names affixed.

As Santa reached deep into the tree to grab a gift, the cotton trim on his coat caught fire from one of the candles. It spread quickly, so Santa ran to the nearest window and dove out into a snowdrift below!

Some of the men ran outside and made sure Santa was okay, but the youngest children began to cry, thinking it was the end of Santa Claus.

Our teacher assured us Santa had only headed home to change his coat, and he would quickly recover from the incident with the help of Mrs. Claus and the elves.

I guess our teacher knew what she was talking about, because our gifts were there under the tree at home on Christmas morning. And Santa has never missed a Christmas since!

—Vernon Nielsen Salt Lake City, Utah

Tale About the Donkey Lives on in Memory

WHEN I WAS in the fourth grade at our country school, our class acted out the Christmas story. I was chosen to be Mary, and the story began with Joseph and Mary traveling to Bethlehem on a donkey.

Two older boys were the "donkey". Covered with a blanket, they had ears, eyes and a tail to look authentic. We had to climb a set of steps up to the stage, and I would always hang on for fear I'd slide off.

Joseph was to lead the donkey across the stage and knock at the door of the inn. After talking with the innkeeper, we were to exit out the door.

We had practiced many times, but stage fright does strange things. The night of the program, we crossed the stage, but Joseph forgot to knock. He started leading the donkey on through the door.

When the teacher realized what was happening, she hopped up on the stage and caught the donkey by its tail and pulled it back out. We ended up redoing that part of the play as everyone laughed uproariously! *—Gloria Stutzman London, Ohio*

Chocolate Drop Melted In Front of Crowd

WHEN MY SISTER was 6, she was cast as a chocolate drop at our church Christmas pageant. I was made an angel because I was a tall 7-year-old.

A touring car full of all our relatives, including Grandma, turned out at the Baptist church for the big production.

We angels fluttered about the stage wearing filmy white ponchos and tinsel halos fashioned by our mothers. When we successfully completed our routine, the candies came on to do their part.

Like the rest, my sister wore black cotton stockings on her legs and arms. Her white dress represented her vanilla filling.

All went well until our favorite chocolate drop had to say her line. She stared at the audience with her thumb in her mouth. The audience broke into loving laughter. At that, my sister took out her thumb and retorted, "I was going to sing you a song, but now I won't!"

Oh, yes, she eventually did say her line! *—Deloris Dunham Syracuse, New York*

WINDOW WISHING. **There was no need for a calendar when Christmas came around. Downtown stores fairly sparkled with lights and decorations, and, most important, windows full of toys that Santa had just delivered from his shop at the North Pole... and might end up under your tree.**

SuperStock

Chapter Two

Downtown Was All Aglow

My hometown was a nice place to grow up, but truth to tell, it was pretty plain. Perhaps you recall growing up in such a place, too.

Good old Sterling, Illinois wasn't a destination for tour buses, and its downtown business district had expanded hit-or-miss. Most of the buildings were two-story affairs with a store at street level and a law office or insurance agency upstairs. Not exactly a sightseer's stop.

But immediately after Thanksgiving each year, downtown Sterling was transformed into a thrilling, glamorous, magical place for 5 weeks. That's when the city fathers and the local merchants dolled up the area for the Christmas season.

The six blocks of Main Street were an unbroken canopy of Christmas lights arching up from curb to curb. All of the streetlight poles were wrapped in spirals of tinsel, topped with large gold and white bells. And, if you were lucky, Mother Nature contributed a couple of inches of snow to make everything sparkly and fresh.

What a sight!

On each side of the street, store windows were filled with glittering treasures that would have awed the Oriental princes of old. As a kid, you could hardly handle the excitement.

Look at That!

We pushed up as close as we could, noses pressed against the store windows. All around you, other kids were shoving, pointing and chattering with astonishment. Back then, we hadn't been preconditioned by hundreds of television commercials that started running in October. This was brand-new stuff!

Girls *oohed* and *aahed* over Dionne quintuplet dolls. They quickly decided that Santa absolutely had to bring a Shirley Temple doll, along with a flouncy wardrobe.

Boys stood hypnotized by the newest Lionel or American Flyer train sets that chuffed along, tootling their way through masses of merchandise that included the Giant Deluxe Tinkertoy set that came with enough pieces to make windmills and even a Ferris wheel.

Dear Santa...

We kids moved slowly from window to window and store to store. *Wow*, look at that chemistry set! Just think of the wonderful, stinky things I could invent!

And how about a miniature steam engine heated by an alcohol lamp, generating enough power to run a tiny circular saw. Maybe I could go into the lumber business!

My sister naturally gravitated to the windows filled with doll buggies and cradles, and miniature kitchens complete with dishes and genuine West Bend toy aluminum pots and pans.

The two stores with the best window displays of all were Wynn-Deavers and Sears Roebuck, but you couldn't afford to ignore several other stores with their own Christmas merchandise. If you didn't scout them all, how could you put together the best Christmas list for Santa Claus?

To ensure optimum results, the key last step was to drag Mom and Dad from window to window as you pointed out the merits of the stuff you craved. Call it salesmanship. Or, truthfully, organized whining. Mom was attentive. Dad occasionally grimaced as he kept a running tab in his head.

"Store windows were filled with glittering treasures..."

Oh, it was a glorious scene! Families crowded the streets. The Salvation Army Santa Claus clanged his bell and wished everyone who dropped change into his iron bucket a Merry Christmas. *Oh, Little Town of Bethlehem* floated out from loudspeakers hung above the stores.

If you lived where snow was common but none had yet arrived, the hot question was, "Do you think we'll have a white Christmas?" It was the one time of year when a decent snowfall was really welcome, and never mind a little shoveling or slush on the sidewalks. A proper Christmas absolutely required snow—especially if a new Flexible Flyer sled was on your list.

Nowadays even the fanciest mall at the edge of town can't come close to those downtown Christmases I remember. The exhilaration just isn't there. Exciting window displays are rare, and Santa Claus charges 5 bucks to have kids sit on his lap and have their picture taken. Toys are in cartons stacked to the ceiling. How "good" a Christmas it is will be found weekly in the financial pages of your newspaper.

Perhaps you live where there still is an old-time downtown. Lucky you! Lucky kids! Someday they'll have the same fine memories that you and I treasure today.

—Clancy Strock

Woolworth's Was a Downtown Tradition

By Rita Kayser, Festus, Missouri

ONE CHRISTMAS MEMORY permanently etched in my mind is my family's annual shopping trip to downtown Poplar Bluff, Missouri.

Daddy would park the car down at the train depot and we'd climb the steep steps up to Main Street. For a moment, we'd stand together, awed at the sight of the business district decked out in holiday splendor. Then, after agreeing to meet for lunch at noon, we'd go our separate ways.

For Mama and me, there was only one store—Woolworth's. To walk through those big double doors was to walk into an enchanted forest.

In sharp contrast to the cold outside, Woolworth's was warm and welcoming. Brightly lit by what seemed to be thousands of lights, the store twinkled and glittered.

A myriad of intriguing aromas enveloped us, freshly popped corn mingling with fragrances from the perfume counter. Huge bins of delicious-looking chocolates sat next to cases filled with roasted peanuts, mixed nuts and those golden unaffordable cashews. Bright bolts of material emitted dye aromas while all the plastic toys gave off their own peculiar scents.

Kept Money in Hankie

The few dollars I'd saved from my cotton-picking money were safely tied in a knot in my hankie and buried deep in my coat pocket. I was allowed to look at everything in the store before making my purchases, so I hummed along with the Christmas music as I dreamed and decided.

I took my time but always made sure I was finished shopping by noon. It was then that the most exciting part of the day was about to begin.

At noon sharp, Daddy and my brothers joined Mama and me at Woolworth's lunch counter for our once-a-year meal "out". I still get goose bumps just remembering!

Mama and Daddy would sit in a booth, kind of nervous and stiff, while drinking coffee and waiting for their meal. Meanwhile, my brothers and I could hardly wait to climb up on those round revolving stools lining the lunch counter.

> *"The most exciting part of the day was eating at the lunch counter..."*

My skinny legs dangled as I perched high on a stool and, although Mama always reminded me to "sit like a lady", I never could resist the urge to spin all the way around on my stool at least once during the meal.

And, oh that meal! Everyone else pored over their menus, but I didn't have to. I knew exactly what I wanted—a "BLT". To get crisp lettuce and a juicy slice of tomato in the dead of winter was the most incredible experience I could imagine. The only decision I had to make was whether to have it on plain bread or toast.

If I close my eyes, I can experience it all again.

I see the waitresses, laden with platters and trays, dodging each other in the narrow diner. I smell the strong aroma of coffee, frying hamburgers and browning toast. And I watch Mama frown at the noises my brothers liked to make with the straws in their empty soda glasses.

Then I hear the greatest sound of all: the waitress calling out to the cook, "One BLT, on toast, with mayo!" ▲

Ewing Galloway

FUN AT THE FIVE-AND-DIME. **The local Woolworth store, like the one above, was a great place anytime. But at Christmas, it was a magical place where a girl could spend all day choosing a gift for herself or someone special. And there was nothing better after a hard day of shopping than a bite at the lunch counter.**

Thanksgiving Was A "Field Day"

GROWING UP in Chicago in the days before television, we didn't have football games to watch after Thanksgiving dinner. But on the evening of Thanksgiving Day, Marshall Field & Company on State Street "opened the curtains" on their street-level Christmas displays, and that was better than TV.

After the dishes were done, families like ours piled into their cars and headed downtown to look in the windows. Each had a scene from Clement Moore's *A Visit From St. Nicholas* ("Twas the night before Christmas..."). As you walked from window to window, you followed the story, which was told with animated figures and printed text.

The displays were complete with sleeping mice and an animated Santa who touched his nose. The tree was decorated in the old-fashioned way and all the furnishings and toys were antiques. The whole thing was a delight for young and old alike. *—Jan Stiles*

St. Marie, Montana

***WONDERS IN WINDOWS.* It didn't cost a dime to head downtown and stare into all the store windows decorated for Christmas. Window-shopping was as good as the real thing.**

"Window Nights" Meant Wondrous Sights

BACK IN the '40s, no one began the Christmas season until after Thanksgiving—it just wasn't done!

After Thanksgiving, and only then, brightly colored lights were strung around the lampposts and across the streets, forming colorful arches in my hometown of Traverse City, Michigan. The big introduction to the Christmas season came on "Window Night", and everyone looked forward to this exciting event.

Window Night was a competition between all the businesses in town. Judging was usually done before the parade, which was led by our high school band and ended with the grand arrival of Santa Claus on a fire truck.

Beforehand, store owners covered the windows with plain brown paper so no one could get a peek at their entries before Window Night. As I recall, the Wilson Furniture Store seemed to win the contest year after year. (I guess, being a furniture store, they had a little more to work with than the drugstores did.)

I saved what little money I could and my mother gave me enough so I had at least $1 to spend on Christmas gifts during that magical evening. After the parade, I'd go to Kresge's five-and-ten to buy Mother a large bottle of Blue Waltz perfume for 12¢.

I'd get my father a mug of shaving cream for 15¢, and I used the remaining money to buy treats for myself—some delicious cashews at the candy counter, a tulip sundae washed down with a lime phosphate and maybe a *Mary Marvel* comic book to read on the way home.

Memories of those wonderful nights are among my most cherished.

—Peggy DeLara

Newport News, Virginia

Christmas Began on A Thursday Night

TWO WEEKS before Thanksgiving, colored lights were strung along the telephone poles in downtown Scranton, Pennsylvania. Around the same time, the stores pulled the curtains on their display windows.

We knew that on Thanksgiving night, the lights would all be lit and the curtains pulled aside to reveal wonderful scenes in the store windows. Each year, we eagerly awaited our walking tour of downtown.

One store always set up trains in their window. We loved watching them race through tunnels and over mountains. Some went in figure eights; others chugged around in circles. The biggest department store, The Globe Store, had four windows with different displays featuring movable mannequins nodding, twisting, bending or bowing.

Sometimes, they'd have little elves working at the North Pole and other times they'd show little children playing or hanging up their stockings. It was always worth waiting for and meant the Christmas season had officially begun.

—Suzanne Bevan

Fredericksburg, Virginia

***AND SO TO BED.* Ready for Santa were Suzanne Bevan with brothers Timmy and Charlie.**

Did Santa Come from Philly?

IF SANTA CLAUS was in every store when I was a little girl, my two sisters and I would never have known it. We thought he was only at Wanamaker's Department Store in Philadelphia, because that's where our parents took us to see him. Of all the wondrous displays we saw there, two in particular stand out in my memory.

There was a monorail train we children could ride. It took us high up near the ceiling for a look at the wonderland below and a hearty wave to our parents. And I'll never forget the whistling snowmen. These were larger-than-life figures with whistling boys inside. As the snowmen whistled tunes, their heads rose and necks appeared.

Another highlight of our yearly trip to Philadelphia was lunch at Horn and Hardart's Automat. Dad gave each of us a handful of nickels and we'd wander around the restaurant trying to decide which slots to put our coins in. We loved looking through the tiny doors and seeing the sandwiches, fruit and desserts.

Years later, my husband and I took our daughters on a special trip to Philadelphia to see Santa at Wanamaker's. They were impressed, but afterward, at Horn and Hardart's, they needed quarters, not nickels, for their food.

—Helene Harned, Zionsville, Pennsylvania

Huge Tree Highlighted Christmas Trip

ABOUT A WEEK before Christmas in the late '40s and '50s, my mom and I dressed in our finest clothes, climbed onto a streetcar and made our annual holiday trip to downtown Cleveland.

Downtown was glorious and safe in those days. Public Square and all the stores were decked out with lights and beautiful decorations.

Higbee's Department Store on the square was known for its lavish and extravagant decorations. Meanwhile, bells rang, everyone bustled about and you could smell wonderful fresh-roasted peanuts from the Morrow Nut House.

In those wonderfully innocent days, most kids believed in Santa Claus. I'd have my picture taken with him and tell him all of my wishes for Christmas. After that, Mom and I had lunch, then walked down Euclid Street (downtown's main street) and stared into all the store display windows.

At 13th and Euclid, we arrived at the Sterling, Linder & Davis Department Store, site of the nation's tallest indoor Christmas tree.

From 1927 through 1968, a 70-foot-tall live Christmas tree stood inside and was covered with 75 pounds of icicles, 1,500 yards of silver tinsel and more than 2,500 sparkling ornaments. By taking the store elevator, you could view the tree from all levels. It was a spectacular Cleveland tradition!

Finally, on the way home, Mom and I stopped at the malt counter in May Company's basement for the perfect way to end our trip. In most people's opinion (including mine!), no one's ever been able to duplicate the taste and texture of those frosty malts.

— Linda Sanvido, Parma Heights, Ohio

WERE YOU A GOOD GIRL? **Little Linda Sanvido (above) had that question to ponder when she faced Santa Claus in one of the many department stores in downtown Cleveland in the late 1940s. Linda tells of the wonders of those days in her memories on this page.**

Ewing Galloway

MAIN STREET MEMORIES. **No matter how many times you'd been downtown during the year, when Christmas arrived, it was transformed to a totally different place filled with lights, wreaths and other delights.**

Holiday Window Watchers 'Got the Picture'

By Bob Langbein, Lakeview, Arkansas

IN DECEMBER of 1943, while the rest of the country was singing war songs like *Coming in on a Wing and a Prayer* and Humphrey Bogart was basking in the fame of *Casablanca*, Gerber's Department Store in downtown Memphis, Tennessee had just unveiled its Christmas displays.

Moving along with that "first night" crowd, I went from window to window, soaking up the holiday atmosphere. Then, in the very last window, I saw it—a sight that nearly bowled me over! But that's getting ahead of the story...

I'd just turned 18 and would soon join the Army. But at that time, I was working at Gerber's. Earlier in the month, I'd gone to the store's photo studio for a professional portrait that I intended to present to my folks for Christmas.

The picture (at right) depicts a lanky young man in casual stance, dressed in a new long-sleeved maroon shirt, which, as an employee of Gerber's shirt department, I'd enthusiastically sold to myself.

> "Window number four literally made me gasp!"

A prominent feature of my Christmas portrait was the Kaywoodie pipe that idly rested in one hand. I must say, the portrait delivered the man-about-town impression for which I'd hoped.

Wonders in the Window

The day of the Christmas window unveiling had been busy in the shirt department. Despite the war, the holiday spirit was certainly upon people. As I left the store that night, I couldn't help but notice the people marveling at the Christmas windows and the merchandise displayed inside.

Joining the crowd at the first window, I saw Santa seated on a pedestal surrounded by a half dozen boys and girls. His head was thrown back in the "ho-ho-ho" position. Beside him, a little girl stood flashing a smile, minus her two front teeth.

The second window was full of toys like Flexible Flyer sleds, erector sets, Red Ryder BB guns, bikes and a heavily ornamented Christmas tree.

Threading its way through the toys was a magnificent Lionel electric train. The three children standing beside me filled the air with *oohs* and *aahs* as their "Little Orphan Annie eyes" took in the scene.

***PIPE DREAM.* At age 18, Bob Langbein was the star of the local department store window display.**

Window number three was the family window. Mom and Dad, Grandma and Grandpa and three children were seated at a large table. Dad was preparing to carve a beautiful turkey, and through the dining room on the far side of the set, you could see and hear carolers singing *Silent Night*. It was a scene few could resist.

Shock Among the Stockings

But it was window number four that literally made me gasp. Still dressed in their nightclothes, Mom and Dad were seated on the sofa, while Junior proudly held up a brand-new sweater for all to see.

Clutching her new dolly in one hand, Betty was handing little Billy his new Erector Set. Amid the wrapping lying on the floor was the family dog, chewing on a Christmas bone. But the part of the display that caught my eye was the fireplace.

Christmas stockings marked Mom, Dad, Junior, Betty, Billy and Spot hung from the mantel. Atop it were three photographs, Mom and Dad, Betty and Billy, and Junior. Except "Junior" wasn't Junior—he was me!

The store photographer had placed my picture in the window for all to see. It was a proud moment for a young man not many months out of high school and soon to enter the armed forces.

So, here I sit, more than 50 years later, examining that same picture. I remember a happy time in my youth—and wonder whatever became of Billy and Betty, Mom and Dad, and that handsome young fellow who stares back at me from Christmas of 1943. ▲

Ewing Galloway

***SHOPPERS' PARADISE.* When all of your shopping could be done in one store, that store went all-out to present its best to the customers, especially at Christmas.**

15
9
2
Santa Claus
1
11
7
14
5

The Downtown Joys of Christmas Toys

TURN-OF-THE-CENTURY TOYS **in this store window were made to last. James and Bonnie Ziolecki of Menomonee Falls, Wisconsin collected these toys and enjoy them each Christmas. The German bisque doll (1) has a body made of kid leather, while the teddy bear (2) and pull horses (3) are covered in mohair. The bank showing a dentist pulling a tooth (4) is made of cast iron, and the 1903 train (5) and boy and girl teeter-totter (6) are tin. Other items shown here include: a Belsnickle candy container (7), Magic Drawing Cards (8), McLoughlin Brothers blocks (9), *Christmas ABC's* book (10), die-cut German Santa book (11), Daisy "trick pony" bell toy (12), Bradley's toy village (13), cardboard soldiers from "bowling game" (14) and a feather tree decorated with delicate blown-glass ornaments (15).**

J. Anderson/H. Armstrong Roberts

LIGHT BRIGADE. **Thanks to her father, Jack Shannon (seated at far left), Judy Trayle's hometown was aglow from one end of Main Street to the other at Christmas. Her enlightening memory is below.**

Santa and Mr. Peanut Were Part of the Season

IT WASN'T JUST a day, it was a whole season! Christmas began on Thanksgiving weekend, when Mom took one of us shopping in New Haven, Connecticut. We traveled into town by bus early on Saturday morning.

Malley's Department Store always had a wonderful animated Santa Claus display. One year, I recall the old fellow was sitting in a great bathtub, "ho-ho-ho-ing" as the elves poured in water and scrubbed his back. It was also intriguing to watch the cash carriers run on their overhead electric trolley tracks to the cashier booth and back again.

For Mom and me, Malley's was mostly for looking. The serious shopping came when we reached the five-and-tens like Woolworth's, Kresge's, W.T. Grant's and Newberry's. Those stores were where we could really stretch our money to cover gifts for the whole family.

Music wafted around the downtown, people bustled and the silver tones of the Salvation Army bell ringers blended with the rest. The trip wasn't complete without stops at the Fulton Food Market and the Planters Peanut Shop.

The food market had sawdust on the floor, huge wheels of cheese, barrels of pickles and cured meats. At Planters, a mechanical Mr. Peanut greeted everyone from the store window, tipping his top hat and raising his cane. Peanuts, peanut butter, peanut brittle, peanut butter fudge and trinkets in the shape of peanuts could be purchased.

—Rita Roberson, Walkersville, Maryland

Linemen Ensured Small Town's Holiday Glow

MY DAD was line foreman for the public utility in our farming community of Arlington, Washington. Although winter work schedules were arduous, Dad and other volunteers made our little town come to life through electricity at Christmastime.

They hung large bells of beautiful colors and large candy canes on each and every lamppost on Main Street. At night, all of Main Street from one end to the other was aglow with Christmas lights. Some of the larger ornaments played music as well as gave off radiant colors.

I can still remember my awe as I walked in the snow and looked up to behold the flashing colors and beautiful music. Today I decorate my home with over 700 lights, but it's not as beautiful to me as the bells and candy canes that adorned our little town.

—Judy Trayle, Fairview, Oregon

WAITING FOR SANTA. **William Danford of Elmhurst, Illinois and his girlfriend waited for Christmas over 70 years ago at his father's decorated drugstore in McConnelsville, Ohio. Many customers took pictures of the cute tots.**

A Trip with Grandma Held Appeal

By Tom Harvill, Forest City, North Carolina

SOON it will be Christmas again. I can always tell by the scent of apples in the air…

It's been that way for a long time now—all because I once had a grandmother who rode streetcars and buses and peeled apples like no one I've ever known.

My Grandma Jones was small and thin, had pernicious anemia and a bad heart. But what she wanted to do she did—and she had a fine old time doing it!

She never learned how to drive, so if she wanted to visit someone, take in a show or do a little shopping, she nearly always took the bus or a streetcar (she was a real genius at transferring from one to another).

One of my most vivid memories of Grandma comes from the 1930s, when I was a kid and Christmas was coming. In those days, she lived with us in a little house in South Gate, California.

Grandma loved to shop, so, in less than an hour, she could be in Long Beach by bus or Huntington Park by streetcar. To her, these were "one-apple trips".

When something special came along—like Christmas—she'd make a day of it and take a "two-apple trip" on the old "J" car into Los Angeles. Sometimes, if I'd been especially good, she would take me along.

I always looked forward to those two-apple trips, and the one before Christmas was the best of all. Boarding the streetcar, Grandma took a window seat while I sat on the aisle.

A Ribbon of Red

She'd spread a flowered handkerchief on her lap. Then she'd take an apple out of the sack and hand it to me to polish on my shirt while she rummaged in her old black purse for the knife.

That knife had character. It was small, with a mother-of-pearl handle yellowed with age and two blades blackened with apple acid. Looking over the tops of her rimless glasses, Grandma would hold the apple in one hand and begin peeling with the other.

> *"She'd make a day of it—a two-apple trip on the old 'J' car…"*

It was wondrous to watch. Slowly, with the care of a surgeon, she'd slide that blade under the shiny red skin. A slowly lengthening half-inch peel twisted and bobbed with the sway of the streetcar until finally it fell into her lap, all in one piece.

Jack Westhead; inset: Ewing Galloway

***APEELING MEMORY.* When Tom Harvill's grandmother, like the one pictured above, took the bus or streetcar, she measured the trip in apples.**

Then came the slicing. One for me and one for her—sweet white wedges dripping with juice—till all that was left was a sliver of core. Last (and best) came the peel. That was all mine.

It had a flavor all its own—tart and slightly metallic from the blade of that old penknife. For me, that taste had more Christmas in it than all the decorated windows and sidewalks full of people slipping past our streetcar.

I made the peel last as long I could, but it was a long ride. By the time we passed through Huntington Park, Grandma was working on our second apple. Later, coming home from a two-apple trip, I'd be one sleepy kid.

I remember the sound of the wheels rattling on the rails as I thought about the department store windows full of new toys and the sticky candy cane some skinny Santa Claus had given me. But most of all, I remember falling asleep in Grandma Jones' lap while her hand, smelling faintly of apples, smoothed my hair.

Streetcars are no longer around these days and buses are fewer. Grandma Jones has been gone for nearly 25 years now, but whenever Christmas is near, I find myself thinking of her.

Packed away in a box in my closet, I have some of her things: an old wristwatch, a few flowered handkerchiefs and that penknife. They're not worth much, really.

But every year after Thanksgiving has come and gone and I'm feeling a little depressed with all the holiday hustle and bustle, I take down that old box, spread the things out on my desk and suddenly, I'm back on a rickety streetcar heading into downtown Los Angeles.

Outside, the sidewalks are filled with people and packages, and the holiday decorations are up. Next to me, rocking back and forth with the motion of the streetcar, is Grandma Jones, looking over her glasses and calmly peeling away.

There's a scent of apples in the room and, right then and there, it's Christmas the way it used to be. ▲

IT'S ALMOST CHRISTMAS! **When the tinsel went on, and most of the ornaments had been hung, the next step was for Dad to plug in the lights. Then everyone stood back and *oohed* and *aahed* as the room was bathed in soft color, and silver glistened from the tree. It was a magical time.**

Chapter Three

'The Best Tree Ever!'

As you'll recall in the next several pages, every family has its own special way of enjoying the Christmas tree.

First is the matter of when your tree goes up. In some families, this happens soon after Thanksgiving, so the tree can be enjoyed for a whole month. In other homes, decorating the tree is a Christmas Eve tradition. Everyone pitches in while sampling Mom's array of Christmas cookies washed down with eggnog.

Then there are families with little children who wake up on Christmas morning to the miracle of not only presents, but a fully decorated tree that wondrously appeared overnight.

We were a "Christmas Eve" family while I was growing up, but I think it was more out of economic necessity than anything else. Dad would wait until suppertime on the night before Christmas, then drive over to see the tree vendors when they were ready to close up and go home. If they'd been lucky, only a few scraggly, deformed, lopsided trees remained on the lot.

Dad Was "Branch Manager"

Dad would pick out the best of the rejects, offer the man 25¢, tie it to the roof of our Willys and head home. Once there, he'd spend an hour creating a tree we could be proud of. He'd prune here and lop off a branch there, then use a drill to insert them in spaces that needed help. Only God can make a tree...but Oscar Strock didn't shy away from offering a helping hand.

He'd haul the tree into the living room, then slowly rotate it until Mom decided how it looked best. Even with all his work, there was always an ugly side that needed to be hidden.

Dad was also in charge of putting up the lights. If one bulb on the string was loose or blown, the whole works went out. When that happened, Dad set to the tedious task of hunting down the bum bulb, starting at one end and, bulb by bulb, testing each socket with a new bulb.

No matter which end he started with, the dead bulb was always at the other end. To make matters worse, he had wired several strings together. Instead of checking a dozen bulbs, he had to work his way through 50 or 60.

Both Mom and Dad remembered their own childhood trees, by the way, which were illuminated with real candles. Those were some nervous Christmases.

When the lights were in place and working, Mom, my sister and I would hang the ornaments. Mostly they were more fragile than eggshells and shattered into scores of tiny pieces when dropped. The sturdier ones went on the lower branches, and any cat owner knows why. Cats love to practice their tennis serves on Christmas ornaments.

Homemade Ornaments

In those Depression days, people made many of their own decorations. We strung popcorn and cranberries on strong thread. It was slow work, but it kept us kids busy for hours. We also made paper chains with red, green and white paper, gluing each link together with flour-and-water paste.

One year we tried marshmallows for ornaments. As they gradually vanished, Mom blamed Mary and me. We denied everything, pointing out Dad's fondness for marshmallows. He blamed the cat.

Ornaments could also be made from walnut shell halves painted gold or silver, or pinecones with paint-frosted edges. People living near southern-Atlantic beaches collected sand dollars which, with a little paint, became elegant decorations.

One Christmas tree ornament I miss is the old-time tinfoil icicle. Today's plastic stuff doesn't have enough weight to hang right and slips off the tree every time someone walks by. Besides, you can't pick it off the tree and save it for next year.

"If one bulb on the string was blown, the rest went out..."

The final touch was the tall spiky ornament that slipped over the topmost twig to crown the tree. Dad, a veteran of World War I, always called it "the Kaiser Wilhelm" because it looked like the spike atop German helmets from that era.

Finally, we'd plop down in chairs and silently admire the tree. Soon someone would sigh and say, "That's the best tree ever!" And we'd all agree. Until next year. *—Clancy Strock*

Grandpa's Magic Planted Lifelong Memory

By Gene DuVall, Eureka, California

EVERY CHRISTMAS, my hometown of Rising Sun, Indiana erected a huge Christmas tree in the bandstand area downtown.

The tree was tall and bushy, but it wasn't clear to a boy of 4 just how it got there. For several years, I believed some of Santa's elves placed the tree there and trimmed it for us to look at.

Back around 1929, Grandpa would take me to town for an ice cream soda every Saturday afternoon in his old Dodge four-door sedan. It had iron wheels, a radiator cap like a huge gun sight and a tinny horn I loved to blow whenever Grandpa wasn't looking.

One December Saturday as we passed the bandstand and Christmas tree, I asked how the tree got there.

"Didn't you know I plant a magic pinecone there every year 2 weeks before Christmas?" he asked. "It grows overnight!"

My eyes grew wide and I begged him to let me help plant the magic pinecone next year.

"Certainly," he said. "But that's a year off. Are you sure you'll remember by then?"

Reminded of Promise

Winter snow melted, spring flowers bloomed, summer's hot days ripened into fall, and before I knew it, Christmas was 2 weeks away.

Grandpa picked me up to get our ice cream sodas, and on the way, I reminded him of his promise. He had a hunch I was going to ask him.

He produced a beautiful fat pinecone from his coat pocket. "When we finish our sodas, we'll go plant this," he said.

"Great!" I enthused. "Can we watch it grow, Grandpa?"

"I'm afraid not," he answered. "It grows overnight and it's much too cold to sit out there at night.

"Besides, the tree may not grow if it knows someone is watching. And if it doesn't grow, no one would get to look at the beautiful lights and tinsel. You wouldn't want that to happen, now would you?" Grandpa inquired seriously.

"Oh, no," I replied. "Can we come back tomorrow morning to see if it grew?" He promised me we would after breakfast.

When Gus, the fountain owner, brought our sodas, I told him Grandpa and I were going to plant the magic pinecone for the new Christmas tree.

Scott Anderson; inset: Gail Denham

***TALL TALE.* A "downtown" Christmas tree like the one above made memories for Gene DuVall, who recalls trees that brightened his hometown whenever he sees a pinecone.**

Grandpa looked at Gus and winked, "See, I have the magic cone here in my pocket."

Gus laughed and said he hoped the tree would be as nice as the one last year. "It will be," I promised him, "maybe even better."

After finishing our treat, Grandpa took a small shovel out of the car and we walked to the bandstand. In the center of the bandstand area was a large flowerpot in which someone had previously planted daffodils.

Among the bulbs, Grandpa dug a hole large enough for the pinecone. He let me take the cone out of his pocket and put it in the hole.

We both covered it and tamped it down.

Standing back and observing our handiwork, Grandpa remarked, "Now all we have to do is wait until tomorrow to see if the magic cone works."

He never told me that the town's street crew would be there that afternoon to put up the real tree.

On Sunday morning, I was so excited I could hardly finish my breakfast. Mom and Dad were all smiles when I told them what Grandpa and I had done.

What Would They See?

We bundled up and headed for Main Street. As we approached the bandstand, there, as big as life itself, was the beautiful Christmas tree.

"Grandpa!" I shouted, " the magic cone worked!"

There were at least 20 people standing around the tree and admiring it.

Fortunately for Grandpa, the workmen had put the flowerpot under the bandstand and out of sight. I told the crowd how Grandpa and I planted the magic cone the day before. He was grinning from ear to ear and no one let on it didn't happen that way.

For the next 3 years, Grandpa and I planted the magic pinecone that gave our town a fully decorated Christmas tree, and I felt like a hero.

In the summer of the fourth year after the first planting, my grandpa died. From then on, the city had to erect its own tree.

I often think about Grandpa. And every year about 2 weeks before Christmas, I wonder if he's still grinning from ear to ear somewhere up there, at the memory of a little boy and the magic in a simple pinecone. ▲

J.C. Allen and Son

TREE SHOPPING. **Years ago, the search for the perfect Christmas tree started with a drive in the country. Trees grew in the woods, not city lots.**

Tenacious Teen Tackled Tremendous Tree

By Margaret Dalton, Huntsville, Alabama

DADDY ALWAYS took us out to the country to select just the right tree. Then he'd cut it down, bring it home and we'd all have the pleasure of decorating it. I always admonished him to get one that would touch the ceiling. I liked a lot of tree.

One year, when I was a teenager and driving the family car, it seemed Daddy was especially busy. "Come on," I told Momma one day. "We're going out to get our tree. It'll be a nice surprise for Daddy," I said. "That way he won't have to worry about it."

My mother was aghast at such a thought, but I had a lot of confidence. Hadn't I been with Daddy all those other times? It seemed simple enough to me. So I put Momma in the car one snowy afternoon, gathered up Daddy's hatchet, his saw and some rope and confidently started for the country.

Cedar Looked Perfect

I had no idea where to look. So I watched for trees as I drove along. Soon I spotted a beautifully shaped cedar on top of a hill along the road. It looked perfect, like it could touch the ceiling. There was no need to look further. Mother was still nervous about the whole thing. "Just sit in the car and I'll chop it down," I said. "Don't worry."

I got the hatchet and saw and scrambled up the snowy hill to the tree. With hatchet in hand, I took a mighty swing. Was I ever shocked when my teeth clattered and my whole body vibrated!

I was all of 5 feet tall and weighed a hefty 94 pounds. All that I had done was put a little scar on the tree trunk. After a little thought, I decided to use the saw. It bounced from place to place so much I couldn't seem to make any headway. I finally made a slit and began to saw back and forth. But then the saw stuck dead tight in that tree.

By that time, the tree didn't look quite as pretty as it had at first, but I was determined not to admit defeat.

I hacked and hacked and finally got the saw loose. I was sweating and praying as hard as I'd ever prayed in my life. After what seemed like hours—I still don't quite know how it happened unless God got on the job in a hurry—I pushed that tree over.

The tree was too big to carry, so I rolled it down to the car. I looped the rope around the bottom branches and secured it to the bumper. We started slowly home, dragging that tree behind us. The road was muddy and full of slush. When we finally rolled into the driveway, the tree

"I gathered up Daddy's hatchet and headed for the country..."

was caked with dirty slush from top to bottom.

When Daddy came home, he was so surprised all he could say was, "Why, honey, how did you do that?"

I didn't really know how I had done it.

He made a stand for the cedar and shook out as much mud as he could. Then he had to cut off several feet of the tree in order to get it into the house. We turned the dirty side to the wall and played Christmas carols while we decorated it.

Now and then all through the holidays, we could hear particles of mud trickling onto the packages beneath the tree.

Daddy's saw ended up rusted. His hatchet was somewhere out there in the country. My mother had been taken on a strange outing. And I felt like every bone in my body was broken.

Yet that was the prettiest Christmas tree we ever had. ▲

H. Armstrong Roberts

HOMEWARD BOUND. **This youngster will haul the tree home on his Flexible Flyer—not behind an auto, as eager Margaret Dalton did!**

'Hi Ho, Hi Ho, A Giant Tree To Go!'

By Mary Anne Putnam
Urichsville, Ohio

IN 1960, we purchased an abandoned strip-mined 140-acre farm in southeastern Ohio. The coal company had mined part of the property and made rudimentary reclamation on the rest. This included planting a mixture of pine and black locust trees, which flourished.

My husband and I are the parents of 11 children, and back then, he was working long hours to provide for us. He usually came home in the dark, and the children began to worry when he'd be able to get our Christmas tree.

The Saturday before Christmas, they decided to "help Dad" by going for the tree themselves. After giving me many assurances that only the eldest would use the ax, the five older children marched out in the gently falling snow and up the hill to where the prettiest pines grew.

I tended the younger ones and watched the others troop up the hill and into the trees. Large feathery flakes were falling, so I bundled up the children and took them outside for a romp in the snow. All the while, though, I kept the piney hillside in view.

Worry Set in

After an hour or so, we came back inside, where I divided my attention between the younger children and the pine woods beyond the window.

Another hour passed, and the littlest children snuggled in for a nap. I started supper, still keeping an eye on that hillside. I was becoming worried, alternating between self-blame and prayer as I turned the pot roast.

I shouldn't have let them go! What on earth could have happened to them? Wouldn't one come back for help if something was wrong? I would have rushed out to look, but the houseful of smaller children kept me back.

Should I call the neighbors? My husband?

I took one last look out the window before calling my husband home. Suddenly, I sighted the children's bright knit caps, scarves and mittens! But barely.

Archive Photos/Lambert

SANTA'S HELPERS. **It only took two to handle this tree, but when Mary Anne Putnam's kids headed for the woods to bring back a tree, they brought back a *tree*! Dad admitted it was the best tree they ever had. But, aren't they all?**

The children were almost obscured by the branches of the gigantic tree they were lugging.

They formed a line with the youngest carrying the smallest part of the tree. The children struggled valiantly down the hill, pausing several times to rest. When they finally made it to the front yard, they all just sat down in the snow—exhausted and so proud.

"The children struggled valiantly down the hill..."

I couldn't believe my eyes! That tree was enormous.

"Look, Dad!"

The children were bustled inside, warmed, rested and waiting when our pickup pulled into the driveway. They rushed to open the door. "Did you see the tree, Dad?" they chorused.

Their father made a grand production out of inspecting the entire length of the tree, studying it carefully. "Why, I believe that's the prettiest Christmas tree I've ever seen," he pronounced. "How did it get here? It would take a giant to carry this."

"We did it, Dad!" the oldest proclaimed.

"That's sure a load off my mind!" their father declared. "I didn't know how I was going to get our tree this year."

Three times, he had to cut off sections from the bottom of the tree before we could squeeze it through the front door. The only spot in the house where it would fit was by the curving staircase to the second floor.

For the remainder of the evening, the children paused often to admire "their tree", envisioning what it would look like in the glory of its holiday decorations.

That year, the tree didn't come down for 3 weeks after Christmas. And even then, the children hated to see it go. So my husband stood it in the backyard, where it served the birds all winter with popcorn, suet and cranberry treats. ▲

These Decorations Were Delicious

By Rose Guarino Cianchetti, Wading River, New York

THE PIRROTTAS were the lone merchants on an otherwise residential street in the Bensonhurst section of Brooklyn back in the early 1940s. My family and I lived on that street, right next door to their fruit and vegetable store. Each morning at 4 a.m., Mr. Pirrotta would trudge to the market in the city to carefully select his wares for the day.

Each year, a couple of weeks before Christmas, a supply of freshly cut trees would arrive, and Mr. Pirrotta would arrange them in front of the store, leaning them against the rail fence of our house. The overwhelmingly fragrant scent of the pine needles would magically turn the cold brownstone of our homes and the concrete street into a neighborhood of warmth and good cheer.

Fragrant Fruit Lent Scent

The Pirrottas lived in back of the store with their three daughters and two sons. A welcome was always extended to me when they decorated their tree. Records of jolly carols blasted from the phonograph as they picked the plumpest and most colorful fruits from the stand in front of the store.

Pears, apples and grape clusters were hung by their stems on the tree. String was threaded through each tangerine, releasing a sweet aroma. Gingerbread cookies nestled in the branches. Popcorn and cranberries were draped in loops.

Cornucopias, cone-shaped holders fashioned by the children, were filled with nuts, raisins and hard candies. Hot chestnuts were roasted in the oven for all the young tree-trimmers to enjoy. There was lots of sampling of the "ornaments" in the process of decorating. Friends poured in to admire the tree that was so rich in its simplicity.

It was a tree decorated in the true spirit of Christmas—a tree that offered gifts for all to enjoy. ▲

ORNAMENTAL SALAD. **When Rose Pirrotta (offering grapes to Rose Cianchetti) and her family decorated the tree, it was a tasty time. Bob Cianchetti already knew that, as he gobbled up a sample in Brooklyn in 1947.**

Hide-and-Seek at Tree Lot Left Fragrant Memories

LOTS O' TREES. **A city lot became a magical playground when Christmas rolled around.**

IN 1955, I was 8 years old, and my family lived in the south suburbs of Chicago. This year, my 5-year-old sister, Nancy, and I were going with Dad to pick out our Christmas tree. We waited impatiently for him to come home from work, and as he ate his supper, we asked every 5 minutes if it was time to go.

Finally, Mom bundled us up and off we went into the night in search of the perfect Christmas tree.

The lot was decorated with multicolored lights strung across the front and sides. But the back portion of the lot was dark and mysterious, and the trees back there were still bundled up with twine.

Dad wasn't a fussy person, except when it came to picking out a Christmas tree. He'd look at 10 to 20 trees before he made his choice.

So, while Dad looked at the trees, Nancy and I played among them, hiding from each other. The greenness of the trees, the scent of pine and the colored lights reflecting off the snow were magical.

We ran from tree to tree, burrowing into the soft, cold, fresh-smelling branches. When Dad finally made his choice, we took a small branch with us in the car to enjoy its aroma all the way home. *—Michael Scott*
Brevard, North Carolina

Grandpa's Tree Lights Were a 1920s First

WHEN I WAS a child in the 1920s, my grandfather had the first electric-lighted outdoor Christmas tree in our small Connecticut town.

There was a tall pine in his yard. He mounted colored lights on a long board, climbed a tall ladder and nailed it high in the tree. It was just a single line of lights, but it could be seen almost all over town, causing quite a bit of interest and comment.

—Mrs. Robert Collett
Piscataway, New Jersey

Tumbling Tumbleweeds Made Terrific Tree

WE HAD an odd but beautiful Christmas tree in 1953.

My folks had a farm then, near Kingsburg, California. My brother had just married and he and his wife, Betty, were temporarily living with the folks. Betty had severe allergies, including all types of cedar and pine.

So it looked like we wouldn't have a Christmas tree that year...right? Wrong!

Mom sent us out to round up three different sized tumbleweeds, which she stacked atop each other and spray-painted white. We then decorated it like any other tree.

It was different, but it looked wonderful. That taught me to never underestimate the ingenuity of a loving mother!

—Jo Crane
Jamestown, California

Ingenious Dad Mops Up Christmas Cheer

IN 1932, my dad recruited me and my 8-year-old sister to help with the annual tree hunt near our apartment in New York City.

Like everyone else during the Depression, we had little money. But from experience, Dad had learned that tree prices were always marked down late on Christmas Eve.

On this particular night, however, we were too late. We walked in vain for blocks to find a tree...any tree. There were none left—everything had been sold. All that was left at the deserted lots were twigs and shavings left over from trimmings. Undaunted, Dad filled our arms with some of that leftover greenery and we hurried home.

He called to Mother, "Say, where is that floor mop of yours?" Mom produced the mop and Dad drilled holes in the handle, which we carefully filled with boughs.

During my life, I've enjoyed scores of Christmas trees. But the one I best remember is that 4-foot beauty my dad fashioned in the kitchen of our New York City apartment...the one with the yellow trunk.

—Kenneth Larkin
Punta Gorda, Florida

Meager Tree "Sticks" in This Couple's Memory

OUR FIRST CHILD was born in 1960, just weeks after I graduated from college and started my first teaching job. A student loan for summer school left my wife and me with only enough money to rent a trailer to move.

As the holidays approached, we could see no way we could afford a Christmas tree. But one morning in December, as I was leaving for school, my wife asked me to cut across the nearby football field on my way home and drag back a fallen tree branch she had seen there. She said that would be our Christmas tree!

I thought she was fooling and didn't bring it home. But she was serious, so that night after dinner, I went into the field and dragged the branch home. I was too embarrassed to do it in the daylight.

My wife, bless her, used an artist's brush to painstakingly paint the branch and twigs white. When decorated, that branch turned into an attractive, but certainly unique, Christmas tree.

Many Christmases have passed since then, but this tree is the one that remains clearest in our memories.

—Robert Pearson, Fort Dodge, Iowa

WELL, IT'S REAL. **Don Condon of Janesville, Wisconsin "built" this Christmas tree years back for his daughter who gave him a hard time about his artificial tree. Nothing like Christmas to stir the imagination.**

FAMILY TRADITION. **Helping get the Christmas tree provides a youngster with precious memories.**

Christmas Tree Trek Was A Great Time with Grandpa

WHENEVER Christmas approaches, my mind travels back some 75 years and thousands of miles to my boyhood in rural Wisconsin. Much of my time was spent on my grandparents' farm.

At the end of summer, Grandpa would take time from his farm duties to lead me into the woods to find and mark our perfect Christmas tree.

Grandmother would pack us a lunch of bread, cheese and chunks of sausage wrapped in a white dishcloth and placed in a 2-quart syrup pail. We tramped through the woods inspecting many potential trees, until we were hungry.

Grandpa would build a fire, then go to a nearby stream and fill the syrup pail with water. He pulled a cloth sack of coffee from his pocket and brewed coffee so strong I couldn't drink it! I was content with the fresh cold water.

After we ate, Grandpa would lean back against a log and I rested my head in his lap. He told of his experiences coming to Wisconsin from his homeland of Germany. Gradually, his voice would fade and we'd both fall asleep. Sometime later, we would awake and resume our tree search.

As those afternoons waned, I wondered whether we'd ever find that perfect tree. Then, magically, there it was! Our search was over, and we could head home. Months later, just before Christmas, Grandpa would cut the tree and pull it through the snow to the house.

The two of us made our late-summer expedition from the time I was 5 years old until I was 9. It wasn't until years later that I realized he always knew beforehand exactly where that tree was located.

—L.A. Wincentsen, Vallejo, California

Kids Needled by Dried-Out Tree

EACH DECEMBER, my sister and I would pester our dad to search the back 40 for our Christmas tree. There were always a few small cedars growing somewhere on our 300-acre farm, generally trees that had been planted by birds or wind.

One particular year, Dad tried something different. He'd dropped into the local co-op and found an unbelievably low-priced imported Christmas tree. He brought it home and surprised us.

This tree was not our usual fluffy-branched cedar. It was short-needled, just built for decorating. My sister and I hung lights, icicles and many shiny balls on the branches. We were extra-attentive and never forgot to check the water level, hoping to keep it fresh longer.

But after a few days, we noticed needles dropping off. As we skipped through the living room, we could hear a shower of needles falling on the tissue-paper tree skirt. As the days went on, even the dog trotting past caused an avalanche of needles.

By December 23, we could have counted the remaining needles. The family became more depressed as that tree turned more and more ugly. Finally, Dad could stand it no longer.

He donned his sheepskin coat, his caps with earflaps, his boots and gloves and set out into the cold blowing snow. Meanwhile, my sister and I "undecorated" the bare branches of the store-bought tree and set the decorations aside.

Dad returned with a cedar and set it in place, then we again hung the shiny ornaments on the branches. It would not have won a prize in a "beautiful Christmas tree" contest, but our family appreciated it more than any other tree.

—Louise Beehler, Anderson, Indiana

HOMEGROWN. **Dad's "store-bought" tree didn't measure up, so he headed to the back 40 for this beauty, and it was, of course, the best tree ever.**

"The Perfect Tree" Was Boyhood Quest

A DENSE CLOUD of poverty covered southwest Washington during the 1930s, and everyone I knew owned a thick slice of it.

Poor as we were, we always managed to put up a nice Christmas tree. As a boy, I always remained on the lookout for the perfect Christmas tree while hiking in the woods, no matter what time of year.

One spring day amid the scent of fresh evergreen, I finally discovered the perfect tree—a small cone-shaped white fir with perfect symmetry. I coveted it so much that I pulled it up like pigweed and took it home. Much of the root broke, but I knew it would grow. Perfect trees don't die.

When I got home, Mom called us for lunch, so I dropped the tree in the yard. There it rested through lunch and the next 3 days. I rediscovered it and went for a shovel.

"It won't grow," said my father, and a tiny voice in my conscience told me he was right—I'd been lazy and left the job half done. Chagrined, I planted the little tree in my mother's iris bed and watered it. I watered it again the next day and then turned it over to the tender care of neglect.

It survived. Uncrowded, the symmetrical growth continued. In 2 years, the 18-inch seedling was tall enough to support a string of lights. We added strings of lights annually, and after a few years, we needed a ladder to decorate it. The tree stretched higher and higher, towering above the roof.

My perfect Christmas tree was never brought indoors to stand over brightly wrapped presents, but it remains my all-time favorite. *—Dale Shearer*
Valley, Washington

Two Trees Did Double Duty

BACK IN the 1950s, our family got larger and our living room seemed to be smaller. So, one Christmas, we went out in the country and found two trees that looked alike. We brought them home, and I cut the branches off half of each tree.

I put one tree inside the front window and the other one outside, making it look like one tree. We decorated both sides. This gave us much more room in the house—and it drew a lot of comments from those who saw it!

—Roland Rentz, Hector, Minnesota

GREAT TREE HUNT. **Sean Cullen really got into the 1958 Christmas season when he searched for the perfect tree at Bob's Market (below), says Mom Leona of Melrose, Massachusetts. Sean, then 8, found what he was looking for and pulled it home on his sled (left) along the snow-covered streets of Melrose. The search for the perfect tree is a tradition for many families.**

Measuring Mother Made A Picture-Perfect Tree

By Cynthia Young, Monterey, California

OUR LIVING ROOM framed our Christmas tree like a picture. Each year's tree had to be just the right height and width, and back in the early 1940s, Mother saw to that with a special measuring technique.

From tree lot to tree lot we'd go, and Mother would hold her hand a couple of inches above her head to gauge the height of the trees she examined. For the width, she'd extend her arms. The widest branch tips should reach no farther than her wrists.

"The tree doesn't have to be perfect; we can fill in the bare spots," she'd say. So we always came home with extra branches. Mom drilled into the trunk and inserted a branch where needed. With a little garden tape and a supporting wire here and there, our tree could have won a contest for symmetry.

Decorating Soon Began

Once this perfect specimen was placed on a low box and the stand wedged level with folded newspaper, the decorating began.

I learned early that each ornament was placed according to color, size and shape. My first attempts were with unbreakable ornaments and foil-covered papier-mache bells. From Dad's arms, I'd clip a bird on the topmost little branch below the spire.

> *"We can always fill in the bare spots..."*

Then the real fun began. Starting from the lowest branches, the fragile tinsel was very carefully hung so it wouldn't touch the branch below. This took several evenings to complete, but when we were finished, the colored ornaments peeked out from behind the hundreds of silver strands.

Everyone Rushed Outside

Then Dad would set up his floodlight (we never had strings of lights on the tree), and the blinds were raised. All of us hurried out to the sidewalk to see the finished masterpiece. It was beautiful!

The process was reversed on New Year's Day. Every strand of tinsel was removed, carefully looped over the cardboard holders and slipped back into the narrow boxes.

Mother lives with us now, and I put up a small tree in her room each year. Among her tissue-wrapped ornaments lay the flat boxes of much-tarnished tinsel. "It just didn't seem quite right to throw it away," she said. ▲

NOW, THAT'S A TREE! **When Cynthia Young (above) helped decorate the tree, things had to be done just so. After Mom got through creating a veritable symbol of symmetry, Dad hung the tinsel, strand by strand, making sure none touched the branch below. When the tree came down, the tinsel was removed, strand by strand, and saved for next Christmas.**

THAT'S MOM? **A brief modeling career when she was a teenager in Scranton, Pennsylvania led Suzanne Bevan to pose for this 1960 ad promoting genuine Reynolds aluminum Christmas trees. Suzanne, of Fredericksburg, Virginia, says her kids laugh at the ad today. "The joke's on them," she says. "I think these trees are coming back!"**

Search for Tree Was Summer-Long Project

By Lee Misner, Anderson, California

MY DAD was a lumberjack in remote Upper Michigan, and because of his occupation, he could search all summer long for the "perfect tree".

Just before Christmas Eve in 1950, Dad decided it was time to trek into the woods to cut our tree. It was tradition in our house to put up and trim the tree on Christmas Eve, and this year would be the first time we kids were allowed to go along to help Dad cut the tree. Dark came early, and the night was cold and crisp.

A full moon filled the evening with shadows and made light dance across the snow. After bundling up in long johns, jeans, long-sleeved shirts, heavy boots, hats, mufflers and mittens, we started off to cut the perfect tree that Dad had staked out earlier.

I can still hear our boots crunching in the snow and see our breath making fog. I remember feeling scared of the shadows, and yet being filled with awe at the beautiful winter night around us. After trudging for some distance, Dad led us off the path through the quiet, deep snow. We whispered as we walked, because no one wanted to break the spell.

"With three excited children cheering him on, Dad cut it down..."

Standing before us, with snow-covered branches in the moonlight, was the perfect tree. Dad shook it to knock off the snow, and with three excited children cheering him on, he cut it down.

Whoosh, down it came, onto the soft snow. Dad tied a rope around the trunk and off we started for home.

Dad pulled the tree along on the snow, and every step of the way, we begged to put up the tree that night. Even though it wasn't Christmas Eve, Dad agreed—perhaps because he was sorry there would be no presents to go under it.

That tall wonderful-smelling tree dripped melting snow all over the floor. Bushy branches waited eagerly for the few Christmas ornaments that we had managed to accumulate over the years.

Many trees and better Christmases have come and gone in the years since then, but my memory of that tree and the wonderful walk in the woods will always remain with me. ▲

German "Pyramid Tree" Complex Yet Fun

I HAVE wonderful memories of childhood Christmases, but the most fun I ever had at Christmas came after I was married.

My husband, Ed, had a wooden Christmas tree that was handmade in Germany in 1911. Called a "pyramid tree", it consisted of more than 1,000 pieces, and I always loved to set it up with Ed.

All the pieces were individually wrapped, and it took 2 days just to unpack everything. In a week, we'd have it all up, including the train moving around its base. Since it took so long to put that complex tree up, Ed and I never dreamed of taking it down until February 1. Much as I loved to assemble the tree, the fun went away in taking it down.

When the candles on the tree are lit (see the photo at right), the vanes on top turn.

—Helen Neumann, Sun City, Arizona

ASSEMBLY REQUIRED. **It was a real project putting up this German "pyramid tree", says Helen Neumann, but the results made it worthwhile.**

Christmas Trees "In the Bag" for Prairie Relatives

IN THE late 1930s, when I was a child, there wasn't much money to spend for Christmas. I'm sure our holidays then were pretty meager by today's standards, but to me, they were joyful and wondrous. Perhaps it was because of the sharing.

We lived in northern Minnesota, where fresh fragrant pine trees were plentiful for the cutting. When we went out to cut our Christmas tree, Dad always cut two more.

Mom would wrap the trees in burlap and sew the burlap shut with her darning needle. She would attach a tag and send them by mail to our grandma and an aunt and uncle who lived on the western-Minnesota prairie. Trees were not abundant there, so my parents made sure the relatives had a nice Christmas tree for the holidays.

Even though we didn't have much money, I often marvel how rich we were in things that counted. My parents were generous with those types of things, and I've tried to pass this feeling of wonder, joy and sharing down to my children and grandchildren.

—Louise Thomsen, Marble Falls, Texas

***TOUCH OF HOME.* His little tree lit up Howard Maddux's Christmas.**

Pacific Christmas Brightened By Tree from Home

DURING WORLD War II, I spent quite some time on Saipan in the Pacific. Christmas always meant a lot to me and I was really thrilled when, in December 1944, I received a small Christmas tree from home. I decorated it and placed my presents under it. Even though I was about 7,500 miles from home on Christmas Day, that little tree sure brightened my holiday. It truly was the best tree ever. *—Howard Maddux St. Peters, Missouri*

❄

Victorian Ornaments Contributed to Magic of Tree

ON CHRISTMAS MORNINGS during the 1920s, I was not allowed to come downstairs until Santa Claus blew his horn prior to leaving via the living room fireplace and chimney. What a marvelous surprise once I came down! What an unbelievable sight! The tree and gifts had appeared like magic.

Our ornaments had been handed down from Victorian times. The most unusual and precious were a pear, peach and banana made of real fruit skins somehow stuffed with a kind of cotton. Today, these ornaments are well over 100 years old and still look very good.

Not only did Santa bring the tree when I was young, he also made it disappear after the holidays. But when I was about 6 or 7, a mysterious written message arrived giving me special permission to *undecorate* the tree because I had been so good.

It was quite an idea to provide an extra pair of hands for a task that lacked the excitement of the previous preparations! *—Margaret Bacon Williamsville, New York*

It Was Tinsel Time When Dad Did His Decorating

OF ALL my Christmas memories, the most wonderful are of our trees and Dad's painstaking work to beautify them.

First, he'd pick out the tallest, most fragrant, bushiest evergreen he could find. The piney aroma would permeate the house, blending with the delectable baking in the oven.

And then would come Dad's careful decorating. Tinsel was the cheapest ornament and, I still believe, the most beautiful. It was usually 10¢ a box and even cheaper on sale. Dad liked it in abundance, and he insisted it be draped just so...strand upon strand with no careless tossing. It took hours!

When completed, the tree was a silvery sparkling forest. We didn't have many colored lights, but the beauty of the ones we did have was mirrored in the tinsel...and in the eyes of Dad's three adoring daughters.

—Marjorie Smith, Peoria, Illinois

***TINSELMANIA.* Her dad liked lots of tinsel, says Marjorie Smith.**

Secret Sleigh Bells Signaled Start Of Christmas Fun

***CHRISTMASES PAST* live on when Lynn Kemp celebrates the season.**

IT WAS Christmas Eve in 1947. We had just moved to an area of northern Wisconsin that had not yet received electricity. Money was scarce, and my sister and I knew there wouldn't be many presents under the tree.

We decorated the tree as best we could with shiny ornaments that had belonged to our grandmother, but without colored lights, the tree looked rather sad.

After supper, we cleaned up the kitchen. Daddy went out to get some firewood and came back shortly to announce that he had "heard" sleigh bells and reindeer hoofbeats.

When Dad heard those sounds, it meant it was time to see what was under the tree. As I stepped through the doorway, the most magnificent sight greeted my 14-year-old eyes. Our sad little tree now stood bathed in the warm flickering light of many tiny candles.

I can't tell you what was in the packages that year, but the tree will be engraved in my mind forever. Some of Grandmother's ornaments now adorn the branches of the tree in my parlor. Yes, the candles are on it, too.

I often wondered as a child why our father was the only one who ever heard those Christmas sounds. But after I had children of my own, I found that I had acquired this mysterious sense of hearing as well.

—Lynn Trier Kemp, Milton, Wisconsin

'Noisy Tree' Made a Snappy Christmas

By Brenda Jackson, Rogersville, Missouri

DAD, MOM AND I were quite a trio. We did everything together—movies, drives in the country on weekends and plenty of cross-country trips. I was included in all their plans. One of my most cherished memories of those days is one special Christmas.

We always got our Christmas tree early to enjoy it through the whole month before the holiday. In 1959, though, Dad must have been real flush, because we splurged and bought our tree from a lot that'd just opened. The beautiful tall pine fell open to perfection when the man cut the cords that had bound it tightly.

Dad Untangled Lights

It was unusually cold that winter, so Dad set up the tree in our living room next to the fireplace. He untangled the strings of lights and stretched them out across the floor. This was his special job each year. The lights were tested and bad bulbs replaced before he carefully strung them on the tree.

Meanwhile, Mom and I unwrapped the ornaments. Each year, new ones were added, but some of my favorites were old and just a little worn. Fragile glass balls and other ornaments in shapes of Santas, trees, stars and angels were placed just so on the limbs.

This tree was so big it needed even more decorations, so popcorn was strung and silver tinsel strands draped over every outstretched branch. As the additional trim was added, the limbs seemed to open up, as if asking to be made festive.

I could only reach so far, so I took special pride in the lower portion. I crawled under the boughs and wrapped the base in white cotton. The few gifts we already had were carried out of hiding and placed under the tree.

Admired Handiwork

When the tree was finished, Dad lit a fire in the fireplace and started the Christmas music on the record player. Mom served hot chocolate, and she and I sat in the dark as Dad plugged in the lights. It was beautiful! We gazed at our handiwork, sipping our drinks. I was content, warm and cozy.

But after about 30 minutes, the peace was suddenly broken by a loud *crack*. We sat up and stared at each other. What was that? Another pop! And another! Dad turned on the lights and we searched for the source of the noise. It didn't take long, because the pops continued and we just followed the sound.

The warmth of the room had caused the pinecones on the tree to start opening. They had been closed so tightly that I hadn't even noticed them. Nature gave us a wonderful Christmas present that year. The cones were as pretty as any of the ornaments.

> "Nature gave us a present that year..."

On Christmas morning, when I could stay in bed no longer, I'd call to Mother. No matter what time it was, she and Dad would get up and start the day. The first thing was a phone call to my grandparents, who lived only a few houses away. They were early risers, too, and as soon as they arrived, Christmas began. The presents were opened and the day was filled with visitors and cheer.

Pinecones Saved

On New Year's Day, we usually took the decorations off our tree and put them away. Dad gathered the strings of lights and put them in a box to stay tangled for 11 months.

This very special year, I saved some of the pinecones and put them away in tissue, just like the treasured glass ornaments. Each year after that, we always included them in some way.

Years later, after I was grown and Mom and Dad no longer put up a tree, they gave me the boxes with those special Christmas decorations. The first time I used them, I opened a box of ornaments and found wrapped in tissue… a pinecone.

CONIFEROUS CHRISTMAS. On Christmas 1959, Brenda Jackson and her parents got up at the crack of...well, it wasn't dawn! That's Brenda at right, wearing a new formal. She appears above, too, in later photo with her parents. Read Brenda's Christmas story and enjoy a "snap-happy" memory.

TREE OF GIFTS. **The tradition continues, says Jo Soldoff, and granddaughter Natalie enjoys it.**

Landlord's Generosity Led to Tasty Tradition

TIMES WERE TOUGH in December 1940. My husband was 22, I was 19 and we had a baby. Hank worked long hours for short pay, but still, I wanted a Christmas tree.

When Hank asked our landlord if he could cut a limb from the tree in front of our dwelling, he was told to go ahead. We put the branch in a bucket of dirt and decorated it with cars, trucks and boats Hank had carved out of balsa wood and painted.

Meanwhile, I baked colorful cookies and made candy. After some experimenting, I learned how to wrap and seal these goodies in scraps of cellophane by using a flat iron covered with towels.

We hung all our goodies on the "tree", and it really looked nice! The neighborhood children loved it most. On Christmas, they were allowed to take what they wanted, and it was a huge success!

Every year since, we've decorated a tree with tiny toys, candy and cookies. Our grandchildren and children of our friends and neighbors love our special Christmas tree because it's unusual and a long-standing tradition they're happy to be part of. *—Jo Soldoff*
Canyon Lake, California

Candlelight Warmed Young Girl's Heart

MY FIRST recollection of a Christmas tree dates back to 1910 or '11 when I was 4 or 5 years old. On the day before Christmas Eve, my brother and I were forbidden to enter the parlor, where the door was tightly closed.

The day of Christmas Eve was spent greeting all the family as they gathered for our celebration. At long last, the door was opened and the children were allowed to enter this secret room. What a marvelous sight!

There was a glowing gorgeous tree reaching to the ceiling, with a shiny ball on the topmost branch. Beautiful colored balls and tinsel garlands hung all over it. A lighted candle on the end of each branch bathed the tree and the room in warm light.

After my wonderment and surprise subsided a bit, I noticed Papa standing near the tree with a bucket of water close by, but the significance of this didn't register with me until I was much older.

No other tree ever looked as good to me as this candle-lit wonder that I remember so well. *—Dorothy Butcher*
Valley Stream, New York

Mom Made Sure Kids Had A Plum-Good Christmas

IT WAS the height of the Depression, but our home felt far from depressing as we prepared for Christmas. I didn't realize until many years later how bravely and creatively our parents worked to provide us with a happy and secure childhood. My mother's special Christmas tree was a perfect example.

There were no pines or cedars on our farm, and we had no cash to buy a Christmas tree. So my resourceful mother took a small ax and headed for the wild plum thicket. She selected a well-shaped bush with many small branches.

Bringing it into the house, she painstakingly wrapped each little branch with green crepe paper. I can see her yet, carefully cutting strips of the paper, which she then wrapped and pasted until each brown branch was green.

Mother popped a big pan of corn and we gathered 'round the cozy heating stove to string the fluffy kernels. Next, we made paper chains from the shiny pages of the Sears Roebuck Catalog.

In the years since, I've seen many beautiful Christmas trees. But Mother's tree made from nothing more than a wild plum bush, green crepe paper and lots of love will always be the best tree ever. *—Evelyn Russell*
Holdrege, Nebraska

Castor Bean Plant Saved the Day

CHRISTMAS was a bright spot amidst the snowy, windy days in Nebraska for my family during the Depression years of the 1930s.

One Christmas Eve, Mom and Dad took us kids to look for a tree, but the only two lots in town were sold out. All that we found were a few straggling needles on the trampled snow. How could we have Christmas without a Christmas tree?

The dejected looks on the faces of us little kids was more than my big sister could stand. This artistic 13-year-old came up with a solution to our problem. She asked Dad to help her cut down a dried, bleached castor bean stalk that stood 6 feet tall at the corner of our house. They brought it in and stood it in a bucket.

We carefully arranged strings of lights, green and red rope and silver icicles from the bottom to the highest branch. At the very top, we even found the perfect place to attach the tin star.

An old sheet was used to disguise the bucket stand and represent a blanket of snow. We placed our presents on the "snow"...*then* we could have Christmas! *—Tillie Bottenberg*
Los Gatos, California

Little Sister Always Knew Big Brothers Could Accomplish Miracles

DURING the Depression, Santa sometimes ran out of gifts before he got to our house, or he couldn't find where we lived. Yes, we had some lean Christmases, but one in particular remains my favorite of all.

One year during the '30s, my big brothers decided that we should have a tree like the ones they'd seen in store windows in town. On Christmas Eve morning, they insisted on going to the pasture to look for one. No evergreens grew in our area, but that wasn't about to deter them.

My mother didn't try to discourage them either. She helped button their mackinaws, fastened the chin straps of their aviator caps and saw them, somewhat reluctantly, out the door. They picked up the hatchet from the corner of the porch and marched into a skin-chapping wind, across the yard and beyond the barn. My heroes.

I believed they could accomplish miracles, and they didn't disappoint me. With numb fingers and frozen smiles, they trudged back triumphantly, dragging the dead branch of a persimmon tree.

In an already crowded front room that served as a living room and bedroom, Mother helped them set the tree in a bucket of red dirt between the bed and the stove. The narrow space it left forced us to shuffle sideways.

We decorated the naked limbs with buttons, yarn and trinkets. I found a strand of red beads and draped them across an empty branch. No ornaments have ever looked more dazzling to me.

Santa didn't come that year, but we had a tree. And I had two brothers who gave me a Christmas that I remember more vividly than any other. *—Betty Gay*
Lindsay, Oklahoma

The Weather Inside Was Frightful

By Judith Wainwright, Eagle River, Wisconsin

I'M NOT CERTAIN what prompted Mom and Dad to decide to flock our Christmas tree that first time. I suspect Dad admired a prototype in the window of a home where the tree was put up just after Thanksgiving.

He delivered capons to Milwaukee during those weeks just before the holidays and always returned home with some new decorating scheme in mind. His plan for the Christmas of 1954 was to flock our tree.

First, he brought home the cut tree. I was skeptical about the plan because the tree was a long-needled pine instead of our traditional short-needled spruce. "Your ordinary evergreen wouldn't hold the flocking as well and wouldn't be as pretty," he assured me.

"The floor, the walls and Mom's red hair were powdery white..."

Dad carried the tree to the basement, where he placed it in the stand. The next step was to spray the tree with water. Mom brought her vacuum cleaner to the basement and plugged it in. I quickly informed her that she had attached the hose to the wrong end of the cleaner.

"Nope," Mom replied optimistically. "I'm going to spray the tree white with the flocking powder. This end of the vacuum cleaner blows air out of the machine and it will blow flocking on the wet tree."

Basement Snowstorm

I wasn't sure if Mom was a bad aim, if the tree was somehow not cooperating or if the vacuum cleaner was too powerful. But the floor, the walls, the tree and even Mom's red hair were soon a powdery white. The vacuum cleaner was noisy, the flocking powder smelled like wet diapers and the air in the basement was turning snowy.

From my supervisory position on the basement steps, I began to cough.

Finally, the flocking compound was gone. The spruce was white, as was our entire basement. Our tree now reminded me of a lone evergreen laden with snow, standing erect and proud in a wintry forest.

We allowed the tree to dry. But Mom and Dad tracked a trail of new "snow" throughout the house when they brought the tree upstairs.

Dad proudly showed off two strings of tiny lights. Those and two dozen red balls were the only decorations to adorn our tree that year. The final step was to plug in a spotlight.

We turned off all the lights in the house and sat on the living room floor admiring in awe our first flocked tree. It was beautiful!

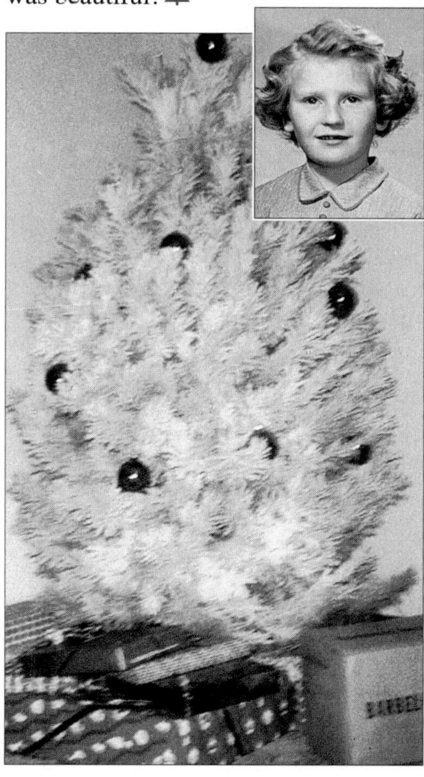

IT SNOWED! **Nope, it was just their first flocked tree, says Judith Wainwright. But it *was* an event.**

HOLIDAY HOUSE OF LIGHTS. **When Christmas rolled around, it was time to dig out the lights and decorations and make the house a lighted showplace. Good-natured competition turned the block into a great bright way that often drew folks from all over town.**

H. Armstrong Roberts

Chapter Four

Decorating Made Homes Bright

Every family has its special holiday traditions. They're what make Christmas "our" Christmas. Like precious antiques, they're handed along from generation to generation.

Some of the most memorable traditions have to do with decorating. Nearly every family I know has hand-me-down ornaments for the tree. Each one is packed with memories of happy Christmases gone by.

Many of the special ornaments my wife and I enjoy today were handmade by Peg's beloved Aunt Ella. Hours of painstaking work went into each one.

We received our first batch while living in Spain over 20 years ago. Who but thoughtful Aunt Ella would have boxed up a score of those beautiful baubles and shipped them across the ocean? We hung them on the tree and suddenly we were home again!

Last Christmas when they were hung on the tree, Aunt Ella was very much in our hearts again, along with memories of our months in Madrid.

Memories by the Boxful

Every year we dig out the boxes of Christmas gear, and the memories return. Here's a hand-knitted holiday hanging Mom made for us years ago...and an elegant door wreath created by daughter Terry...and dated tree ornaments from grandchildren...and holiday candle holders from Peg's mother.

By the end of the day, all the precious bits and pieces transform the house into our special holiday home. No one else on earth has one just like it.

Men are generally shooed away while this is going on, so their contribution happens outdoors. And, being men, they inevitably become competitive. It seems to start with festooning the fir tree in the front yard with lights. "Hey, that's really pretty! Everyone, come on outside and admire our tree!"

But halfway up the block, a neighbor not only has lights on his tree, he's outlined the roof eaves with lights, too. The competition is on!

Next year it's lights on the tree and the house *plus* an illuminated Santa in the front yard. But the neighbor cannily anticipated the move and *he's* added a Santa plus a sleigh and reindeer on the roof!

King of the Block

In every neighborhood we've ever lived, there has been one man who simply refused to be outdone. This sort of fellow has computerized lights that chase each other around the roof, a Santa that waves as he gets ready to go down the chimney, a Rudolph with blinking red nose, giant glowing candy canes, colored floodlights, twinkle-lights to the top of 60-foot pine trees and carols played over a dozen loudspeakers.

Usually the evening TV news does a special feature on his handiwork, along with the statistics about how many thousand bulbs illuminate not just the home but the entire block. The neighbors complain about the traffic, while the other men on the street sulk in their Barcaloungers, hopelessly defeated.

Each year, Peg and I reserve one night during the holidays to drive around town and see the handiwork of all these Yule-time decorators.

In Lincoln, Nebraska, there's a neighborhood in which every house has an illuminated 5-foot candy cane near the sidewalk—jolly sentries all in a row. North of Dixon, Illinois is a farmstead so lavishly decorated that people drive from 20 miles around to see it.

No matter where you are, "going out to see the lights" is the best free entertainment of the year.

Someone I know lives in a neighborhood where the men got together once a month to play cards. A new family moved in and the husband joined the card group. During the family's first fall, he casually inquired about how much outside decorating went on at Christmas in the neighborhood.

> *"When we dig out the Christmas boxes, the memories return..."*

"We have a longtime tradition here," explained one of the old-timers. "We use nothing but blue lights." The others around the table nodded in agreement.

So the new homeowner did all his outside lighting with nothing but blue bulbs. His, of course, was the only house in the neighborhood with blue lights.

As you'll read on the following pages, no matter how humble the home or poor the family, we all find a way to make home our own very special place at Christmas. Once again, we're "home for the holidays".

—Clancy Strock

'Twas the *Long* Night Before Christmas

By Patsy Potthast, Phoenix, Arizona

IN OUR FAMILY during the 1940s, it was tradition that our trees, gifts and decorations were always unseen by the children until Christmas morning. Pop would then light the tree and shout, "Okay!"

The scene was magical, but for us parents, it took a ton of work. Our long night's labors would begin with Pop balancing a plywood platform on two sawhorses. The cold fragrant tree was hauled in from beneath the cellar door, screwed into the metal stand and hoisted atop the platform.

Archive Photos/Lambert

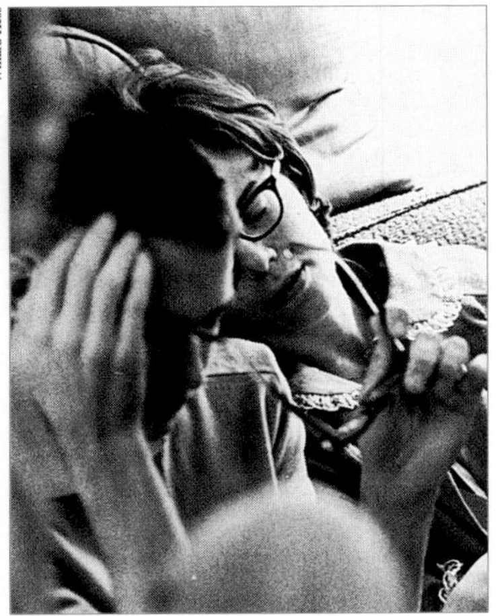

Willard Hess

***MERRY CHRISTMAZZZ.* Mom and Pop were all smiles when they finally bought all the presents, like the happy couple above. But by the time everything was ready for the kids, there was usually precious little time to sleep on Christmas Eve, and it was a weary set of parents, like those at left, who ushered in another Christmas morning. How about a nap after dinner?**

The electric lights were strung around the fluffy pine. Colored bulbs, bells and special handmade ornaments were hung one by one on the branches. Next came the tinsel, painstakingly separated and patiently hung on each branch. Candy canes were then hooked onto the branches where little hands could reach them. Finally, the angel was positioned atop the tree.

Humming carols of old, Pop tacked the train tracks to the platform as I arranged the faded cardboard houses and tiny figures to form a village. We made roads from artificial dirt and modeled salt into snowdrifts and mountainsides. The vision of our three kids' delighted faces helped us carry on.

The red brick paper was thumb-tacked around the platform to give a finished look to the village. After hiding all the empty boxes, we turned out the lights for a trial run. The tree twinkled, tinsel sparkled and the little train huffed and puffed through the village.

"Thoughts of our kids' delighted faces helped us carry on..."

Two o'clock was closing in when we tiptoed to the attic and brought down the colorfully wrapped gifts. Then there were the challenging "put-together" gifts. Nuts, bolts, wheels and handle had to be assembled into a wagon. The bicycle was an even bigger challenge. Wearily, I fumbled through the directions while Pop screwed and pliered the pieces.

Oh, for Some Sleep!

At last, drinking Santa's milk and taking a bite of his cookie, I handed Pop a reindeers' carrot to chew. Giving each other a satisfied look, we dragged our aching legs to bed. "Oh, Lord, let them sleep a ways past sunrise," was our prayer.

As Pop snored and I relaxed into my pillow, a loud crash startled me. Shaking Pop awake, I pulled him along to the stairs. As we reached the bottom step, our hearts sank.

"Oh, no!" I cried. The tree had toppled—lights, ornaments and all! An avalanche of pine needles had buried our neat little roads, and water from the tree stand had flooded the train tracks.

I began to cry, but Pop put his arm around my shoulders, reassuring me we could fix it all in time.

It was 4 a.m when Pop firmly secured the tree to the wall with rope. We picked up the ornaments and rearranged them on the tree, and I tucked the broken candy cane ends under the tinsel and camouflaged the rope with garland. By the time we dried the tracks and touched up the village, the hallway clock was striking 5 a.m. Restoration was complete!

Up the long staircase we trudged. Sleep came fast but only for a few minutes...then, there they were! Smiling, expectant faces peered down into ours. Six restless feet lined up at the stairs as Pop and I went downstairs. He reached for the switch to light the tree.

"Okay!" he called, then gave me a weary, loving wink.

***TRADITION LIVES* ON. The elaborate outdoor scene created by her father, Willie Stewart, in 1958, still gives joy to the children, says Helen Davis of Pascagoula, Mississippi. Her son Parish and his friend Ashley Parker enjoyed the decorations in 1977 (left). Helen says the tradition is being continued, now creating memories for her grandchildren.**

The Year Dad's Display Took First Place

By Carolyn Schiro, San Jose, California

EVERY CHRISTMAS from my childhood remains a wonderful memory, thanks to my dad. Christmas was his time of year, and back in 1942, he went all-out building a front-yard display like no other. A lot of people in San Francisco enjoyed it.

It all began in summer, when Dad asked if he could borrow some of my dolls. I was upset when I saw him drill holes in their bottoms so he could install electric motors to make them move.

***DADDY BOY.* That's what Carolyn Schiro called her dad, as she gave him a big smooch in 1942.**

He cut out a Victorian-style house from plywood and made furniture to go in the rooms. For the rooftop, he made a sleigh, reindeer and a Santa ready to head down the chimney.

As the months went by, Dad kept at it. Since Mom didn't sew, a neighbor friend made clothing for my dolls, transforming them into a mother, father, boy, girl and a baby.

December 1 was the night of the big unveiling, and all of our neighbors eagerly waited out front. When Dad thought it was finally dark enough, he turned on the display. It was just wonderful!

Made Mechanical Marvels

Through the parlor window of the dollhouse, we could see the mother rocking her baby. The father was sitting at a table reading the paper, his head moving from side to side. Sitting on the floor was the little boy, who was reading *The Night Before Christmas*. Nearby, his sister enjoyed a lollipop, with her hand moving the treat up and down to her mouth.

Standing at the fireplace was a little brown dog looking up the chimney and wagging his tail.

Meanwhile, up on the rooftop, Santa was about to come down the chimney. His head moved side to side and he waved his hand to passersby. Slung over his back was a big sackful of toys. Behind Santa, his lead reindeer was moving his head, eager to continue on the route.

Dad had done all the lighting, along with music—it was his best display ever!

As it grew closer to Christmas, more and more people stopped by to visit our display. One night, we heard people laughing and Dad went out to see what had happened. Santa's hand was stuck, with his thumb right on his nose!

> *"When it was dark enough, Dad turned on the lights..."*

These days, you can buy computer-synchronized lighting and all sorts of other electronic gadgets that move, talk, dance, sing or blow bubbles. But back in 1942, our simple front-yard Christmas displays were something everyone in the neighborhood enjoyed and looked forward to.

Families couldn't wait until the newspaper came out with the list of displays to visit. And at the top of the list in San Francisco in 1942 was "Joe Costello, 39 Cain Avenue". To be listed first was a real honor! ▲

TREE OF MEMORIES. **The ornaments on all the Christmas trees Irene Slyter knew as a child magically appeared for the 1948 season (above), her first Christmas away from home. The doll was there, too (right).**

Familiar Ornaments Held Cherished Memories

WHEN I WAS growing up in Chicago, Christmas was such a joyful time, though we didn't have much money. Our holiday decorations were one reason.

Every year, our old familiar ornaments would come out of storage, along with the many wonderful memories attached to them. My favorite ornament of all was a little broken celluloid doll from my childhood, oddly outfitted with a pair of pipe cleaners for arms.

When my husband and I were married in 1948, we moved to his hometown of Seattle, Washington. I was homesick as the holidays approached and wondered what our first Christmas together would be like.

On December 22, I returned home from downtown and found a fully trimmed Christmas tree standing in our apartment. It was decorated with all my favorite familiar ornaments! My parents had sent a box from home to my husband so he could surprise me. Did he *ever.*

Tears came to my eyes when I saw that celluloid doll with the pipe cleaner arms. I could almost hear my big brother reassuring me, as he had when I was a girl, "Don't cry, Irene. I'll make some new arms for your broken doll."

—Irene Slyter
Longview, Washington

Century-Old Ornament Remained Favorite Decoration

MY FAVORITE ornament is 100 years old, and I treasure it because it was enjoyed by my father when he was a youngster.

Father was the youngest of six children, and his parents emigrated from Germany in 1876. The holidays were always special for his mother, so, knowing this, her second youngest son saved his pennies to buy an ornament for her.

This special ornament became even more meaningful when that older brother of Dad's died at age 19.

Grandma lived to be 90 years old, and she never lost her love for Christmas. Every year, when she helped decorate the tree, she would place her special ornament where it could best be seen. Then she would stand back and sing *O, Tannenbaum* in German. Each year, we do the same in her memory.

—Audrey Nieman
Cedarburg, Wisconsin

CHRISTMASES PAST **live again in charming old ornaments owned by Ernestine Bong of Phoenix, Arizona. The "Happy Hooligan" ornament (left) is about 100 years old and was in her husband Jim's family, Ernestine says. The fish ornament (above) is about 60 years old.**

A 'Flame of Love' Glowed Brightly

By Charlotte Adelsperger, Overland Park, Kansas

MY CHILDHOOD Christmases were filled with simple but delightful surprises.

I'll never forget the Christmas Eve when I first saw a candle in the birdbath in our backyard. A magical flame flickered from a large red candle covered with a hurricane lantern. My sister, Alberta, my little brother, Wally, and I pressed our noses to the frosted window in awe.

Joining in our excitement, our parents quickly explained: "Santa has marked our house. That candle must mean he's coming back tonight when everyone's asleep." We children flew straight to our beds that night!

Of course, we awoke early on Christmas morning and scampered into the living room. There we saw a fully decorated tree surrounded by all kinds of presents.

"Santa came!" Alberta cried out.

"And look at the tree he brought—and the toys!" I added. For a glorious moment, I just stared at the wonderful sight, my heart pounding. The air around me seemed to crackle with excitement and I felt very loved.

Jack Westhead

Later on Christmas morning, our father gently took each of us to the kitchen window. "See, the candle's still burning out there," he reassured us. Hearing those words caused a wave of joy to ripple through me.

Our unique family tradition of the birdbath candle continued throughout our childhood. After we'd outgrown our belief in Santa Claus, we learned that our father, so creative and loving, had slipped outside and placed the candle while Mother kept us distracted.

For us, that candle came to symbolize our family's closeness and a sense of God's love and light in the world. Today, our own children are grown ...but if you look outside our house on Christmas Eve, you'll see a glowing red candle covered by a lantern.

Special love still marks our home. ▲

BATHED IN LIGHT. **The tradition of a candle in a birdbath, like this one, lives on for Charlotte Adelsperger.**

Discarded Items Made Holiday Sparkle

MOTHER couldn't afford to buy Christmas ornaments, so she taught us how to make our own. We gathered spools from thread, dried wishbones from chickens and turkeys, pieces of cardboard and sometimes a small wheel from a discarded toy truck or windup train.

We covered these items with bright foil that Mother had set aside during the year. Then a piece of colored yarn would be attached to each item as a hanger. They all made for a very attractive and interesting Christmas tree.

—Charles Martin
Bartlesville, Oklahoma

Family Flocked to Puny Poplar Tree

FIR TREES weren't plentiful and were rather expensive during the Depression. So my parents always cut a bare-branched poplar tree and stood it in the living room.

Mother "flocked" the tree by whipping Lux Soap flakes with a little water until they made a stiff foam that could be put on the branches.

We cut some tinfoil Mother had saved in long strips to represent icicles, and we made ornaments by covering milk bottle tops and cardboard shapes with foil, too. We also enjoyed popping big bowls of popcorn and stringing it to hang on the tree.

Father made 12 wooden soldiers that stood around the base of the tree and he carved a wooden star to crown the top. I always thought we had the most beautiful tree in the world.

—Joan West
Battle Ground, Washington

Tiny Santa Has Seen a Century of Christmases

By Edna Bronson, Placerville, California

HE'S JUST a little stuffed Santa—about half a hand high—but he has always meant Christmas in our family.

In 1896, my mother, Edna, was 5 years old. She and her 7-year-old sister, Maude, were sent to a boarding school in Reno, Nevada. They had to stay a week at a time because it was too far for the little girls to hike back and forth to school.

On Fridays, the homesick sisters would press their noses to the windowpane at school and wait for "Grandpap" to roll up with his freight wagon and take them home for the weekend.

One year as Christmas approached, Edna and Maude were so looking forward to their vacation and 2 weeks at home. They had little handmade gifts for everyone and had them stowed in their travel boxes.

They looked out the window for a long, long time, but no one came to pick up poor Maude and Edna. Grandpap, it turned out, was very ill.

Had to Wait at School

All the girls could do was wait at school while most of the other pupils went home. The remaining few children were taken to see the community Christmas tree, where each received a 4-inch-tall doll. It was Maude and Edna's first doll!

To pass the time until Grandpap came, they stitched tiny hats, underclothes, dresses and shoes for their new dolls. Maude then set about making a little red stuffed Santa as a gift for her sister. She made a red felt suit, a white stocking face, black boots and belt and a fluffy wool beard.

She quietly wrapped him in cloth and hid him in her travel box.

After 4 days, Grandpap recovered and made the trip for Edna and Maude. Nearly delirious with happiness, the little girls sang all the way home.

On Christmas Day when gifts were exchanged, that little Santa was every-

"She made a little stuffed Santa as a gift for her sister..."

one's favorite. Eventually, Edna was persuaded to hang her treasure on the tree.

So began a family tradition. Every year, Little Santa is lovingly taken from the same cloth that he was originally wrapped in. No one seems to notice that his beard has mostly disappeared and he has a rather moth-eaten look. After all, he's been around for 100 years!

Today, our Christmas decorating is not complete until Little Santa takes his customary place of honor on the foremost limb of the tree to oversee the holiday frivolity.

We wait until everyone has gathered and then call out, "Here comes Santa!" Four generations join in the clapping and singing—first my brother and I, then our children, our grandchildren and our great-grandchildren. It's Christmastime once again. ▲

GIFT KEEPS GIVING. **The Santa in Edna Bronson's family really is a jolly old elf...he's 100!**

TRADITION LIVES ON. **Maria Cassano's father built this *prescipio* in 1928, and the family has decorated and enjoyed it almost every year since.**

She'll Never Forget Pop's 'Prescipio'

By Maria Cassano, Staten Island, New York

WE NEVER had a Christmas tree in our house, but I didn't miss the scent of pine. That's because we had a *prescipio*, a manger about 5 feet wide and 3 feet deep. It had fresh fragrant Christmas tree branches layered over its top.

My father built this homemade grotto in 1928 (he maintained that Christ was not born in a wooden barn, but in a grotto). There were hills and houses, each with lights in them. On the lower level were ponds with ducks, bridges and a complete village from the Holy Land with cast-iron figures set in their place.

We all helped decorate our *prescipio*. I can recall sitting at the kitchen table making paper chains and using flour-and-water paste to glue them together. I especially remember the silver foil milk caps that we'd flatten with the back of a spoon before we cut little stars out of them.

Pop would save Christmas cards that we'd received the year before. From them, he'd delicately cut out angels to hang under the canopy. Every so often, he'd add another wise man he'd come across somewhere.

"Pop, there were only three wise men," we'd tell him.

He'd laugh and say, "No, there were many!"

Christmas Canopy

Each year, kindergartners and first graders from P.S. 11 in Dongan Hills would come and visit our *prescipio* as part of a holiday class trip.

Mom would serve them from a 5-pound box of candy that Pop bought especially for the occasion. To this day, when I come across peach cream chocolate, it reminds me of those wonderful years.

My father died in December of 1976. That year, Mother refused to set up the *prescipio*. Next year, though, we convinced her to set it up in his memory. For some reason, though, we couldn't find the Baby Jesus that my father had so sacredly placed in the manger each Christmas Eve.

For the next few years, we used a plastic Jesus. After my mother died in 1981, I took the *prescipio* to my home. As I set it up the next Christmas Eve I couldn't help but wonder once again what had happened to that missing Infant Jesus.

That very afternoon, my sister, Lucy, asked my husband to check out a leak in the basement at the house where Mom and Pop had lived. To his surprise, there, in a box carefully tucked away close to the leaking pipe, was Pop's Baby Jesus!

That was one Christmas I've never forgotten. I felt Pop's presence all around me...and each year at Christmastime, I still do. ▲

ANTIQUE CHRISTMAS CARDS. **Mrs. Kenneth Hoffman of Oxford, Pennsylvania saves holiday greetings and shared these.**

Jeff Ethell

NIGHT OF LIGHTS. **Christmas, more than any other time of the year, is a celebration of illumination.**

Electricity Had This Family Dreaming of a "Bright Christmas"

WE DIDN'T have electricity in our little log house until I was 10 years old.

It was Christmastime, and Father had wired the house in anticipation of the great event. The power company was to turn on the main switch on Christmas Eve. In the meantime, and with eager anticipation, we'd sent away to Montgomery Ward for a radio and some lights for our Christmas tree. I carried them home from the post office and couldn't wait to see and hear the magic.

Finally, the big day arrived! On Christmas Eve, we all sat around our kerosene lamp, as usual. Suddenly, the whole room lighted up as if it were day! The tree became a blaze of sparkling, twinkling colors—we couldn't believe our eyes.

After countless *oohs* and *aahs*, we finally looked around the room. All the dark corners were gone! We could see each other's faces *so* clearly.

Then, suddenly, the most wonderful thing happened. The strains of *It Came Upon a Midnight Clear* began drifting out of our little radio. As we sat silently listening to that beautiful Christmas carol, we knew in our hearts that this would be our very best Christmas ever!

—Beth Carter
Salt Lake City, Utah

WHAT A TRAIN! **Filling the family sun porch, this 1930s' Christmas display included a standard-gauge train that was 9 feet long. Dick Stiffler of Altoona, Pennsylvania is still amazed that his parents put up this entire exhibit on Christmas Eve!**

'Berry Shack Kid' Made Christmas Festive

By Jim Davis, Burien, Washington

UNPAINTED gray shacks stood beside the berry fields of Washington's Pullayup Valley in 1935. During summer, they buzzed with activity, housing the migrant workers who swarmed in from all over the country to pick berries, peas, beans or other ripening crops. My family was among the pickers.

As the workers followed the harvests toward the apple and pear orchards east of the mountains, the shacks would once again become dark and dormant.

My mother was a very good picker, so the field owner wanted her to work the next year. To stay, she was offered free use of a shack through the winter. Mother jumped at the chance, because it enabled me to attend the same school for a year.

Our berry shack home was basic, constructed of rough boards with a tar paper roof. There was one window, but it didn't open.

A pull cord hung down in the center of the room, providing both light and power for a hot plate—there was no stove. We could also use that single socket to plug in our old Philco radio. The bathroom was a one-holer out back.

Other families were living near us, and as Christmas approached, we berry shack kids became eager. We got together and made swags and wreaths of cedar and holly to sell for spending money. Sometimes we made as much as a dollar.

Mother had found work in the local cannery, so I was entirely on my own. It was my privilege to decorate our shack, so I got to it!

Our Christmas tree would need decorations, so I made paper chains using colored scraps from school and flour-and-water paste. I cut ornaments out of old wrapping paper and formed them into interesting shapes. Cut-up tin cans made good ornaments, too.

Jeff Ethell

BE IT EVER SO HUMBLE. **It might have been just a shack, like the one above, where Jim Davis spent Christmas 1935. But after he got done decorating, it was a warm and joyous place that was a real home, full of lasting memories.**

I strung popcorn with a needle and thread, then dipped the white strings into some of last year's Easter egg dye to make festive colors. A glass star for the top of the tree had been given to us a long time before and was carefully preserved from year to year.

About 2 weeks before Christmas, my friends and I searched the woods for a very small tree. I cut one down and hauled it home. We had no electric lights to put on the tree, and Mother wouldn't let me use candles on it, but I could light larger candles near the tree.

"It was my privilege to decorate our shack..."

I suspended the tree from the ceiling, and after it was decorated, I could give it a spin and it would twist back and forth for a long time, shimmering brilliantly.

When Mother paid our grocery bill that month, she received a free bag of candy. Some of that colorful candy was also hung on the tree.

On Christmas morning, there was a stocking on the wall—a gift from the berry field owner. After dumping out its contents, we berry shack kids couldn't wait to open our other simple presents. They were usually practical gifts like shirts, knit caps and socks, all made by the berry shack mothers. We kids exchanged simple homemade things, such as rubber band guns, wooden boats and crayon pictures.

These modest gifts were gigantic to me back then, a poor boy who never considered himself poor. I look back now and see a youngster wild with joy at receiving a shirt or pair of boots... and happy to decorate a crude cold berry shack to celebrate a festive, warm Christmas with his mother. ▲

Robin Rudd/Unicorn Stock Photos

HOMEMADE. **The best decorations were those made by the family.**

TOKEN OF LOVE. **The visit to the folks' house on Christmas, the sharing of memories of past Christmases, the beginning of memories for the grandchildren—these are the true gifts of the season. Of course, there are the boxes of gaily wrapped gifts.**

H. Armstrong Roberts

Chapter Five

The Joy Is in the Giving

You can learn a lot about Christmas by sitting back to watch faces while the presents are being unwrapped.

Little kids' eyes brighten with anticipation. "What am I going to get? Did Santa get my Christmas letter? Did Mom and Dad remember that special toy I want most of all?"

Many adults, meanwhile, wait to see how much joy their gifts bring to the ones they love.

My own spouse is a perfect example. Peg prowls the stores for hours and hours, day after day, not to find gifts, but to find *the exactly right* gifts.

Here's a nice blouse for granddaughter Katie, but it's not the *perfect* blouse. So the search goes on, even though Peg's countless hours of mall crawling will later demand a long hot soak in the tub to ease her aches and pains.

Last Christmas, she canvassed every music store in town in an unsuccessful search for a particular recording I want. Apparently it's no longer available, but she persisted anyhow.

Better to Give Than Receive

Peg is one of those people who says she'd rather give than receive, and really means it. Her gifts aren't simply *things.* What she's giving is love.

It's obvious to me as I watch her face on Christmas morning. She loves the gifts she receives, but what makes the day special for her is to see the joy her gifts bring others.

Years ago, an exchange student from Peru was living in our home during the winter. Besides feeling the isolation that's always part of living in a country where everyone speaks a different language than your own, Roberto was desperately homesick.

He had more than his share of gifts under the tree, but the one he treasured most was the simplest of all—a telephone call to his family thousands of miles away. Nothing else could have given him as much joy.

During the dark days of the Depression, our family was forever living on the brink of total poverty. The low point for us came in 1934, when Dad farmed from dawn till dark 7 days a week and still ended up the year losing $500.

There wasn't much money for Christmas gifts that year, but my parents were resourceful.

I was 10 years old, and my special passion at the time was the game of chess. Using lumber scraps, Dad made me a chessboard. Then Mom found a set of chessmen. The price is still on the bottom of the wooden box they came in: $2.95.

Fit for a King

I'm sure I received other gifts that year, but the one I'll always remember was that chessboard. Bone-weary from his workdays, Dad labored far into his nights to make that gift for me, long after I'd gone to bed. Never have I received a greater gift of love.

During those tough years, Mom's relatives always gathered on Christmas night. Everyone was scratching hard just to keep food on the table, yet they continued to draw names and exchange gifts.

As best I can recall, the limit was a dollar per present. Though it *was* the 1930s, a dollar really didn't buy very much—even if you confined your Christmas shopping to the five-and-dime.

It's no big trick to find the right gift if money is no object, but finding it when you're limited to a dollar takes considerable ingenuity. Somehow, though, they pulled it off. The thank-you's were sincere, not merely polite.

Never mind fancy wrapping paper. Never mind a box that announces a present from a pricey, famous store. Never mind even the present itself. What it cost has nothing to do with love.

"What really matters is the love and thought that go into a present..."

What really matters is the care and thought that went into it. Part of being a good parent, I think, is teaching that important truth to your children as early as you can. Love is not measured by how much you spend. It's measured by how much you care.

The stories on the pages that follow are, in the end, not about *things* nor about *receiving.* Instead, they are about love and the joy of giving. Reading them brought back many happy memories for me, and I know they'll give you just as much joy. —*Clancy Strock*

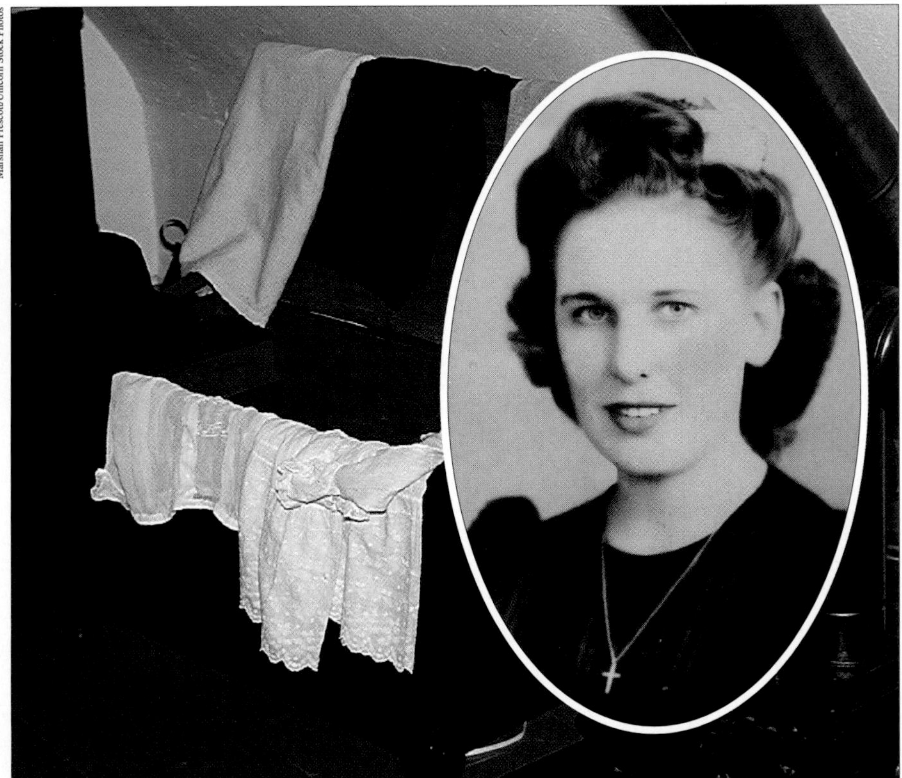
Marshall Prescott/Unicorn Stock Photos

MIRACLE CHRISTMAS TRUNK. **The war years were hard times. But when a young lady had a chance to date a handsome captain, she thought first of her family and used her meager wages to buy them needed Christmas gifts. It was, however, the Christmas season, when miracles can happen. One did, in an old wooden trunk.**

Formal Dilemma Taught Lesson About Giving

By Verla Mooth, Goodman, Missouri

AS CHRISTMAS 1943 drew near, I planned how I could make life a bit brighter for my family. I was 23 at the time, living with my parents and working for the quartermaster at Camp Crowder in the Ozark foothills.

We lived about 10 miles from camp. My older brother was a lieutenant in England, flying bombing missions over Germany. Another brother was ill in a Coast Guard hospital on the East Coast and my sister's husband had been wounded on Guam.

In addition to my 13-year-old brother at home, we were taking care of my older brother's 3-year-old son. My sister had a 9-year-old son, and I wanted the holidays to be bright for all of them.

I 'd put enough money aside from my mid-December paycheck to buy gifts. Then my father became ill and couldn't work. This only left my salary and the money Mama received as an allotment for taking care of my brother's child.

Around this time, a handsome Signal Corps captain invited me to be his date for the officer's club New Year's Eve dance. Guy Lombardo's band would be performing!

I began making plans to buy a beautiful formal I'd seen in town. Twenty dollars would be enough for the dress, a new pair of shoes and an evening bag. I could hardly wait!

Plans Fell Flat

But my car tires were worn out and I had flats almost daily on my way to work. A few days before Christmas, one tire completely blew. I needed a set of four retreads, which took all but the $20 I'd put away for Christmas presents.

I kept thinking of using the last shoe rationing stamp for my new pair of dancing slippers. But Mama showed me the hole in my younger brother's shoe. How could I justify getting new shoes when he didn't have a warm pair for winter?

I reluctantly took my $20 and went Christmas shopping. I bought balls and toys for the children, dress material for Mama, a work shirt for Daddy and a lace collar and beads for my sister.

"It's a Christmas miracle, honey..."

Then I managed to get some extra sugar and lard from the camp bakery so Mama could make cookies to send to my brothers. After I'd bought wrapping paper, tree ornaments and a turkey, I had only $2 left.

What to Wear?

Seeing the joy on my family's face on Christmas morning made it all worthwhile. Still, my quandary over what to wear to the New Year's Eve party kept me awake nights.

Then I remembered three or four formals packed away in an old wooden trunk in the basement. I went downstairs to investigate, but when I removed one dress, the hem caught on an upholstery tack behind the trunk's cardboard lining. Reaching behind the lining to free the dress, I touched a wrinkled piece of paper.

To my amazement, when I removed it, I discovered it was an old yellowed $20 bill! I cried with happiness!

When I rushed upstairs to tell her, Mama didn't seem surprised. "It's a Christmas miracle, honey. You were unselfish in your giving, so you were rewarded," she said.

I finally got to buy that lovely formal, and the party was all I'd dreamed it would be. The band was out of this world and we danced the evening away! Afterward, my handsome captain leaned down and kissed my cheek.

A week later, he was shipped overseas and I never saw him again. But life went on and I got over my heartbreak, eventually marrying a soldier from Chicago. In the ensuing years, I've never ceased to marvel at the joy in our children's eyes at Christmas.

With the passing of time, I realized that Mama was right. The miracle of Christmas *is* in the act of giving. ▲

Secret Photo Session Mystified Mom

CHRISTMAS OF 1934 was close at hand, and my sister and I were wondering what we could give our parents. We had six little brothers, so this is the idea we came up with.

Without telling Mother, we made a date with the local photo studio. It was important, however, to let Daddy in on our little secret in order for everything to work out.

We needed his help in getting the boys from our house to the studio and back home. It was also important to have someone in authority warn them they were not to tell anybody about the plan because that would spoil the surprise.

One Saturday, when Mother went downtown shopping alone, we quickly changed the boys into their "Sunday best" and, with Daddy's help, got them to the studio. We also carefully laid out their play clothes for them so that they could dress in a hurry when they got back home.

We could hardly believe everything went so smoothly. Everyone was outside playing in their old clothes when Mother returned—and not a peep was made about the quick trip to the studio.

On Christmas morning, a special package was delivered to our parents. Even sweet Daddy acted "surprised". With tears on her cheeks, Mother said, "I know these are our boys. But when? And how? And why didn't I know about it?"

It was great! *—Vivian Coday, Eldon, Missouri*

PHOTOGRAPHIC PHENOMENON. When Vivian Coday's mother saw her six sons all clean and neat in this Christmas 1934 photo, she was really surprised. Well, Vivian says, that was the whole idea!

Grandfather Demonstrated Importance of Sharing

MY GRANDFATHER owned a grocery store in Salisbury, Maryland in the 1950s. To help out before the holidays, we spent several evenings placing fruit, nuts and candy in bags. They were gifts for everyone in the neighborhood who came to a gathering at the store just before Christmas.

Grandfather knew families in the area who could use a free bag of groceries in order to make their holiday more enjoyable. This certainly demonstrated to us that it was better to give than receive.

A local farmer would bring a flatbed wagon to the party so the adults and children could share their talents. We'd sing, dance and perform comedy skits, and there was always a musical group. The evening ended with everyone singing carols and a visit from Santa. Those were some memorable Christmases. *—Sandra Tyndall Delmar, Maryland*

Little Sis Just Had To Thank Santa

MY MOTHER was left a widow with five children to raise, so Christmas at our house meant few frills. There were homemade gifts under our tree, and an occasional article of clothing from a catalog.

Our Christmas celebration started with a church program on Christmas Eve. One year, I spoke "a piece" while my 3-year-old sister sat quietly on Mother's lap.

After the program, everyone was told to be very quiet and listen for Santa's sleigh bells. The room fell silent, then, sure enough, we heard the bells and Santa's jolly laughter. He was coming closer and closer.

When Santa came through the door, my little sister leaped off Mother's lap and dashed down the aisle after him. She hugged Santa's leg and said, "Thank you, Santa, for my beautiful red shoes!"

She held out one foot to display a little red slipper she'd picked from a catalog some days earlier. Mother had told her that Santa had given permission for her to wear them to the church program.

Santa took my sister back to Mother, then started passing out the Christmas goodies. I don't remember the presents I got or anything else about that Christmas—but the sight of my little sister and her genuine joy and appreciation of her gift seemed to me to be the real essence of Christmas.

It still does. *—Dorothy Rogers Rancho Cordova, California*

Jeff Ethell

***FAVORITE DOLL,* like the one this girl is holding, became lesson in giving.**

Hard Lesson Finally Appreciated

MY FATHER practiced medicine in the small town of Rogersville, Alabama in the 1930s. There were seven of us children in the family and we all loved Christmas. But the holiday I'll always remember was in 1933, when I was 8.

Father was delivering a baby that Christmas morning, so we had to wait until he came home to open our gifts. After he returned and we opened our presents, I made the mistake of saying my new doll with real hair was my favorite toy of all.

Right after that, Father announced that we would all take our favorite gifts to the home where he had just delivered the baby and give them to that family. I was really angry but grudgingly went along as we piled into two cars with turkey, cake and our gifts.

The home we visited was awfully bleak. It had only two rooms and a dirt floor and was heated by a cookstove. Although there was a younger child there, there was no sign of Christmas until we came.

I didn't appreciate the lesson then, but many years later, I had to admit to my parents that particular Christmas was the best one ever.

—Virginia Cobbs, Blackstone, Virginia

Unselfish Sons Made Mom Proud

IT WAS one of the coldest winters on record in Boston. About a week before Christmas, my husband and I and our two boys, Danny and Sean, were seated in our warm living room, the aroma of the buttery popcorn we were eating blending with the fragrant scent of our Christmas tree.

The TV news had just covered the tragic story of a fire that had destroyed the home and all the Christmas gifts of a family with five children. They lived around the corner from us.

The newscast mentioned the Salvation Army was asking for donations and toys for the children. After the news ended, our two boys left the room for a moment.

When they returned, they told us they wanted to give the children their ages a toy (the story mentioned two boys the same age as them). Since they'd already spent all their money on gifts, they each picked one of their own wrapped gifts to bring to the Salvation Army, never even asking what was in the packages.

Since that Christmas so many years ago, my children have done much to make me proud—but nothing ever made me as proud as that night when, of their own accord, two little boys decided to give up a couple of their toys without knowing or caring what they were giving away.

—Doris Reynolds
Foxboro, Massachusetts

J.C. Allen and Son

***FOOD FOR THOUGHT.* Mom's baked goods, like these, helped the needy.**

Bighearted Parents' Kindness Never Forgotten

THERE WERE 10 kids in our family and we were not well off. When Dad was injured in a farm accident and couldn't work for a year, things got even tougher.

One Christmas in the early '60s, when I was about 10, we kids came home from school and found Mom busy baking cakes. She was decorating them with peppermints and other delicious treats we hardly ever saw. In particular, I recall a beautiful coconut cake. We couldn't wait to taste all those goodies.

J.C. Allen and Son

***POOR FOLKS* had a good Christmas because of family's concern.**

But then Mom explained that none of it was for us. In the next valley was a poor family, she explained. She said the family's father was out of work and the mother wasn't able to take care of her family because of nerve problems.

I got to go with Dad to deliver our truckload of goodies. The kids were as excited as if we were Santa himself.

About 25 years later, I was driving a school bus and saw the mother of one of my riders in her yard. I recognized her as part of the family my parents had helped so long ago and mentioned to her daughter that I used to know her mom.

The next day, the woman was waiting for me. She told me that she had never forgotten our family. "If it hadn't been for your mom and dad, we would've gone hungry that Christmas," she explained. At that moment, I was awfully proud of my poor but bighearted parents.

—Vivian Webb
Knoxville, Tennessee

First Shopping Trip Taught Simple Lessons

By Anita Perna Bohn, Bloomington, Illinois

THESE DAYS, when Christmas shopping sets my head to swirling like the inside of one of those little glass snow globes, I don't worry. Despite all the hype, frenzy and glitter, the memory of my first Christmas shopping trip will carry me through the season.

The year was 1955, and I was 5 years old. My sister, 17 years old and newly employed, delighted in buying gifts from her own earnings. Returning home with bulging department store sacks and humming carols, she'd shut herself in her room.

Pressing my ear to the door, I heard the rustle of wrapping paper and the rasp of a scissors blade against curling ribbon. Later, I'd sneak into her room to note the mysterious new packages added to the "off limits" shelf in her closet.

Begged to Shop

My sister's obvious delight in shopping for presents really attracted me. Whatever she was getting from the Christmas shopping experience, I wanted some, too.

At first, Mother dismissed my pleas to go shopping, telling me 5-year-olds didn't need to buy anything.

When she saw my supplications wouldn't let up, she finally gave me a dollar and asked my 11-year-old brother to take me downtown. Quick to recognize the possibilities of an unsupervised outing, he agreed.

We bundled up in winter coats and leggings and scratchy woolen mittens that smelled slightly burnt from drying on the radiator. Then, linking spongy thumbs, my brother led the expedition out the back door.

Clutching my dollar in my fist, I held it to my chest the whole way. Finally, we reached the shopping district. I was right: Christmas shopping *was* an adventure!

Found Great Bargains

We went to Woolworth's, of course. Depositing me at the gift counter, my brother went off to investigate the toy department. No Rockefeller ever felt more flush than I did as I stepped up to the counter with that dollar bill in hand.

Soon I found the perfect present for Mother: a glass rosary with each bead encasing a tiny statue of the Virgin Mary. At 39¢, its unbelievable elegance was easily within my means.

Then, for my golf-playing father, I found a wonderful tie clasp with a small painted picture of a golfer in mid-swing. I can remember turning it over and over in my hand, relishing the purchase almost as much as I did my own wedding ring years later. At 29¢, it was another bargain.

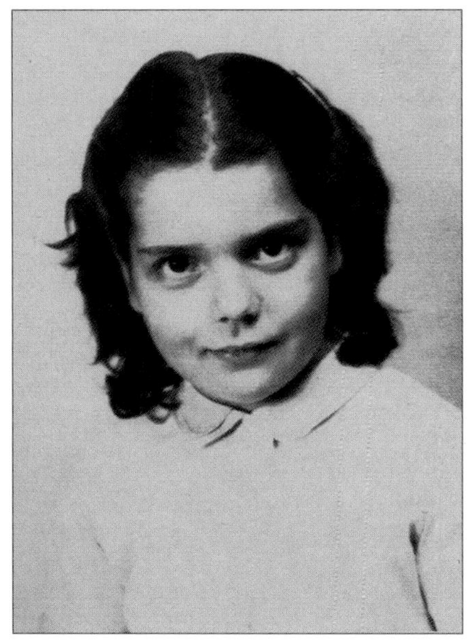

HAPPY SHOPPER. **Five-year-old Anita Bohn learned the joy of giving.**

Locating my brother, I asked him how much I would have left if I bought both items. Thirty-two cents, he figured.

I discovered a lady's hanky with yellow roses embroidered on one corner. It seemed just perfect for my sister and it was only 15¢. Next to the lacy ones were men's handkerchiefs, all crisp and snowy white and neatly folded. Perfect for my brother! I made my last selection.

At the checkout counter, there was good news. The handkerchiefs were two for 29¢. The grand total was 97¢. Leaving the store, we encountered a Salvation Army bell ringer.

Without hesitation, I tossed the three remaining pennies into his red kettle. "God bless you, sweetheart," the smiling man said to me, "and have a Merry Christmas!" At that moment, there seemed little doubt about either one.

No Christmas shopping trips have held a candle to the pure joy of that first one. Now, whenever the pressures of the season threaten to overwhelm me, I try to keep in mind what I learned about Christmas gift-giving my very first time out:

> *"No Rockefeller ever felt more flush..."*

Keep it simple. Stay within your means—the real gift is wanting to give. Show the people you love that you care about them...and don't forget to share your good fortune with those who have less than you do. ▲

CHRISTMAS OF '52. **Anita, above with sister Ginger and brother Michael, enjoys opening presents as only a child can. But in a few years, she would learn from her older sister that buying and giving gifts was more fun than receiving them.**

My Dad Was a Real Holiday Hero

THE CHRISTMAS I'll never forget was in 1939, when I was 12 years old. Father, Mother and I went to Sears Roebuck so I could pick out a doll.

While browsing, we noticed a boy about 13 who was also looking at dolls. He picked out a pretty doll with dark curls and a bonnet, then asked the sales clerk how much she cost. When he learned he didn't have enough money, he looked so disappointed we thought he might cry.

KIND FATHER. Ruth Steffy's dad made a little boy happy in 1939.

"Who do you want the doll for?" my father asked. The boy said it was for his little sister. His father was out of work and the family couldn't afford much.

"Wrap up the doll," Dad told the clerk. He paid for it and gave it to the boy.

That youngster's face lit up like a Christmas tree. "Who should I say it's from?" he asked.

"Santa Claus," said my father.

With that, the boy dashed out of the store. I'm sure there was one very surprised little girl and a very happy little boy in that home on Christmas morning. My dad—who was always great in my eyes—became a real hero that day.

—Ruth Steffy, Boca Raton, Florida

Young and Old Enjoyed The Gift of Time

JUST BEFORE Christmas in 1949, my grandma fractured her hip and had to be placed in a nursing home. Spending Christmas away from her family would have broken Grandma's heart so, on Christmas, Mum, Dad, my sister and I took Christmas to her.

We gathered around Grandma's bed and had a wonderful time, telling tales of Christmases past and even singing carols. Grandma was thrilled, but Dad noticed few of the other patients had visitors.

He excused himself and returned with ice cream cups from the cafeteria. While Mum stayed with Grandma, the rest of us went visiting.

A shy 11-year-old, I was nervous at first, but the heartwarming smiles and kind comments I received gave me confidence. I especially remember my last stop. The occupant of that bed was a frail-looking woman. I sat beside her and said softly, "Merry Christmas. Would you like some ice cream?"

She looked up at me and said hesitantly, "But, I don't have any money."

"That's okay," I replied, "they're free."

"Oh," she said with a twinkle in her eye, "then I'll have two!"

I can still picture those sparkling blue eyes and recall the wonderful feeling that came from giving the gift of my time.

—Carol Forrest, Orillia, Ontario

Dimples Led to Smiles

ABOUT a week before Christmas of 1925, Mom explained her plan at the dinner table. I was about 6 years old then, the youngest of four daughters. All four of us attended the two-room country school where Mom was a teacher.

"You girls have too many dolls," she said, "more than you can take care of. Most of the girls at school don't even have one doll. It'd be nice to give some of your dolls to your less fortunate classmates."

We protested at first, but Mom was firm. "You may pick your favorite doll to keep and the rest we'll take to school and let the girls choose one for Christmas," she said.

All the next week, my sisters and I tried to decide which dolls we'd keep. I changed my mind several times but at last narrowed my choices. I finally decided that Dimples, a porcelain-faced baby doll, would join the 12 dolls to be given away in my class.

Soon, the day of the special Christmas drawing arrived. All the girls at school were excited except me—I still had some mixed emotions about Mom's plan.

The dolls were lined up on the floor in the front of the room. I can still see them, all scrubbed and wearing their best dresses, waiting to go to their new homes. Each girl in class drew a number, came forward, hesitated a moment, then picked a doll and returned to her seat all smiles, eagerly clutching her new baby.

When someone chose Dimples, my tears dropped onto my school papers. She was such a beauty!

I was dejected about losing Dimples until Christmas morning. There, under the tree, was the most beautiful baby doll I'd ever seen. She had eyes that opened and shut and, when you turned her over, she said, "Mama."

As I cradled my new doll in my arms, I thought of Dimples. Now I was happy she had a new home, helping another little girl share the joy of this morning. Mom helped me realize that sharing was the true spirit of Christmas.

—Belle Brown, Bristol, Connecticut

Archive Photos/Hirz/Falco

NEW FOR OLD. The gift of a doll makes all little girls happy at Christmas.

I Was Mama's Little Stocking Stuffer

By Grace Salerno, Ballston Lake, New York

MY MOTHER is a "Christmas person". Even today, at age 80, she decorates her house just as I remember from childhood—and her joy in watching each new grandchild experience her treasures is immeasurable.

Early on, I must have sensed the special euphoria Mama got from Christmas. I appreciated all the trouble she went through to make each holiday memorable—her excitement was contagious, and it set the whole show in motion!

Every year she tirelessly shopped, decorated, cooked and baked. Christmas morning was her triumph, and our squeals of delight made all the work worthwhile.

So how do you give Christmas joy to such a person? How can you top what she's already done? I'll never forget the year I tried.

At Christmas, we hung our stockings on the fireplace mantel. When I was about 10, it occurred to me that Mama didn't have a stocking hanging there. I knew she was the one who filled them for everyone else, so this year, I decided to rectify the situation.

Using my weekly allowance, I bought a red stocking with fleece around the top and printed her name on it with a blue marking pen. Unfortunately, I starting printing "ELIZABETH" with letters that were far too big. Realizing I was running out of room, I scrunched the rest of the letters in as best I could.

It looked funny, but to a child's eye, all that mattered was that Mama now had a stocking with her name on it. Next, I started buying small items to put in it, like packages of sewing needles and spools of colored thread.

"All eyes swung to the mantel..."

I included an orange, too. I remembered Mama saying that oranges made her think of her childhood Christmases, so an orange *had to* be in the toe of Mama's stocking.

In our house, the gifts weren't put under the tree until all the children were in bed on Christmas Eve. Usually I'd try to force myself to sleep so Christmas morning would come sooner. Instead, though, I'd end up lying there listening to Mama and Daddy whispering as they moved about, trying to keep the wrapping paper from rustling.

How to Sneak a Stocking?

Somehow, I had to secretly hang Mama's stocking without having her hear me. I decided to get up in the middle of the night, around 3 a.m.

But how would I wake myself up? I shared a bedroom with my sister and couldn't use an alarm because it would wake her, too.

I hatched a two-step plan that involved water and prayer. I prayed real hard that God would make sure I woke up...and I drank gobs of water to make sure I'd *need* to wake up! My plan worked marvelously.

In the morning, the whole family assembled and we opened our gifts. After saying our "thank-you's", we made a beeline to the stockings. We kids gave Daddy his, and each of us took ours—but no one noticed there was one left hanging there.

When everyone was seated on the floor dumping out the contents of their stockings, I proclaimed, "There's one stocking left!" All eyes swung to the mantle where "Elizabeth" was still hanging.

Mother gasped and said this just couldn't be. One of us handed her the stocking and she sat there for perhaps 2 or 3 minutes, tears in her eyes. She said this was the first stocking she'd received since she was a child.

I still recall my excitement as I watched her go through it and exclaim over each item. When she got to the bottom and pulled out the orange, I knew I had succeeded.

Finally, I'd given back to her some of the magic that she had put into our Christmas for years. Even better, I learned that there can be more joy in giving than receiving. ▲

Jean Higgins/New England Stock Photo

TURNED THE TABLES. **Every Christmas, Grace Salerno (inset) would find her stocking filled with wonderful things. One year, she realized Mama, who filled the stockings, didn't have one of her own. Grace fixed that and made Mama happy.**

Bread Man Was Santa's "Middle Man"

MY EARLY YEARS were spent in a tiny town in eastern Massachusetts. During the '20s, '30s and '40s, we had a milkman, a bread man and even a "fish lady", who drove her little blue truck all the way up from Rhode Island with fresh fish.

Around Christmas each year, I often remember our bread man. Mother always used to listen to his stories about some of the really poor families along his route. She'd often give him our outgrown clothes for those families. (Dad used to joke that if he didn't wear a suit for 3 weeks, Mother would give it to the bread man!)

Early one December, Mother told my sister and me that she was sure Santa would bring us new dolls for Christmas.

"Wouldn't it be nice if you cleaned up your old dolls?" she asked. "You could wash and mend their clothes and give them to some poor little girls," she suggested. "Santa doesn't bring them dolls because he has to give them food and clothes instead. They might not get a single toy this year, and surely not a lovely doll."

Mother was very persuasive. With her help, we fixed up our dolls beautifully. We even took scraps of material and made a little mattress, sheets and pillows. Then we laid the dolls in their beds and covered them with soft warm blankets.

Just before the holidays, we gave the boxes to the bread man, who thanked us, promising to give the dolls to little girls who would love and care for them as we had.

***BREADWINNER.* Clifford Hayden (above in 1937) supported the family with his bread route in Rochester, New York, says his daughter, Anita Sinkler of Brandon, Florida.**

It wasn't always easy to part with a favorite toy, but with Mother's urging and her reminders of how much such a gift would mean to a poor little girl, we very early learned a priceless lesson that has enriched us all our lives.

—Geraldine Binder, Pittsfield, Massachusetts

Mom's Gift Not What It Seemed

ON A warm December day in Baton Rouge, Louisiana, our family sat around the kitchen table for an important meeting.

My father had finally landed a job at Standard Oil Company and he'd decided this would be a special Christmas. We were going to have a tree with lights! And my sister and I would each get one dollar so we could go Christmas shopping.

To an 8-year-old in the mid-1930s, a dollar was a bonanza. Mom, Pop, my sister and seven cousins would all get presents. I figured there was enough money to go around and still get Mom something extra.

Walking to the dime store, list in hand, I thought I had the world at my command. After picking out all of my other gifts, I had a quarter set aside for Mom.

I looked hard for the perfect present and finally found it—a little basket made in China. The lady said that not only was it made in a faraway land, but it was made of split bamboo. Wow! There was no doubt in my mind now. This was Mom's gift.

On Christmas Eve when we opened up our gifts, Mom was ecstatic. She hugged and kissed me and said she would always cherish that basket.

She meant what she said because she immediately installed it on the back of the commode in our bathroom and filled it with kitchen matches to light the space heater there.

As the years passed, we moved into four different rental houses. But, no matter where we lived, in each one, the little match basket always found its place on top of the commode in the bathroom.

It wasn't until after I got married that Mom explained to me exactly what that basket meant to her. She said, "You know, when you gave it to me, I knew you didn't know what it was. But it was from you and that made it special."

It turned out that I had actually given her *one* of a set of drinking glass sleeves!

—Ray Couvillon
Houston, Texas

Santa in Sneakers?

AS A SCHOOLTEACHER, I've taught many memorable classes, but I'll never forget a very loving and giving group of sixth graders in Pecos, New Mexico.

As Christmas rolled around, several of the boys asked if they could adopt a family and buy presents for them, instead of having a $2 class gift exchange.

I readily got the name of a family with four children and the kids hopped to it. On their own, they organized gift, food and decoration committees. The day before vacation, the kids loaded my car with their presents and tied a tree on top.

As I drove four of the students to the home of the family, we all felt the Christmas spirit. We were setting up the tree when a tiny girl looked up at one of the boys and asked, "Are you Santa Claus?"

It didn't matter to her that he was wearing jeans, sneakers and a T-shirt. With moist eyes, we finished placing the presents under the tree.

That year, I felt humbled by a group of 12-year-olds who lived the true meaning of Christmas.

—Maria Mathes
Santa Fe, New Mexico

Mother Bowled Over by Thoughtful Gift

IN THE EARLY 1950s, I was a teenager working my first job. I had been accepted for a gift-wrapping position at Wellan's Department Store, and I felt very grown-up with my new Social Security card tucked in my purse.

I earned a $15 Christmas bonus, which was more than enough to buy a special gift for Mother. After work, I hurried to Schnack's Jewelry Store and bought a pressed-glass pedestal punch bowl set that I'd admired through the display window. It was perfect for Mother—she'd never buy something that extravagant for herself.

Mother loved her gift. And that elegant old bowl served at many family occasions over the years, from weddings and showers to Christmas celebrations. Today, it has been passed down to me. I hope it will continue to be used in the future by my children and theirs! —*Margaret Tarver, Alexandria, Louisiana*

HOLIDAY HEIRLOOM. **The punch bowl Margaret Tarver gave her mother in the '50s (above) is still a treasured part of the family's Christmas and will be passed down. That's Margaret as a teen at right, and Mom at far right.**

Lincoln Logs Made Toyland "Joyland"

WHEN I WAS 8, we lived across the street from a big department store in Chicago. It was 1926, and about a month before Christmas, the store's entire sixth floor was turned into a toyland.

I stood in front of a counter each day watching a lady build cabins and schoolhouses out of Lincoln Logs. I was there so often that she finally asked if I'd like to help her build some of the cabins.

That was wonderful, because I knew I'd never have any Lincoln Logs of my own. They cost $5 and $10 per set, and those were lean years for my family.

On Christmas Eve day, I said good-bye to the lady and thanked her for letting me help. Then she reached under the counter and presented me with my very own set of logs—and a $10 set at that! I thanked her over and over. I couldn't believe those Lincoln Logs were mine!

I never saw her again, but I'll always remember that wonderful lady who made my Christmas of 1926 so unforgettable. —*Marion Zingsheim, Chillicothe, Ohio*

WINDOW MAGIC. **Department stores became a kid's heaven at Christmas. Photo of this 1935 display was sent by Michael Reilly of Morristown, New Jersey.**

Knock on Door Turned Bleak Christmas Bright

CHRISTMAS of 1940 will always hold special meaning for me. It came only a few days after the death of my mother from a long illness.

As you might imagine, Christmas Day was less than festive, but Dad and I were determined to have a good Christmas dinner anyway. We were going to try our best to celebrate the occasion. I'd been given a turkey by my employers (although only 17, I had a job as a bookkeeper), so we had a wonderful dinner, "turkey with all the trimmings".

What neither Father nor I had realized, though, was that we wouldn't have an appetite. When we sat down at that table without Mother, we looked at each other for a moment, then decided to put the food away.

Just as we started to clear the table, we heard a knock at the back door. Standing there were two very tired, sad, hungry-looking men. As anyone who grew up in the Depression knows, there were plenty of hoboes then, and these two were obviously down on their luck.

When they asked if we could spare any food, Dad and I exchanged glances again. We immediately invited the pair into the house and Dad showed them where they could wash up.

Then we showed them to the table and told them to sit down and help themselves. They didn't believe us at first, but after Dad explained the circumstances, they realized this was no joke. They didn't take long to start demolishing that feast!

The thankful expressions on their faces provided me with a memory that will remain bright and clear in my mind as long as I live. I think that was the day I found the honest and true meaning of Christmas: the joy of sharing and giving. —*Jeanette Breitmayer, Forest Grove, Oregon*

No Bones About It, The Book Had to Be Found

By Frances Wykes Searcey, Norman, Oklahoma

KAREN, our book-loving third-grade daughter, was just crazy about horses. Her love sprang from the dozens of horse books she toted home from the library, as well as movies featuring her favorite animal.

In December of 1964, her teacher began reading a story about a horse that Karen could not get out of her mind. The book was *Old Bones* by Mildred Mastin Pace, and Karen wanted her own copy in the worst way. She specifically requested it for Christmas and was really looking forward to finding it under the tree.

Without Karen's knowledge, her dad and I contacted every bookstore in our area. None of the stores had the book, nor could they order it. To our dismay, we learned it was out of print. We didn't know what to do—our daughter had her heart set on that book for Christmas.

We weren't ready to give up. Long-distance phone calls were a rarity in our house during those years, but this was an emergency. My husband called the New Whittlesey House Books for Young People at McGraw-Hill Book Company in New York.

He explained our predicament and asked if anyone there could help. The person he spoke with must have been a book lover and a kindred spirit, because he promised to personally check their warehouse to see if he could find a copy of *Old Bones*. This was our last chance—Christmas was only 2 weeks away.

Thrown a Bone

Only 4 days before Christmas, to our delight and relief, a package arrived from McGraw-Hill. Inside was a precious copy of *Old Bones*.

On Christmas morning, Karen opened her gifts, showing delight with each one. But we could see her eyes continually searching under the tree, as though she were looking for one package in particular.

When the last gift was handed out (and before too much disappointment could set in), her dad reached for a package hidden on an upper branch in back of the tree. When he handed it to Karen, her face brightened and her eyes widened in anticipation as she eagerly grabbed that special package and tore off the wrapping.

> *"Her eyes widened in anticipation and she tore off the wrapping..."*

"*Old Bones*!" she cried. Hugging the book tightly, she jumped up and danced around the room. At that moment, you could say that the joy was equally divided between the givers and the receiver.

Today, Karen shares her love of books with her four children, and *Old Bones* still occupies a special place of honor on her bookshelf. A second copy, found at a garage sale, stands alongside the first. She's corresponded with the author in the years since, and she's even mailed her books to Mrs. Pace to be autographed.

We shall remain forever grateful that a stranger in a New York publishing house willingly went out of his way to find an out-of-print book—just to please a horse-loving little girl in Oklahoma. ▲

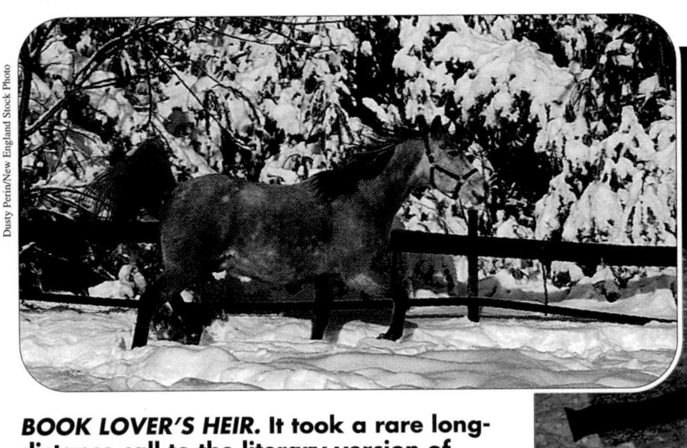

Dusty Perin/New England Stock Photo

BOOK LOVER'S HEIR. It took a rare long-distance call to the literary version of Santa's workshop to find a daughter's favorite book. And now the daughter's daughter (Shylan Bearden, right) gets to enjoy the book, just as her mom did.

Ewing Galloway

NOT HOME FOR THE HOLIDAYS. Although their soldier boy had to ship out, as these GIs are doing, Goldie Buckner's family was able to help another get home for Christmas.

'Miracle Ride' Brightened Bleak Day

By Goldie Buckner, Albuquerque, New Mexico

THE YEAR was 1944, and I was 14 years old. Being so young, I thought World War II would never end. For 3 years, it had been on our minds, especially since my brother had been right in the thick of it, slipping back and forth across the Atlantic on a destroyer.

Now he was home on leave. But why, oh why was he scheduled to head back to duty the day *before* Christmas? Why couldn't it have been the day after?

The day before Christmas arrived all too soon. Our old gray Dodge with the smooth tires was about as ready as it would ever be for the 100-mile trip to the nearest train station. Although the heater didn't work well, we did have blankets to keep us warm.

We made the trip safely and then, amid plenty of tears, left my brother standing on the station platform.

As we started back home, it began to snow. The snowflakes were huge white feathers that seemed to be floating down without a care. But my heart was heavy.

A Sad Ride Home

It would have been a picture-postcard Christmas if we hadn't been so sad. As darkness descended, we crept down the deserted highway, now white with a blanket of snow.

Suddenly, along the side of the road, there seemed to be a form...yes, it was—a man in an Army coat with his suitcase. He was running, wildly swinging his arms at us to stop and pick him up. We had heard stories about people who dressed like servicemen and were "no good".

Was this one of them? Would Dad stop the car?

We'd already passed by the figure when Dad finally stepped on the weak and worn brakes. It took us an eternity to stop. It was nearly dark now as the soldier sprinted up the road toward us.

> *"At that moment, my heart swelled with pride..."*

Knocking on the window, he pleaded, "Oh, mister, please, please let me ride with you. I'm going to Baxter and no one has come along at all and it will take me hours to walk it."

I held my breath. Then Dad nodded his head and told the man to get in. Mom got out of the front seat, and the soldier helped her into the rear with my sister and me. After we were all settled and on the move again, the fellow related his story.

"I didn't think I'd get a pass to come home and then I did. I didn't think I would get on the train and I did," he exclaimed, marveling at his good fortune.

"Mister," he continued, "I had to go to war and then my dad died. My mother lives all alone and this would have been our first Christmas apart." On and on he went, explaining his situation and his joy at returning home.

A Super Christmas Surprise!

"If you can just take me to the Kerber corner, I'll walk the rest of the way," he added. As we approached the intersection where the two roads connected, Dad spoke up. "We'll take you all the way home, son," he said.

At that moment, my heart swelled with pride that we could make this soldier so happy. Maybe we couldn't have my brother home, but at least this young man's mother would have him—and she didn't even know he was coming. What a miracle!

At last, we got to an old house at the edge of town. Before he got out of the car, the soldier took down our name and address. His mom came to the door and we watched them embrace. They waved happily as we drove off. It was going to be a good Christmas after all!

A few weeks later, the soldier's mother sent us a doily she'd crocheted and a lovely letter of thanks. That doily is on my dresser today. For over 50 years, it's been a reminder of my father's gift to that boy and his mother.

GOOD READING. **Kids in the '20s and '30s enjoyed Christmas books like these.**

Family Heirlooms Grew In Importance

By Sallyanne Waldinger, Brewster, New York

CHRISTMAS was the time for my paternal grandparents to revel in their Welsh heritage. Their huge old home in Providence, Rhode Island was always the focus of our family's celebration.

We'd enjoy a delicious dinner of roast beef and Yorkshire pudding, with plum pudding and hard sauce for dessert. Just like the adults, we children ate from the best china at the "grown-up table". We dared to exhibit nothing less than the best table manners.

Our Christmas gifts always reflected our grandparents' sense of Yankee practicality. Money was used to buy things that were necessary and was never tossed about casually.

For Christmas, we nine grandchildren each received a pair of the mittens that my grandmother knitted industriously throughout the year. These new mittens were always a timely replacement for the ones we'd lost at school or had worn holes through.

Other gifts followed: a classic book, clothing, a board game or toy. Then,

"These boxes contained a single piece of our family's past..."

each grandchild was given one special package, which we opened more ceremoniously than any other, as if we sensed its importance.

These boxes contained a single piece of our family's past, an item accompanied by a letter carefully typewritten by our grandfather explaining the gift's history and significance.

The item might be a small piece of jewelry worn by a great-grandparent or an artifact from an ancestor's missionary work. As we opened the gifts, our parents read to us the origins of these treasures, always stressing their importance. They'd explain that one day we would appreciate these items much more and would come to truly understand their value.

Young as we were, we respectfully demonstrated our gratitude. But we were more thrilled with our new games and toys.

Now those same treasured heirlooms sit in my home next to faded photographs of the family member who carried them here from across the world.

My parents were right. Gone are the toys, lost are the pieces of the games, and the books remain shelved in hopes that my children will read them one day. But now, the heirlooms that I didn't appreciate as a child remind me daily of tradition, of the past and of family. They remain the most meaningful Christmas presents from my childhood.

PRICELESS PRESENTS. **Sallyanne Waldinger knows now how precious were the gifts her grandparents gave her as a child. Among her heirlooms are those pictured at left: a dinner gong and brass box from Burma, a brass hand warmer and bowl from China, and her great-grandmother's cutting board from early in the century.**

NOEL NUPTIALS. **When Donald and Edna Bronson were married in 1939 (right and below), Christmas was just 8 days away. So, of course, they had to do their Christmas shopping almost as a part of their honeymoon, even though Donald wasn't sure they'd have enough money left over for food. But all the presents were bought, and Christmas dinner at the in-laws' provided plenty of great leftovers for the young hungry couple.**

Small Gift Remains Most Memorable

By Donald Bronson, Placerville, California

MY WIFE, Edna, and I were married on December 17, 1939. A week later, it was almost Christmas, and I'd spent most of my small savings on our wedding and honeymoon. I had no prospect of income anytime soon because I worked for a lumber company that was closed down for the winter.

Nevertheless, Edna and I went shopping for everyone on our list. It was a cold day, but we were young and enthusiastic, scampering in and out of stores, picking up gifts here and there. I even dropped a small donation in the Salvation Army kettle.

It was getting late. My wallet wasn't fat when we started and now it was very flat! At least the list was finished. Then my new wife reminded me that we still needed wrapping paper and ribbon.

Well, okay. The dime store was the place for that. Off we went (as I wondered to myself how we'd eat for the next week). Afterward, with our packages securely stowed in the back of my roadster, we crawled into the front seat, grateful for the warmth.

One Major Omission!

Before driving home, we scanned our list one more time to be sure we'd not forgotten someone. Edna then said to me, "You'll never guess what I bought for you!" I didn't answer immediately, mostly because I was thinking that we'd just spent the last greenback in my wallet on those wrappings.

Then it hit me! I hadn't bought anything for Edna! Catching my breath, I muttered, "I'll be right back" and shot out the car door before she could ask where I was going.

Pyle & Vans' Pots and Pans was still open, so I ran in. All I had was 59¢. The store had a good selection of kitchenware, but what could I get for half a dollar?

Poor But Pleased

Then I spotted it, a little brass rack with six glass custard cups fitted into it. I bought it and they even gift-wrapped it for me. Hurrying back to the car, I confessed to Edna that I'd almost forgotten her gift. We both laughed about that, and although I only had a nickel and a couple of pennies in my pocket, everything was okay again.

"Then it hit me—I hadn't bought anything for Edna!"

On Christmas, we went to Edna's parents' house, and things were looking great. We'd managed a present for every family member and hadn't gone into debt. Even more importantly, a big worry was off my shoulders.

We'd be able to eat the rest of the week, because out in the kitchen, Edna's mother was wrapping up leftovers for us to take home.

Those custard cups are still in use, and we've had many a chuckle over that first shopping "spree". What could anyone buy today for 50¢ that would last for 57 years? ▲

Dad's Secret Arrived on a Sleigh

MY DAD'S GIFT to my mother for Christmas in 1924 was the highlight of all my holidays. It was a handcrafted kitchen cabinet that he'd made for her. In those days, cabinets were not built-in—they were personal property and went with you whenever you moved to another house.

Dad's gift cabinet contained storage bins for flour and sugar. It was covered by a sheet of zinc and had a pullout kneading board. It was a real gem!

My sister and I were sworn to secrecy and were really excited when he told us about his gift.

After our noon dinner on Christmas Eve, Dad mysteriously announced that he had to go to the feed mill. It was a mild December day, so my sister and I were asked to go along.

Country roads were not plowed then, so we took the horses and the sleigh. We arrived back at the farm with the gift in the rear of the sleigh, covered by a horsehide robe. Dad called Mom from the house. With a flourish, he flipped off the robe, revealing the new cabinet. Mom cried and we kids did, too!

Sharing Dad's secret that day made Christmas of 1924 the one I remember best in all of my 80 years.

—Dan Britts, Nekoosa, Wisconsin

SuperStock

ONE-HORSE OPEN SLEIGH. **Dashing through the snow with bells on the old bobtail, like the couple above, was the only way Dan Britts and family could get to town for Mom's homemade Christmas present.**

Kind Act Was Unforgettable

CHRISTMAS of 1937 was shaping up to be a sad occasion at our house because of a tragic accident that had claimed the lives of my father and brother earlier in the year.

Then, unexpectedly, there came a knock on the door on Christmas Eve. A man handed my older sister a box and I heard him say, "This is for Carol."

When I opened the box, the most wonderful doll that I had ever seen looked up at me. Her eyes opened and closed and she had beautiful golden hair. I immediately named her "Goldie".

After my father had been killed, a kind neighbor, Sam Arneson, had heard me say, "Now I won't get any more dollies." He'd walked nearly a mile in the snow and cold to bring happiness to a little 3-year-old girl.

That was one Christmas gift I will never forget.

—Carol Patchak
Boscobel, Wisconsin

Neighbor Did Duty As Branch Manager

WHEN I was 6 years old in 1916, Dad worked mighty hard to keep food on the table for his eight children. We were poor, but we didn't know it.

We kids always looked forward to the children's Christmas party at the local Moose lodge. We played games and received an orange and a small bag of candy.

This was to be our Christmas, but when we returned home, we found a surprise. There in the living room stood a Christmas tree. It was small but beautiful, decorated with ornaments and real candles burning brightly.

The neighbors knew that we wouldn't have a tree, so each one donated a branch from their own tree. Using the cuttings, one man actually made a tree for us.

Some 80 years later, I still choke up when I remember our wonderful neighbors and the surprise they gave us.

—Edna Biringer
Bella Vista, Arkansas

FAMILY TREE. **Roger and Robert Biringer had a nice Christmas tree in 1944. The one their mom had in 1916, although humble, was a real gift of love.**

H. Armstrong Roberts

CANDY CANE CAPER. **Barbara Hoch (center, with siblings Helen, behind, Joanne and Russell) surprised everyone with a Christmas treat.**

Double Surprise Awaited Secretive Gift Giver

By Barbara Hoch, Naperville, Illinois

DURING the rationing days of World War II, I often did Mother's marketing, and I learned how to use ration stamps. Sugar was one scarce commodity, as was candy.

An elderly couple ran the corner grocery where I shopped, and they were always very kind to me. The week before Christmas, they received an order of coveted candy canes.

Since they knew I had two older sisters and a younger brother at home, they saved six candy canes so I could give one to each member of our family. I was ecstatic and decided to keep this my little secret until Christmas.

As the big day drew closer, our parents explained to us that we didn't have much money, so presents would be sparse this year. It was also unlikely we'd see a Christmas tree, because money was just that tight.

Naturally, we kids were disappointed, but we tried our best not to show it. At least our stockings would be hung near the fireplace, like always.

Had to Be Quiet

I shared a big double bed with my sisters, Helen and Joanne, so on Christmas Eve, I made sure it was my turn to sleep on the outside.

Before it was even light, I crept quietly out of bed and tiptoed downstairs. I quickly put one precious candy cane in each stocking, then scurried back upstairs to bed.

I couldn't go back to sleep because I was so excited about my surprise. Soon, everyone was waking up and putting on robes, and our parents gave us permission to go downstairs.

Waited for Exclamations

I hung back so I could see the surprised expressions on the faces of each family member. But then *I* was surpised when my little brother, Russell, exclaimed, "Look at what Santa brought last night—a Christmas tree!"

Sure enough, there in the opposite corner of the room was a beautiful tree, all decorated for us. I hadn't noticed it when I made my trip downstairs. Our parents had planned all along to surpise us with it.

But the bigger surpise came a moment later when my parents turned and saw the special candy canes in our stockings. They knew these treats were almost impossible to come by during the war.

Since I did the shopping, Mother guessed I was the one behind the surprise. I had a hard time convicing her that I hadn't seen the tree, but I was just as surprised that morning as everyone else. ▲

J.C. Allen and Son

***PERSONAL TOUCH.* Like these two girls, Florence Lay learned that a little of ourselves is the best Christmas present one can give.**

Holiday Verses Were Gifts with Heart

IT WAS Christmas of 1917, and I was 10 years old. Money was tight in our household, so our clever mother inspired us to make our own presents or, as she liked to put it, "to give something of ourselves".

After my regular chores were done, I earned a few pennies by doing odd jobs around the house. By Christmas, I had 19 pennies. That was the exact price of a gallon of gasoline—so I giftwrapped my pennies and gave them to Father with this verse:

Here's 19¢ for a gallon of gas.
Put in your tank,
It will make your car pass,
Every old tub
That comes into view.
Merry Christmas and
Happy New Year, too.

When Father was young, he'd been taught to sew on his own buttons and thought my brother should do the same. My brother hated this task, so my present to him was this verse:

I'll sew on your buttons
For one whole year,
Beginning with
New Year's Day.
This is my Christmas
Gift to you,
So you'll never have to say,
"Give me a pin,
This button's gone,"
Because I will already
Have sewn it on!

To my parents, I gave cards promising to shine their shoes every Saturday night for the next year. I don't remember writing any verses for them, but I *do* remember what a lot of shoes I shined!

The love and joy we shared by "giving something of ourselves" made it a blessed and memorable experience. Now I'm 88 years old, and memories of the Christmas of 1917 still warm my heart. *—Florence Ramer Lay*
Dowling Park, Florida

Georgia Clay On Christmas Day

THE CHRISTMAS that stands out most in my mind happened when I was 11. Dad was in the veterans hospital in Dublin, Georgia. Things were even tighter for our family than usual.

All I knew was that I wanted to give Dad a Christmas present, and the only way I could was to make him one.

I went out and found a big handful of Georgia red clay. Then I punched and slapped and poked at that wad of clay.

I ended up with an ashtray...of sorts. When I finished, I set it up on an old corner fence post to dry. I found some of the most gosh-awful-looking green paint and painted it. But I was proud of my ashtray.

I can still see my dad's face when he came home from the hospital just before Christmas and saw my ashtray. I suspect now that he must have wanted to laugh at that lump of green clay, but instead you would have thought it was made of silver and gold! He acted as if it were the most beautiful thing he had ever seen.

Looking back, I often wonder if the joy on his face was from the gift (which he knew came from the heart) or if it was from being home with his family. I'd like to think it was both.

When I recall those times, I realize we didn't have much...yet, somehow, we also seemed to have everything.
—Jan Allen, Alma, Georgia

"Trolley Sisters" Made Two Special Purchases

IT WAS a crisp December day and Christmas was on my mind. Mother had said we could ride the trolley the 5 miles to the five-and-dime to shop for Christmas gifts. Dad gave us a quarter to spend, my two younger sisters were put in my care and off we went.

When we got to the store, a counter with glassware caught our attention. We knew Mother liked to set a nice Christmas table, so we decided we'd get something there.

We chose a pretty round butter dish with a top that had a small handle, like the stem on an apple. It was only 10¢. There was a larger one that cost 25¢, but we decided on the one for a dime.

To tell the truth, we wanted the cheaper dish because it left us 15¢ so we could buy candy! Our ride back on the trolley was a happy time because we'd done our Christmas shopping and the chocolate we'd bought lasted most of the way home.

On Christmas Day, Mother and Daddy were proud to put the new butter dish on the table. However, it was a long time before we told them how we'd spent the money. *—Vera Riley*
Blythewood, South Carolina

***SWEET SISTERS.* Vera Riley (right) and her younger sisters thought candy was dandy.**

Brother's Unselfishness Was a Lesson in Love

By Marianne Brechler, Naples, Florida

MY FONDEST Christmas memory comes from the year my husband and I moved into our new house. Our three girls had left the nest and we had far too many books, dolls, games, puzzles and other toys to move.

We invited our girls to pick out what they wished to keep, then we put an ad in the local paper:

"CHILDREN WANTED—Toys, games, books and many other items too numerous to mention will be given away at the Brechler Insurance Agency 2 weeks prior to Christmas. Each child may select one gift."

Our office was only one block from the grade school, so you can imagine the children we had coming in. We piled all the items in two back rooms so that the kids could go back and take all the time they needed in making their selections.

It was fun seeing their delight as they stopped at my desk in the front office to show me their choices. Although all of our children were girls, most boys seemed to find a puzzle, book, ball or game to satisfy them.

There was one toy that any boy would like. It was an electric train that

"My sister needs a gift more than I do..."

my husband had bought for our oldest daughter when she was only 6 months old.

Having been raised in the Depression, he'd always wanted an electric train. Of course, it was my husband and my own dad who ended up playing with the train each Christmas.

The train was still available when one boy walked into our office. I knew his family wouldn't be enjoying an elaborate Christmas, and I directed him to the rooms full of toys. Like many of the children, he spent considerable time looking at the array.

Finally, he came out and asked if he understood the ground rules correctly—only one gift per child?

I replied that he was correct. He went back to try and decide, and another half hour went by. At last he reappeared, and I was surprised to see him carrying a baby doll.

"Why did you select a doll?" I asked.

His little sister was at home and couldn't come in, he explained, but he knew she'd want a doll.

I asked him what *he* would have liked.

Breaking into a grin, he said, "The train! But I know we can only pick one gift and my sister needs it more than I do."

Trying very hard to keep the tears from spilling down my face, I led him back to the roomful of toys. Yes, you can be assured, we gave that little unselfish boy a train for Christmas! ▲

J.C. Allen and Son

H. Armstrong Roberts

TRAINS AND DOLLS were the two favorite Christmas presents for boys and girls.

CUTTING CHRISTMAS COOKIES. **It all began right after Thanksgiving, when Mom started bringing home the luscious ingredients for our favorite cookies. The pile of boxes filled with holiday delights grew with each passing day until finally—Christmas was here!**

J.C. Allen and Son

Chapter Six

The Festive Flavors of Christmas

It has been said that the ultimate in self-control is for someone to eat one salted peanut and stop.

Wrong! It's for anyone to say "no thanks" when a trayful of Christmas cookies and candy is set before them. (I'll even include the much-slandered holiday fruitcake in that—but only if it's homemade.)

My list of favorite Christmas foods isn't especially long, and nearly every one dates back to my childhood. Plain old sugar cookies rank No. 1. But they must be crisp, and I don't mind at all if they were left in the oven a couple minutes too long.

I prefer my Christmas cookies unfrosted. Whoever decided to add pink frosting, colored sprinkles and those little silver ball bearings that break your teeth did so, I'm positive, to give overly excited children something to occupy their little hands for the afternoon.

Next on my list of favorites are double-decker cookies filled with raisins and chopped dates and walnut bits. Mom made these treats during the Depression. The dough is similar to what's used for sugar cookies. You cut them out in circles, and the top is made with a doughnut cutter so there's a nice hole in the center. They taste *wonderful*.

If there's time to spare, it's okay to stir up a batch of pecan sandies and another of raspberry meringues with tiny chocolate bits in them.

That's my list of Christmas essentials. But I know your family's list is different.

Bakers' Time to Shine

I'm annually astonished at both the labor and the artistry that go into Christmas cookies and other treats. Let's admit it: Christmas is show-off time for every woman who enjoys baking.

In the course of a couple of centuries of swapping recipes, American homemakers have collected the best from Scandinavia, Russia, Denmark, Germany, England, Greece and everywhere else in the world. The result, I contend, is that our Christmas goodies are the best anywhere on earth.

The whole process kicks off soon after Thanksgiving, when Mom comes home with 375,000 calories worth of flour, white sugar, powdered sugar, brown sugar, shortening, candied fruits, nuts and chocolate, all packed into eight heavy grocery bags.

Then, for weeks, the entire house smells like a bakery. What's bad about it is no one's allowed to sample the freshly baked stuff, under penalty of death or worse. Oh, sure, you can lick the mixing spoons and the pans, but that's hardly the same thing.

The cookies go into boxes and tins that Dad retrieves from the shelf in the garage. When filled, they're safely stored until Christmas.

Watch That Step!

My wife, Peg, has a childhood memory that will chill the heart of any homemaker. Her dad was on his way to the basement, arms piled high with freshly packed containers. But he missed a step and tumbled to the bottom, where his fall was cushioned by hundreds and hundreds of mashed cookies spilled out from crushed boxes and cans.

The dog was close behind. It was a Christmas he happily remembered for years.

Some families specialize in holiday candies—hand-dipped chocolate-covered pecans, frothy divinity, homemade peanut brittle and dozens of other irresistible temptations. I try to avoid them, but the spirit is weak.

"Mom comes home from the store with 375,000 calories worth of sugar..."

Which brings us back to homemade fruitcake. My mother-in-law has an old family recipe that reads, "First get a large clean washtub..." This is followed by hours of slicing, chopping and mincing a long list of exotic ingredients. The only easy part is pouring in a few glugs of brandy and then hand-blending the whole mess together.

Many moons later, when it's deemed ready to eat, the result puts to rest all those scurrilous jokes about fruitcake. It is a confection fit for the angels.

Ah, the flavors of Christmas! Ask anyone who served in the military. We didn't sit around hoping for handkerchiefs or a picture of the family cat. What we prayed for was a great big box of Mom's Christmas cookies, candy and fruitcake.

Suddenly, for a day or so, we weren't 5,000 miles from those we loved. A back-home Christmas was as near as that jealously guarded box in our footlocker. Thanks, Moms everywhere! *—Clancy Strock*

Lutefisk a Swedish Christmas Surprise

By Jeanne Malmberg, Norman, Oklahoma

I WAS RAISED in Oklahoma, and though I have mixed ancestry, I never gave any thought to different ethnic holiday traditions...until I married a full-blooded Pennsylvania Swede.

We were 8 years into our marriage before we made it to my Pittsburgh in-laws' home for the holidays. My husband cautioned me about the different ways his family celebrated Christmas, but he didn't mention some of the minor details. As a result, I committed a few blunders.

For instance, on Christmas Eve morning, I walked into the dining room and found candles burning and seven kinds of cookies arrayed around them. Later in the morning, thinking someone had forgotten about the candles, I blew them out.

Swedish Social Blunder

A little later, my young brother-in-law yelled, "Who's blowing out the candles and eating the cookies?"

I had to admit I was the culprit, but I was only trying to be helpful in saving the candles, and I thought the cookies were put out for everyone to enjoy.

Drawing in his breath and raising his eyes to the heavens, he explained, as if to a child, that it was Swedish tradition to have cookies out and candles burning as a welcome for guests. No one in the family was supposed to eat the cookies.

The main meal was served Christmas Eve, not on Christmas Day. Just before dinner, I smelled this terrible odor from the kitchen. My mother-in-law was fixing lutefisk, which is dried cod that has been soaked in water and lye before cooking.

Nobody else seemed to want it, but she emphasized, "It's tradition. You *must* have lutefisk on Christmas!"

Then there was the language—*ragbrod* bread, *pepparkakor*, *risgrynsakaka* and *lingonberries* (which I thought they were calling "Lincoln berries"). I wondered if Swedes ever served anything like ham or turkey and dressing!

That night, I watched my Russian, Polish and two German brothers-in-law fill their plates with boiled potatoes. They covered them with a mixture of cream sauce and lutefisk. Six of my husband's eight brothers and sisters passed the dish by.

Knowing my mother-in-law was watching me, I decided to try it. I dipped some potatoes onto my plate and covered them with cream sauce and lutefisk. Forking a small potato, I rolled it around in the sauce, closed my eyes and popped it into my mouth.

Much to my surprise (and my mother-in-law's delight), I liked it! Then I moved on to pickled herring and *risgrynsakaka,* which is rice pudding, covered with lingonberries.

A silver ring was stirred into that pudding. If a single person found the ring, tradition held he or she would be married in a year. If a married person found the ring, no weddings would be held in the coming year.

After church and until 3 a.m., many visitors dropped by the house. Each carried a small wicker basket, which was presented to my mother-in-law. She handed them a similar basket in return.

"Mothers in the family exchange gifts," she explained. "We fix the food we make best. Mine is rye bread."

Now I knew why there were little wicker baskets all over the house. It seemed like a wonderful tradition, but I wondered why it had to take place at 3 in the morning!

Dead on my feet, I watched the sun come up while washing piles of dishes. Then, the kids came tumbling downstairs to see what Santa had brought. Struggling to keep our eyes open, we grown-ups shared in their excitement.

"How do Swedes celebrate Christmas Day?" I asked my youngest brother-in-law a little later. He was slouched over one chair with his tie loosened and his shoes off.

Slowly opening one eye, he said, "Sleep!" ▲

Robert Cushman Hayes

LOOK, DON'T TOUCH. **When Jeanne Malmberg visited her in-laws, she learned about cookies and candles.**

> *"My mother-in-law was watching my reaction closely..."*

Holiday Meals Ranged From Soup to...Headcheese!

OUR NOON MEAL on Christmas Eve day was always the same when I was growing up in the 1920s. It was vegetable soup, which became the lifetime nemesis of my little sister, Maggie.

It only reminded her that she had to wait until after the evening meal to open her presents. Her three older brothers and three older sisters, however, enjoyed that homemade soup.

Our Christmas Eve supper consisted of *lutefisk,* which is a Scandinavian dish made from cod soaked in lye. We also had meatballs, headcheese, rice pudding with lingonberries, mince and pumpkin pie, dark fruitcake and dozens of cookies. *—Phyllis Smith Olympia, Washington*

'Candy Day' Nearly as Exciting as Christmas

By Adrian Nader, River Edge, New Jersey

WHILE most mothers in our 1920s neighborhood were baking Christmas cookies, my mom was busy shopping for the ingredients needed on Candy Day.

My sister, Gladys, and I looked forward to this day almost as much as Christmas!

On that magic morning, Gladys and I would wake early and dash downstairs to the big kitchen, where the wonderful aroma of boiling syrup greeted us. After a hasty breakfast, we'd start the day's production.

First came the popcorn balls. I did the popping on the old gas stove using our long-handled popper while Mother prepared a thick syrup, adding peanuts and green food coloring.

When all was ready, Sis and I poured the syrup over the two dishpans of popcorn, then buttered our hands to form the balls.

"Powdered" Their Hands

Next came the vinegar taffy, which had been cooling on the back porch since breakfast. First we'd dip our hands in powdered sugar *(...and don't lick your fingers!)*. Then Mother gave each of us a patty of taffy she'd been kneading on the bread board.

Our job was to stretch and fold the taffy over and over until it was too stiff to work. We'd then roll it into a thin tube between our palms, cut that into 2-inch pieces and wrap each one in waxed paper.

After lunch, we helped stir the fudge that had been boiling on the stove. When it was just the right thickness, Mother quickly added the black kernels and poured it into pans...then we got to lick the spoons.

Next came the task we most enjoyed—making fancy fondants. The night before, Mother had made a big batch of fondant in regular, peppermint and wintergreen flavors.

Now she'd give us each a portion to work with. Sometimes I would make small neat patties and stick a walnut kernel on each, or I'd stuff dates with the creamy fondant while Gladys made the patties.

The most fun of all was making chocolate drops and peanut clusters by dipping the fondant into melted chocolate *(...and don't lick your fingers!)*.

The day before Christmas, the mouth-watering results of Candy Day were artistically displayed in dishes and platters on the large buffet in our dining room.

Alongside was a dish of peanuts (Dad's favorite) and a bowl of store-bought ribbon candy. Christmas was almost here, and we were ready. ▲

Early Birds Earned Sweet Treat

MY PARENTS emigrated from Germany in the 19th century and brought with them many of the "old country" ways of celebrating Christmas. I was born in 1896 and well remember the family celebration we had in the early years of this century.

Our Christmas tree was cut on Christmas Eve (never before) and a requirement was that its tip touch the tall ceiling in our living room. We had some paper and tinsel ornaments, but we also decorated it with fresh apples and spice cookies which, along with the cedar tree, gave off a wonderful fragrance.

In addition, we hung special candies that had little hangers attached to them. During the night, the candy on the tree would "sweat" with the humidity and slide off the little hangers. Sometimes we could hear them hit the floor with a gentle plop during the night.

We all tried to be the first one up on Christmas morning, because the early birds got to eat any candy that had fallen during the night. *—Vernita Schmalz*
Marlin, Texas

***ORANGE CHRISTMAS?* As a child, Linda Rice's grandpa savored the one orange he got for Christmas. When the family moved West, Grandpa (above) had a treeful.**

Grandpa's Sunny Memories Of Special Christmas Oranges

I LIVED with my grandparents when I grew up and often heard Grandfather's tales of when he was raised on a farm with 10 brothers and sisters.

Every Christmas, he'd tell my brother and me how lucky we were to have so much because when he was a child, there was no money for presents. Usually he received handmade socks, a scarf or hat.

The one special gift he remembered most was a ripe juicy California orange—a rare treat in Ohio during winter. He'd carry his orange around just looking at the vibrant color until the temptation to peel it was too powerful.

He said the first spray of orange fragrance he got when he dug his thumb into the skin was a gift in itself.

Grandpa took his time peeling the orange, tucking the peels into his pants pockets to examine later. He savored each wedge and even saved the seeds to plant in spring, thinking he'd have the first orange tree in Ohio. Of course, they never grew.

Grandpa later moved our family to California and bought a house on an acre of land. There he planted a large variety of citrus trees. Every Christmas, there were bowls of fresh oranges on the tables and around the Christmas tree.

Sometimes on Christmas Day, I'd see Grandpa walk out to his little orchard, pick a fresh orange, then sit on the fence post just looking at it in his hand. I'm sure he was remembering those childhood Christmases and thanking the Lord for his blessings. *—Linda Rice, La Mesa, California*

It's Beginning to Smell A Lot Like Christmas...

WHEN the scent of oranges, apples and bananas prevailed in our home, we knew Christmas was near. That was the only time we got to enjoy all of these fruits at the same time. Somehow Papa always managed to buy them for the holidays, and we were so happy.

Our appetites were also whetted by the aroma of mince pies. Mama baked about three pies and stacked them like layer cakes. They were cut into wedges and devoured.

We also enjoyed two special cakes at Christmas. First there was a mahogany cake—a rich chocolate that beat devil's food by a country mile.

This cake's 7-minute icing was never beaten enough to make it stand in white peaks. Instead, it soaked into the cake to create a taste nothing can compare with today.

The second cake called for fresh hand-grated coconut. (When the coconut was cracked, we kids always got to taste the milk.) Mama saved this cake until December 27 (her birthday), and the 2-day delay ripened the flavor to a sheer delight.

Nothing I've tasted since can equal those two desserts—our holiday grand finales! *—Sue Starnes, Tyler, Texas*

***A LITTLE MORE SUGAR.* Helping Mom make those scrumptious Christmas treats, especially during the taste tests, was almost as much fun as eating them.**

Archive Photos/Lambert

Holiday Flavors Were 'Auld-Fashioned'

By Dorothy Smith, Tempe, Arizona

FOR MY FAMILY, the "auld" (old) country was England. When I was a young girl in the '20s, we lived in the coal mining town of Johnston City, Illinois.

People from England, Scotland, Ireland, Italy and Poland had emigrated there to work in the rich southern-Illinois coal mines, so the area was truly a melting pot.

At Christmastime, each ethnic group celebrated with its own special foods and traditions. In our English family, the plum puddings and fruitcakes were prepared weeks in advance and stored in cool dark places.

The plum pudding was mixed, wrapped and tied up in pieces of clean white cloth, then placed in kettles of simmering water to cook slowly for several hours. When done, they were lifted from the water, left in the cloth wrappings and put away to mellow and age until Christmas.

Fruitcakes were lovingly mixed by hand in a large enamel dishpan, then placed in greased paper-lined loaf pans to bake in slow ovens for what seemed like hours. Oh, what a fragrance!

For days afterward, the house smelled so good! After they cooled, the husky brown loaves were swaddled in clean white cloths and also tucked away in a cool dark cupboard to "ripen" for Christmas (helped along from time to time with a light "baptism" of wine, rum or simple fruit juice).

In our house, no piece of fruitcake was ever served before Christmas Eve. The mystery of just how good this year's batch was remained until supper that night when Mother cut into her cakes and found them moist, sweet and rich.

Our tradition was that each piece of cake had to be served with a piece of very sharp cheddar cheese, a good cup of tea or perhaps a sip of port wine.

Next morning, the puddings, still in their cloth wrappings, were returned to a hot-water bath to steam and heat for several hours, ready to be served up warm as our Christmas dinner dessert.

That dinner featured roast goose, roast beef with Yorkshire pudding, suet pudding, mashed potatoes, mashed rutabagas, gravy, parsnips, peas and boiled onions...augmented, of course, with an occasional American or "Yankee" dish from a new sister-in-law or two. ▲

Memories of Home-Fried Doughnuts Still Ring

RAISED DOUGHNUTS were among the special goodies my grandma prepared for Christmas.

They were always crunchy brown outside, light and fluffy inside, delicately flavored with nutmeg and had just a hint of yeast that made them rise to double or triple their pre-cooked size.

It was quite a trick to transfer them from the rising trays to the black frying kettle without squashing them. Then they had to be timed just right on each side so they'd be a rich brown, with a band of white around the middle. When finished frying, they were shaken in a bag with powdered sugar.

These doughnuts were a special part of our Christmas morning breakfast. Even after I was married and had my own family celebration, Grandma would come and spend the holiday with us—and she'd always bring along a big bag of her wonderful doughnuts.

—Rita Roberson, Walkersville, Maryland

***HOLE IN ONE.* When Rita Roberson's family (above) gathered for Christmas breakfast, there was always a platter of raised doughnuts, covered with sugar.**

Grandma's Fruitcake Was No Joke

EACH YEAR during the Christmas season, I hear friends and comedians tell jokes about fruitcake—but they've never tasted "Granny's White Fruitcake", which comes from our kitchen.

In contrast to the typical dark and heavy fruitcake, this recipe yields a light cake because it calls for a lot of egg whites.

I have no idea where my grandmother got the recipe, so it may have been passed down more than three generations. As a kid, I thought the raw dough scraped from the bowl was best of all!

I'm the only one of her granddaughters now who makes this fruitcake every Christmas, and it's a lot of work. But it's worth every minute of it when we cut into that holiday treat, steaming-hot out of the oven, and bite into a mixture of fruit and nuts in a light cake.

—Ann Snuggs, Pine Bluff, Arkansas

J.C. Allen and Son

TRADITION TO FRUITION. **Homemade fruitcake took lots of time, but as these tasty memories show, it was well worth it.**

Fruitcake Was Team Effort

ONE MONTH before Christmas, Mother would enlist my help with the all-day affair of making a big beautiful fruitcake. First I cut the candied fruit into small pieces, then shelled and picked the walnuts, which were well-chopped.

Mother baked the cake, and when it had cooled, she wrapped it in cheesecloth that had been soaked in wine. This was placed in a tin with the lid closed tightly.

I can still remember how eagerly we looked forward to Christmas, when the tin was opened and the cake was cut. To this day, I've not tasted a fruitcake as delicious as my mother's.

—Marion Wagner, Dover, Delaware

Wood-Range Fruitcake Left Fragrant Memories

ASSEMBLING ingredients for my family's favorite Christmas cake took at least 2 nights. A large china basin from the washstand held the contents of our traditional fruitcake. Almonds were blanched, skinned and slivered before finding their place in the bowl. We chopped raisins, currants, dates and figs, sliced candied pineapple and added whole candied cherries, citron and ginger cubes.

Flour was sifted over the fruits and nuts. On top of that, a pound of butter, 10 eggs, cream, rose water and black currant jelly was added with lemon, orange and pineapple extracts for flavor.

All the ingredients were blended and poured in pans lined with waxed paper. Six long hours of slow baking in a wood-burning stove created aromas indelibly etched in my mind.

When the cakes were finally removed from the oven, we wrapped them in sherry-soaked cheesecloth and hid them until Christmas.

I loved that fruitcake and cherish my memories of making it. *—June Cox*
Boca Raton, Florida

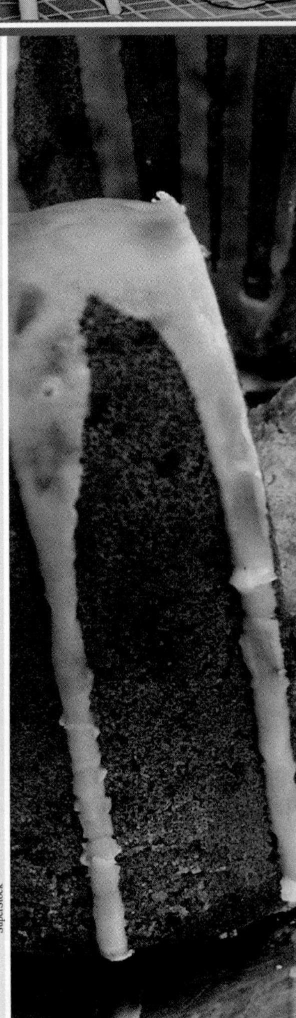

SuperStock

CORNUCOPIA. **No matter how you slice it, and no matter what shape it takes, fruitcake means Christmas, just as surely as cookies, candy canes and Kriss Kringle.**

Christmas Eve Feast Continues

By Rita Woodhull, South Daytona, Florida

PREPARATIONS for my family's Christmas Eve feast began on December 23, when Mother started baking the holiday bread.

We lived in Connecticut, and the temperature during this snowy time of year hovered around the freezing point. My two brothers, two sisters and I were usually outside playing, and as the daylight faded, we would come bursting into the kitchen, where we'd be greeted by the aroma of freshly baked bread, mingled with the scent of oranges and anise. As we took off our jackets, mittens and hats, we began to warm up in anticipation of what was to come. We always sampled the Christmas bread as soon as it came out of the oven.

It was a pleasure to watch my mother cut through the hot, golden crust, then quickly spread each slice with butter that immediately melted.

Sometimes we spread olive oil on the warm slabs and sprinkled each with oregano—a treat learned from our Italian ancestors. The untouched loaves would be placed in a large wicker basket, lined and covered with a white tablecloth—ready for our Christmas dinner.

TRADITIONAL TREATS. **Christmas is the one time a year when all the family gathers together. And what better place to gather than the dinner table, laden with those special treats we've come to associate with the season, and which provide us with so many memories.**

The next morning, Mother would rise early to begin preparing the holiday meal. Getting up early was not one of her favorite things. But on this day, she was happy to be the first one up. She poured some hot coffee and added cream from the top of a milk bottle.

The scallops and fresh fish fillets were washed, breaded and refrigerated until they could be cooked. Then the shrimp were boiled with garlic, lemon and spices before they were peeled and deveined, to be served later with a spicy sauce.

In the meantime, fish stock was simmering on the back burner, to be used later in the Mediterranean meatless stew.

All day long, Mother would sing Christmas carols and other popular tunes of the season, accompanied by the kitchen radio. When the radio was off, she'd sing along with fast-moving Italian folk songs on our phonograph.

> *"On this day, Mother was happy to be the first one up..."*

In the years since Mother passed away, I've tried to prepare the meal just as she did to preserve the family tradition. I'll never forget one year when the whole family pitched in.

Awoke to Surprise

Our son and daughter and their families were with us. And our youngest son came home from college to celebrate the season with our youngest daughter, then a sixth grader.

I was recovering from a bout with pneumonia and went to bed early. I hadn't baked the Christmas bread, but I planned to get up early to do that and prepare the rest of the traditional feast.

When the sun rose, so did I. I dressed and hurried downstairs, but before I reached the bottom step, I was met by the heavenly aroma of freshly baked bread, mingled with oranges and anise. It smelled exactly like our home in Connecticut when I was growing up!

A fire was burning in the fireplace, orange rinds smoldering in the burning embers. When I lifted the white tablecloth covering the wicker baskets on the kitchen table, I found two beautiful loaves of golden bread, their crusts lightly sprinkled with aniseed.

As the warmth of the moment flowed through me, I plugged in the coffeemaker and took some cream from the refrigerator. Then I turned on the radio and got ready to continue the tradition. ▲

Delicious Memories Of a Cake She Wouldn't Eat!

WHEN I THINK of Christmas baking, I recall fond memories of helping Mama prepare her Lane Cake when I was growing up.

I wonder if she considered it "helping", though. I always wanted to be the one who ground the coconut, pecans and raisins in the old grinder mounted on the kitchen counter.

Of course, just as much tasting was done as grinding, and Mama would warn of stomachaches when I sampled too much.

The cracking of the coconuts with Daddy's hammer was done by the grown-ups. I loved sampling the fresh milk from those meaty shells!

The funny thing was, I didn't like coconut and never cared to eat the cake after it was done. Just being part of it all was special. Today, I still have Mama's old grinder.

—Beverly Heartsill, Montgomery, Alabama

***LOCO FOR COCONUT.* For some, eating the cake was the real reward. But when Beverly Heartsill was a child, she loved the making more.**

Marzipan Shapes Made Christmas Sweet

By Ruth Ward, Brooklyn, New York

THE FIREPLACES and chimneys in our old Brooklyn brownstone were purely decorative, but I hung my Christmas stocking anyway.

I knew that when I crept out of bed on Christmas morn, the stocking would be bulging with delights. Best of all, Santa always knew what I wanted most—a marzipan pig.

On the Christmas of 1925, when I was 4, I received my first sugary sweet, melt-in-your-mouth marzipan pig. That candy delight nearly equaled the thrill of new toys and the giant Christmas tree that filled the house with the fragrance of pine.

Part of the charm of marzipan was that it appeared only at Christmas. Easter had its chocolate eggs, Halloween its candy corn and Thanksgiving a chocolate turkey. But all those paled in desirability beside my Christmas pig.

Marzipan paste could be realistically colored and molded into a variety of shapes like flowers, vegetables or fruit. To me, my pig was the most intriguing.

With judicious planning, it'd last for 10 days. I'd eat the ears one night, then one leg at a time, then take five nights to enjoy the rest.

By then it was January 4, my birthday, which signaled the end of the Christmas season.

My pig was now a cherished memory, and the Christmas ornaments and wreaths were packed away for 11 months and 14 days. (Not that I counted!)

Every year of my life since then, I've had marzipan for Christmas. Pigs gave way to vegetables and fruit, but it had to be there. Today, my daughter and I carry on the tradition. Each time I open the tin, visions of merry childhood Christmases dance in my head, along with the sweet memories of marzipan. ▲

***PORK FUTURES?* The pig, mushroom, clover and bag of money all meant good luck for the recipient of this 90-year-old card, says Bonnie Ziolecki of Menomonee Falls, Wisconsin.**

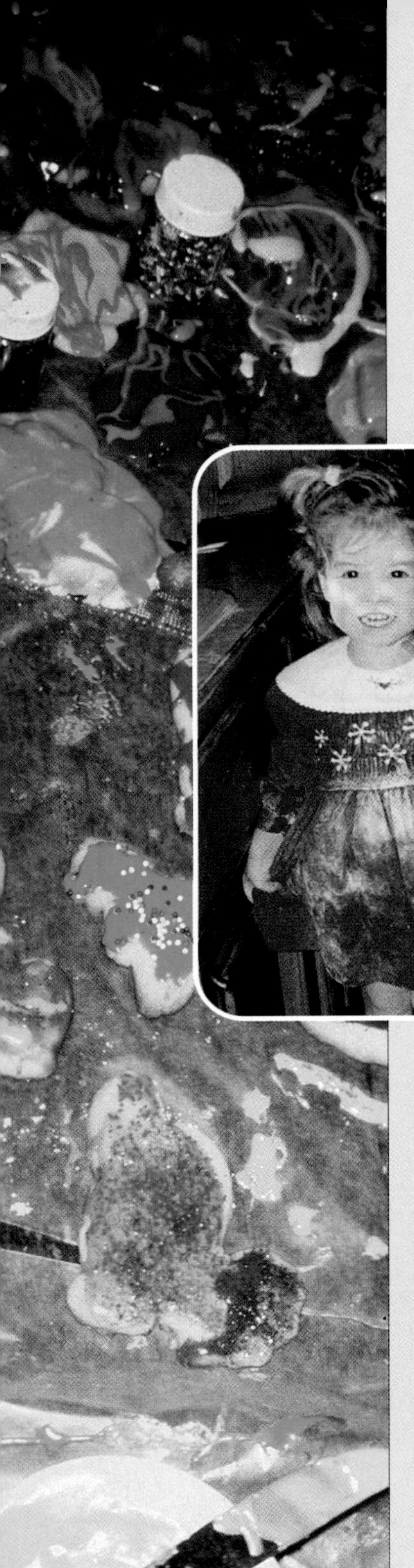

Robert Cushman Hayes

Santa Got the Best Cookies

MY FAMILY'S Christmas celebration began on Thanksgiving weekend, when we kids would mess up the kitchen, and ourselves, making cookies.

Grandpa was a wallpaper designer and block cutter. He hand-carved cookie forms that depicted pets and people we knew.

It was also up to Grampa to mix the dough—he had the muscle for that job. When Grandpa did the mixing, the dough always had a special flavor. We later surmised it came from pipe ashes he accidentally spilled into the batter!

When the cookies were done, they were put in the cookie jar until Christmas. A napkin sprinkled with a few drops of vanilla went into the jar, too.

The best of the cookies were put out for Santa. They were always gone on Christmas morning.

—Florence Lovering
Loganville, Georgia

***FLOUR CHILDREN.* April and A.J. Lovering really got into the spirit—and the ingredients—of holiday baking, says Grandma Florence.**

There's Always Room ...For Popcorn?

WE ALWAYS ENJOYED a big Christmas dinner. But by mid-afternoon, it was popcorn time!

Dad would get several ears of the small white popping corn and we'd all join in the shelling.

Next, Dad would take the shelled corn outside and pour it from one pan to another while blowing away the chaff.

A heat-blackened sheet metal box covered with a screen at the end of a long handle served as the popper. Several poppers worth filled a large mixing bowl with fluffy white kernels, to which lots of butter and sugar were added.

How we could enjoy popcorn after those huge dinners remains a mystery to me to this day!

—Homer Nevermann
Seattle, Washington

Chicken Soup Brought Christmas Dreams

DURING THE 1940s, our family lived with my little round Polish grandmother in Chicago.

I recall the strong fragrance of the Christmas tree, but an even finer aroma was that of Grandma's chicken soup bubbling on the stove.

Noodles Grandma had made earlier hung drying from the backs of kitchen chairs, waiting to be added to the steamy broth and cooked until tender.

Soon it was time to eat. The kitchen came alive with the familiar voices of grown-ups and the chatter of children.

Sitting in my place, I dreamed of a Sparkle Plenty doll and maybe a Lone Ranger coin bank like the one I'd heard advertised on the radio. But my biggest wish was for a pair of ball bearing roller skates with leather straps and a shiny key.

Chicken soup and Christmas dreams were pure excitement on those long-ago Christmas Eves.

—Karen Hanninen
Minneapolis, Minnesota

"The Broken Pieces" Were Childhood Treat

WHEN I was a child, back in the 1920s, it was an annual tradition for my mother and Aunt Grace to get together and make the Christmas candy.

Since my older siblings were in school, I was the lucky one to get in on all the festivities. They made fudge, sea foam, divinity, chocolate drops, peanut clusters and many others.

As Mama and Aunt Grace packed away the goodies for the big day, somehow broken pieces were slyly pushed in my direction. I can still hear my mother saying, "Now, Aunt Grace, you're going to spoil that child."

—Elizabeth Barrett, Holland, Ohio

Baking Aromas Made Holiday Memorable

By Barbara Buehner, Milwaukee, Wisconsin

SHORTLY AFTER Thanksgiving, Mama's friends arrived at our house to help her bake Christmas cookies, all the while talking, laughing and enjoying themselves.

My siblings and I knew it was baking time when we pushed open the back door after school to the tantalizing aromas of freshly baked chocolate swirls, triple layer bars, coconut almond bars, round butter cookies with maraschino cherries in the center and, our favorite, chocolate kiss cookies.

Mama held off making the cutout sugar cookies until we were there to help. Stars, bells, reindeer, Christmas trees and Santas danced merrily before us, our busy hands frosting and sprinkling each one.

Most of the cookies were packed in large gold-colored tins.

When the tins were full of cookies, Daddy carried them downstairs, storing them in our big chest freezer to be brought out when friends dropped by.

Tried Samples Early

Once we children grew big enough to open the freezer, a few cookies disappeared before visitors arrived. We snapped frozen chocolate kisses from cookies, plopping them in our mouths to thaw.

On Christmas morning, Mama would *still* be baking. She'd hurry into the kitchen to check her now-risen cinnamon rings, place them on the oven rack, then join Daddy and us children for the opening of gifts and reading of the Christmas story.

The heavenly aroma of those cinnamon rings baking was like torture—we couldn't wait to eat them! After what seemed like an eternity, Mama pulled them from the oven. We followed the fragrance to the table, leaning on our elbows to catch a glimpse of the crisp, golden rings.

The rings would be covered with a mixture of brown sugar, cinnamon and butter, followed by plump raisins and a glaze of powdered sugar and milk.

Red and green maraschino cherries topped off the sweet rings, giving them the appearance of miniature snow-covered Christmas wreaths.

After Christmas dinner, we'd enjoy those heavenly cinnamon rings disguised as holiday wreaths. What memories they made. ▲

Depression Christmas Left Indelible Memories

I'LL NEVER FORGET Christmas of 1935. My father was in the weekly newspaper business, and Depression-hit companies couldn't afford to advertise.

But I wasn't aware that times were hard. We received fewer gifts that year, but we were so happy.

Santa left us some small gifts, fruit and, of all things, a fresh coconut! Mama told us she'd make a cake with it for lunch. We watched as she scraped the coconut on a grater she fashioned by driving nail holes into a tin syrup bucket lid.

My grandparents arrived unexpectedly, and we had chicken and dressing and the cake for lunch. I think it was my mother's ingenuity and hard work that carried her through. The times we have so little is when we appreciate what we have the most.

—Carolyn Gardner
West Monroe, Louisiana

Archive Photos/Frederic Lewis

TROPICAL TREAT. **Christmas is a time for goodies not seen during the year, like sweet coconuts from faraway places.**

Delayed Christmas Still a Delight

By Nadia Kaplan, Los Angeles, California

IT WAS PAINFUL to be different.

While most children in our Chicago neighborhood celebrated Christmas on December 25, we had to wait until January 7 to mark the feast.

That was the day we Ukrainians observed the holiday, according to the old Julian calendar. Enviously, we'd watch our Italian, Polish, Hungarian and Irish neighbors in their new clothes and playing with their new toys.

But even during the Depression, we eventually managed to have a great time during our later Christmas, enjoying gifts and special foods.

As January 7 approached, the house filled with tempting scents. Mama's skillful hands braided bread dough, shaped it into round baking pans and glazed it with beaten egg. She always made a little *kolach* in a muffin tin for me. "Put lots of raisins in!" I'd beg.

What excitement we felt when Papa brought home two cases of soda pop—one orange, the other strawberry (soda was ordinarily only a summer treat).

For Christmas Eve, Mama prepared the traditional Ukrainian dinner. Straw was spread on the dining table and covered with Mama's best embroidered tablecloth. The straw reminded us of the stable where Christ was born.

This was a 12-course meal, symbolic of the 12 apostles. The meal, however, was prepared without dairy products or meat. It started with *kootya*, which is boiled whole wheat with honey and poppy seeds. This was followed by *borscht*, sauerkraut soup, *holubtsi* made with rice and buckwheat, dumplings, cooked beans and beets with mushrooms and onions.

> "The magic of their voices filled our home..."

That wasn't all. Mama saved all year so she could purchase pickled herring and other ingredients for a compote of stewed dry fruits. We also had mushrooms with millet seed and onions, and delicious hot doughnut cakes filled with either plum jelly or poppy seeds.

Turning on our front light was a signal for the Ukrainian carolers to visit. Blowing on cold hands and stamping the snow off their boots, they crowded into our flat with greetings of *Christos roduvsha* ("Christ is born").

The magic of their voices filled our home and warmed our spirits. Their departure was the signal to hang up our stockings and crawl into our thick, warm feather beds to await morning.

At daybreak, we'd spring out of bed to see what Santa had left us. A beautiful California orange meant we'd been good. My sister Eleanore was happiest when she got embroidery thread and sewing materials. Melania, being a tomboy, liked baseballs, bats and cars. Natalia loved dolls and I got books.

Once again, Santa had thrilled us, and our previous feelings of holiday deprivation were long forgotten. ▲

***JOY TO THE WORLD.* When the carolers, like these, finished their singing, it was bedtime for Nadia Kaplan.**

Archive Photos/Thomas Muir

SuperStock

GOOD FOOD AND GRANDMA. **That combination is hard to beat anytime, but especially at Christmas, says Delle Gherity. Her grandma is shown above.**

My Childhood Memory Christmas Store

By Delle Gherity, Kingston, Illinois

GRANDMA and Grandpa lived behind their small ethnic grocery store on Dubay Street in Detroit. Christmastimes and the special foods we enjoyed there in the 1930s hold some of my favorite childhood memories.

On the morning of Christmas Eve, my younger sister and I would pester Mom and Dad all day long with, "Is it time to leave yet? Why not? How many more hours?"

When the time finally came, the gifts for the uncles, aunts, nephews and nieces were piled in the trunk of the car. Santa would bring our gifts in his sleigh later. At last, we were off on that *long* drive. (It was all of 20 minutes.)

As we drove up, we spotted the store windows sparkling with their holiday finery. There were mounds of oranges and apples in the front window. The side window was filled with a tree decorated with candy canes, red strawberry marshmallows and red and green sour candies shaped like cherries.

Scents of Christmas

My sister and I would run from the car, fling open the squeaky gate and dash through the door directly into the kitchen, where we were greeted by all sorts of delightful, familiar fragrances.

The aroma of anise oil lingered from some special cookies baked days earlier and set aside in tins to "ripen".

The brandy, raisin and citrus peel scents of "poor man's fruitcake" were also in the air, along with the sweet scent of vanilla from the ribbon candy, coffee brewing on the stove, and a big pot of *czarnina*, giving off the rich aromas of allspice, cloves, prunes, raisins, apples and duck.

To All a Good Night

There were the yeasty smells of just-baked strudel, nut and poppy seed coffee cakes, and jelly-filled Bismarck rolls that I got to shake in the sugar sack as Grandma took them from the bubbling deep fat.

From an oven in the basement wafted the delicious smell of the honey- and pineapple-glazed ham that was baking slowly for the Christmas Eve buffet.

Busy as she was, Grandma always stopped her preparations to give us a big hug and a kiss. My Hungarian grandpa, still wearing his white butcher's apron, would pick each of us up, give us a big swing-around, kiss us and remark how beautiful we were in our dresses, made especially for Christmas by Mom.

When the "groaning board" of the buffet was finally cleared of the Christmas Eve feast, it was time for me, my sister and cousins to be tucked into bed.

The front bedroom overlooked the streets and I could hear carolers singing under the streetlight on the corner. If I peeked out the window, I'd see Mom, Dad, uncles and aunts trudging through the snow to midnight Mass.

Then, finally, I would drift off to sleep, dreaming of Christmas morning and of what Santa would bring. ▲

Long Preparations Paid Off On Christmas Morning

MY MOST memorable Christmases were in the 1950s, when I'd spend Christmas Eve in Philadelphia with Pop-Pop and Nanny, my grandparents.

Nanny and I would spend the day preparing for Christmas. We'd clean the house in the morning, then spend all afternoon making cookies, cake and fudge.

After all that was done, the annual ritual of making Nanny's delicious cinnamon buns began. She mixed all the dough while I watched. There seemed to be enough for a small army!

While the dough was going through its first rising, we'd watch *Heidi* on my grandparents' small black-and-white television. The movie was on every Christmas Eve, and it became something I looked forward to.

When the movie was over, it was time to "punch down" the dough and get ready for midnight Mass. When we returned home, it was time to put the finishing touches on the buns.

Nanny would roll out the dough, and I'd help by adding the brown sugar, cinnamon, nutmeg and raisin filling. I think more of these luscious ingredients found their way into my mouth than into the dough.

By the time the buns were rolled, cut and put into the pans for rising again, my eyes were getting heavy. It was way past my bedtime.

On Christmas morning, I'd wake to wonderful aromas wafting up from the kitchen—the sweet cinnamon buns mixing with the succulent turkey roasting. It was heaven...and I hadn't even opened my presents yet!

—Anne-Louise Bennett
Heflin, Louisiana

JUST WHAT I WANTED! **Most of us can recall a Christmas when there was but one special gift that could fulfill our hopes and dreams. When we found it under the tree on Christmas morning, the excitement and joy were unmatched.**

Ewing Galloway

Chapter Seven

Some Gifts Are Unforgettable

These days, some say we've lost the spirit of Christmas...that it's too commercialized and all the focus is on *things*. ("Gimme, gimme!") There's a lot of truth in what they say.

Grandparents of my age come home from holiday visits and grouse about the excesses bestowed upon kids today. ("Too much, too much!") Things sure weren't like that years ago. We were lucky to find an orange in our stocking.

True enough. But in some ways, times haven't changed all that much. For instance, if you carefully read the wish lists from "Our Town's 100 Neediest Families" that newspapers publish before Christmas, you'll note that many parents today are just as desperate to bring a little Christmas happiness to their children as our parents once were.

Just one doll, just one red coaster wagon. It could be a child's most unforgettable gift 50 years from now. So you can look at a modern Christmas in another way. It's still as much about *giving* as it is about receiving. It's about bestowing joy and making dreams come true. Especially for children.

Santa Came!

It takes a cold heart not to be touched when still-sleepy little ones come from warm beds, tousle-haired in their robes and slippers to gasp and stand wide-eyed before the Christmas tree. Santa was here! The glass of milk by the hearth is empty and the cookies are gone. There are, indeed, gifts under the tree. Santa remembered!

Will they someday recall one of those presents as "the most unforgettable gift I ever received?" Which ones will earn a permanent place in their hearts?

Some gifts can never be forgotten, and often they're the simplest, least costly of things. The memories they make have nothing to do with monetary value. They have everything to do with dreams and love.

For my wife, it was a bride doll. It was the one doll in all the world that she wanted. And one Christmas morning, there it was—complete with a trousseau, a quilt and tiny pillowcase—all lovingly sewn by her mother while her father was in the service overseas. It wasn't Peg's only Christmas present, but it was *the* present! Every year that goes by, she appreciates that gift a little more.

A present that stands out brightly in my memory wasn't for me, but for my children. At the time, I worked for a cranky, unpredictable, seemingly unpleasable man who appeared to be a medical miracle—the first human ever born without a heart. I was terrified of him. Scrooge would have been, too.

But then he arrived at our home one Christmas Eve. He was bent over from the weight of the heavy carton he was carrying. He dropped it on our living room floor with a ponderous *thud*, grumbled "Merry Christmas" and left.

Gift of Knowledge

When we opened it, we discovered a complete brand-new set of Encyclopedia Brittanica! From *him*? How could it be?

When I called on Christmas Day to tell him how thrilled our family was with his generous gift, he grouched, "Well, maybe your kids will have a chance to grow up smarter than you are. Have a nice holiday."

Finding out he really was human underneath all that crustiness was my best Christmas gift that year.

Ask family and friends to name their most unforgettable Christmas gift and you'll get surprising answers. "I'll never forget the Christmas when..." they'll say. Then it's a good bet the present they remember best won't be something that cost a lot. But it was *worth* a lot in terms of the thought or effort someone put into it...like that homemade checkerboard I mentioned in the introduction to Chapter Five.

"The best-remembered present often didn't cost a lot..."

Receiving the perfect gift is a lasting thrill. But so is *giving* the perfect gift. We all have our favorite memories of both giving and receiving, as do the *Reminisce* readers who share theirs with us in the pages that follow.

I think it's a chapter you'll ask your own children and grandchildren to read, or read again yourself on a day when you need to be reassured that there are a lot of truly good people in this world. *—Clancy Strock*

Oh, to Skate Like Sonja!

By Sue Hanson, Mentor, Ohio

SONJA HENIE was my idol back in 1942. I was 10 years old and stood in long theater lines every Saturday to watch the Olympic champion skate in musical extravaganzas. She glided like a swan, and I knew that if I only had a pair of beautiful white skates like Sonja's, I'd be able to glide just like her.

A few days before Christmas, Mother and Father called me into the living room. They said Father would take me shopping for skates rather than taking a chance on buying them as a surprise. They had to fit exactly right. "Remember, the most important thing is that they have extra support for her ankles," Mother insisted. "Hers are so weak."

The following Saturday, I was up early and dressed long before my father. Soon we went uptown to Emery's Hardware Store, the place that seemed to have everything in our northwestern-Pennsylvania oil town.

The second floor had been turned into a winter wonderland. As we walked up the creaky wooden stairs, my heart beat faster. Beautiful Christmas lights welcomed us, and a tiny train tooted its whistle, beckoning us to see all the new dolls, games and, yes, skates in stock for Christmas.

NICE ON ICE. **Every girl's dream was to skate like Sonja Henie, who is seen here with Buff McCusker of Valencia, California. Buff was in two movies with Sonja in the '40s. Sue Hanson never skated like Sonja, but she was a hit with the local kids.**

BLACK AND BLUE. **Sue was sad when she got black skates instead of white. But it all worked out just fine.**

Father told the clerk what we wanted, and she came back with a box. When she opened it, I instantly saw my dream—white soft leather with brilliant blades, just like Sonja's! I could already see myself gliding gracefully across the pond, with all my friends admiring my fine new skates.

I sat down on the floor and tried one on. Dad laced it up and helped me stand. The clerk bent over, felt my foot, then slowly shook her head. Looking up at my father, she said, "I truly don't think you should buy these for her because they don't fit well enough."

"I'd be able to glide on the ice just like Sonja..."

Suddenly, my mother's words echoed in my head: "Be sure they fit exactly right; her ankles are so weak..."

But I didn't care how they fit! I'd be wearing several pairs of socks to take up more room...I *loved* those skates ...they were *so* beautiful...

How About These?

Tears welled in my eyes, and Father put his arm around me. "Don't worry, honey," he said, "I'm sure they have other skates in the store with the support you need."

In seconds, the clerk was back. But when she opened the box, I saw the ugliest sight I could imagine—black skates! She put one on me, then snugged the leather strap that went around the ankle. This extra strap would give me the support I needed.

I stood up and prayed the skates wouldn't fit, but they matched my feet perfectly.

Dad asked if they came in white, but the clerk shook her head. By now, tears were running down my cheeks...but I wanted new skates so badly that I said they'd be okay. Deep down, though, I knew I'd never skate like Sonja.

The day after Christmas was crisp and cold, and the pond was frozen smooth. My best friend had also received skates for Christmas (white ones) and suggested we try them out. I reluctantly agreed, hoping no one would notice my embarrassing black skates.

We huddled near a bonfire and laced up our skates, and I was glad no one else was around to see me. Then three neighborhood boys appeared.

"*Wow*, are you lucky!" one of them marveled as he looked at my skates. "You've got *racing* skates! Those are the neatest skates of anyone out here!"

My frown quickly turned into a smile as I saw the genuine excitement on their faces. Then I said to my friend, "Come on, I'll race you to the other side of the pond." We did, and I won!

I was so proud of my new skates—even if I'd never quite glide like Sonja.

Two-Wheeler Was Double-Good Gift

By Marian Laub, Milwaukee, Wisconsin

I GREW UP in a big family, which meant you didn't always get what you wanted for Christmas. For a long time, I'd wished for a bicycle, but it was never there under the tree. I'd feel sad for a little while, but I knew deep down it was an awful lot to ask for.

On Christmas Eve in 1957, I was a disappointed 10-year-old. We'd opened our gifts, and none of mine had two wheels. Father asked my younger sister and me to take all the torn wrapping paper into the basement. So we gathered it up and

"There, in the middle of the room, stood a shiny new bicycle..."

carried it downstairs. When we came back up, we noticed it had become very quiet in the living room.

We walked in and there, in the middle of the room, stood a shiny new bicycle and a tricycle. My sister knew which was hers and ran straight to it. But I just stood in the doorway, dumbfounded.

My bike was *beautiful*, with streamers of red, white and blue hanging from the handlebars.

Everyone was waiting for me to run excitedly to the bike. Instead, I looked at my father and started to cry! I really *was* happy, but I was so excited I just didn't know what to do. I ran and hid in the bathroom—maybe to hide my tears.

After a few minutes, my brother Butch came and got me. We went back to the living room and then took the bike and tricycle outside. Even with snow on the ground, my sister and I pedaled around the block for hours.

I rode that bike for the next 8 years. It then was passed down to nephews and nieces, ending up in my brother-in-law's grandmother's garage. When she died in 1986, he asked if I wanted the bike back. Of course, I said yes. I put the bike in my attic, thinking that someday I would ride it again.

In 1990, I found the bike when going through things in the attic because we were moving. The tires were flat and it needed repair, but I convinced my husband we should keep it.

On the Christmas Eve after moving into our new house, I got the surprise of my life again. I had taken the wrapping paper out, and when I returned to the living room, there was my bike!

My husband had taken it to a local repair shop to be cleaned and fixed. He even put white and blue streamers on the handlebars. I started to cry...but this time I didn't run from the room!

After nearly 40 years, I still ride that bike as often as I can. Each time I do, I think about what a wonderful Christmas it was—both of them. ▲

RECYCLED CYCLE. **When Marian Laub got her first bicycle for Christmas in 1957 (above), she never dreamed it would be the bike she'd ride nearly 40 years later (top). It was a Christmas bicycle that really was recycled!**

BLAST OFF! Her son was ready to go to the moon on his third Christmas in the 1950s, says Betty Reifeiss of Santa Maria, California. Nice space suit, too.

Wish Book Choice Led to Exciting Wait

By Charles Johnson, Dunnellon, Florida

AN INFLUENZA epidemic in the late 1920s left my mother widowed with four little children. Those were the days before Social Security and children's benefits, so she had no choice but to reluctantly place her three older children in the State Orphan's Home at Corsicanna, Texas.

My two sisters and I rode to the home in a neighbor's Model T on December 28, 1929. I was too late to celebrate Christmas in the Little Boys Building, and everyone else was playing with new toys furnished by the state of Texas. Next year, it would be my turn.

When summer rolled around, my home-appointed "big brother", Ray, talked eagerly about the approaching Christmas.

"Charlie Wayne, Mrs. Hawkins will soon tell us to select our toy for Christmas," said Ray, looking up from our game of marbles. "We'll get to look through the Sears catalog to choose!"

In those days, the Sears and Roebuck catalog was known as "the wish book", and just as Ray said, we soon got our wishes. We were told to break off in groups of six and wash our hands before paging through the catalog. Ray, our group leader, would write down our names, the toys chosen and the catalog order numbers. The state allowed $1 for each boy.

"I wanted everything on those pages!"

It was such a difficult decision! Would it be marbles? A football? Toy cars? I wanted *everything* on those pages but finally settled on a black cast-iron Model T Ford. Maybe it was from the memory of riding to my new home in one the year before. Whatever the reason, I couldn't wait to see my toy, and I looked forward to it for 4 long months.

WISH BOOK. **There were many wonderful things to wish for in the old Sears catalog.**

CHRISTMAS KIDS. **Three days after Christmas 1929, Charles Johnson (above at age 4) sat with sisters (from left) Jewell, Adele and Amalene.**

On Friday, December 19, 1930, several of us younger boys were told to help the older fellows cut a Christmas tree for our building.

We went down to a clump of cedar trees about a half mile from our building, where the trees were perfectly shaped. They were the prettiest green I had ever seen!

One of the senior boys cut down the tree and fashioned a stand in the woodworking shop. We were a proud group as we stood that perfect tree in the hall of our building.

Made Paper Chains

Our matron, Mrs. Hawkins, showed us how to make paper chains to decorate the tree. We went up the stepladder to swag the chains over the tree from top to bottom.

On Christmas morning, Ray ordered us all to get up, wash our faces, dress and make our beds. "It's Christmas morning! We get our toys today!" he said.

Under that special Christmas tree, along with our toys, we found durable beanbags made by the students of Texas Woman's University. From the Red Cross were red and green mesh stockings filled with an apple, orange, banana, nuts and candy.

In nearly 70 years since, my sweetest Christmas memory is of that morning in 1930 at the Corsicanna State Orphan's Home. I'll never forget how excited I was to finally see that handsome black cast-iron Model T Ford with my name on it. ▲

ROCKING AND REMINISCING. **This rocker has been soothing the bodies and minds of folks since it was first a cherished Christmas present in 1903.**

Beloved Chair Will Always Have a Home

By Judi Weber, Carthage, Missouri

I HAD PLACED a newspaper ad seeking an old comfortable rocking chair. The ad was answered, addresses exchanged, and I knocked on a door that was opened by a small elderly woman. She invited me into her old-fashioned living room.

She avoided my questions about the rocker but instead asked about my plans, interests and how I felt about old furniture. After what seemed to be a long time, she became silent. Then she cleared her throat and told me this story:

"When I was a little girl, around 1903, my family lived on a farm. We were poor but happy. The weeks before Christmas all of us kept very busy making gifts and preparing the food.

"When Christmas morning came, everyone had a gift but Mother. She tried to hide her disappointment in not receiving anything from Father. Meanwhile, he donned his winter hat and coat and started off through the yard.

"Morning chores were over, and we wondered where he was going. We wiped the frost from the windows and kept watch for him, and soon my brother called, 'I see Dad coming from the neighbors'...and he's carrying something on his shoulders!'

Surprise for Mother

"Dad stepped into the kitchen and unwrapped the most beautiful rocking chair we'd ever seen—his gift to our mother. After the harvest, he'd ordered the oak rocker from our 1903 Sears and Roebuck catalog. A wagon had delivered the chair to the neighbor's, where it spent the autumn in their barn.

"Mom gently touched the rocker. She moved it close to our wood stove, sat down and began to gently rock. This gift from Father was her most cherished possession, and Mom spent many hours sitting beside the stove, enjoying her rocker along with the aroma of baking bread."

"This rocker must go to someone who will love and cherish it..."

After telling her story, the woman fell silent again, then turned to study me. "I'm all that's left of my family. They've all died and I have no one to care for my rocker. It must go to someone who will love it, cherish it and keep it always."

I paid for the rocker and carefully loaded it into my pickup. As I drove away, I could see the small woman watching from her doorway.

Touched by her story, I stopped to share it with my own dad. He, too, was impressed by the story and offered to reglue the rocker's joints for me.

For the next several years, every time I visited Dad, he was sitting in that old chair. His favorite pastimes of reading and rocking were combined, and not a word was mentioned about returning that chair to me.

When Dad passed away, the rocker came back to me, its golden oak arms worn smooth by the touch of loving hands.

Each year as I decorate my Christmas tree, I pause and settle back in that special chair. Then I slowly rock and think of a snowy morning back in 1903 and a father's gift...and then I remember my own dad.

That old Christmas rocker will continue to have a loving home and its story will live on when I pass it along—very carefully—to the next person chosen to be its owner. ▲

"Adopted Dad" Gave Sweet Gift

CHRISTMAS was always my dad's favorite time of year. In 1959, when I was 11 years old, Dad passed away. I knew the holidays would be especially sad without him.

I spent Christmas Eve with friends that year, and since they hadn't expected my visit, there wasn't a present under the tree for me.

Everyone began opening their gifts and I sat there watching. Then a wonderful man (who years later became my father-in-law) noticed me sitting there empty-handed.

Someone had given him a box of chocolate-covered cherries. But when he thought I wasn't looking, he ever-so-gently rewrapped the candy and wrote on the gift tag, "To Pat, from your adopted dad. I love you."

If I live to be 100 years old, I'll never forget how special and loved he made me feel with a 39¢ box of candy that long-ago Christmas. *—Pat Williams Knoxville, Tennessee*

Lunch Counter Owner Was Big Wheel to His Boys

DURING the early 1930s, my parents bought a small restaurant called The Wonder Lunch in Wichita, Kansas. Our family car was given over as the down payment on some sparse fixtures and for the first month's rent.

Our first year was *tough*. We had no car, lived in a one-room basement apartment and had to work very hard. Dad told my brother, Bill, and me that our family Christmas would be a small one that year. We'd just have to wait for the things we really wanted.

A few days before Christmas, on an unseasonably warm Kansas winter day, Bill and I were playing softball with some friends in a vacant lot.

"Bill, look!" one friend shouted. "Isn't that your dad?"

It sure was! We were surprised to see Dad riding down the street on a brand-new, bright red Western Flyer bicycle with one hand on the handlebar...with the other hand, he struggled to maintain control of a matching blue Western Flyer!

The photo of The Wonder Lunch building (at right) always calls to mind the sacrifices that my parents obviously made for us to have those wonderful Christmas bikes. That unselfish act taught me more about unconditional love than any book, lecture or advice ever could. *—Robert Black Wichita, Kansas*

Lonely Coupled Hungered for A Traditional Christmas

NOTHING could have been more miserable. It was Christmas Eve back in the 1950s, and my husband had just been transferred to Minneapolis by his employer. It was our first Christmas away from family and friends, and it was snowy, cold and dark outside.

Determined not to be alone, we'd invited another lonely young couple from our apartment building to share Christmas Eve supper.

To our dismay, however, my husband's paycheck hadn't yet arrived in the mail. To add to the problem, we discovered that we each had written checks to buy a gift for the other. That left a grand total of $2.03 in our checking account, and the refrigerator was bare!

Heartsick and embarrassed, we debated which one of us had the tact to phone our new friends and explain the problem. We knew that we certainly could survive on peanut butter sandwiches and cereal, but that wouldn't do for dinner guests.

I was about to cry when the doorbell rang. Into my husband's arms the mailman thrust a large beat-up cardboard box sent by my aunt and uncle in central Wisconsin.

We tore open the sorry-looking box and found a treasure: Two freshly dressed farm-grown chickens, a bag of potatoes from the patch down by the barn, onions and carrots with bits of rich soil still clinging to them, a couple of pounds of pork sausage and *lefse*, that glorious flour-and-potato flat bread without which no Norwegian Christmas is complete. Plus there was my aunt's angel food cake, made with 13 egg whites and baked to perfection in a hot wood stove.

This generous gift from my aunt and uncle had saved the day...and it was an anticlimax when the paycheck came by special delivery a few hours later! *—Gudren Conmy Minneapolis, Minnesota*

WONDERFUL TIMES. **The Wonder Lunch restaurant in 1930s Wichita, Kansas had all the amenities, recalls Robert Black. Robert's dad is behind the counter, and his mom at the end. Times might have been tough then, but Dad managed to make two kids real happy with a pair of Christmas bicycles.**

TELL SANTA. If there was one sure way to get that special Christmas present, it was to go directly to the man himself. Santa delivered!

Santa's Promise Made for Glum Mom, Gleeful Daughter

MY daughter Claudia was born after her dad went overseas in World War II. When she was 8 months old, we got word he was missing in action.

In 1946, when Claudia was 2-1/2 years old, she was afraid of Santa Claus but agreed to go see him. I took her to Hornes Department Store, where their Santa never promised a gift unless parents gave an okay.

Had it not been for the huge teddy bear beside Santa's throne, Claudia would never have gone near him. He coaxed her into his lap by promising her (to my surprise and mouthed "*No, no, no*!") that teddy bear for Christmas.

There was no way I could afford that pricey bear, but Santa just smiled as we left. Claudia was ecstatic...I was upset.

On the way home, all she talked about was that bear. I tried to gently suggest that maybe Santa might not be able to deliver such a large bear. Of course, I couldn't change her mind, and that made me even *more* upset with Santa. I knew Claudia would be heartbroken come Christmas morning.

While she napped, the doorbell rang and the mailman gave me a big package from an APO in the Pacific. Inside was the same giant teddy bear that Santa had promised! A note said, "Claudia, I knew your daddy would want you to have this. Merry Christmas, Jerry."

Jerry, my husband's best childhood friend, had ordered the bear months earlier. On Christmas morning when Claudia found that bear under the tree, she said to me, her doubting mother, "I *knew* Santa Claus would!"

Claudia never did get to meet her daddy because he remained missing in action and was never accounted for. But that teddy bear, ordered from across the globe, was literally loved to pieces. We shall always believe in Santa Claus.

—Regina Mueller
Pittsburgh, Pennsylvania

Sleigh Bells Announced Special Delivery

WHEN WE were married in 1938, my husband and I moved from southern Michigan to Traverse City, 180 miles north. The post office there delivered Christmas packages by horse and sleigh complete with ringing bells, and I thought it looked *so romantic*.

No packages on that sleigh were ever for us, though, because we'd planned to go back and spend Christmas with our families and exchange gifts in person.

One day I was surprised when that mail sleigh did stop at our house. The postman stepped up to the door with a good-sized box! When I opened it, I found that my husband had gone to the dime store, bought me a set of plastic measuring cups, took them to the office and asked the girls there to help him wrap them. He then mailed them to me.

How romantic can a gift get?

After nearly 60 years, we're still happily married.

—Mrs. Fred Bishop
Traverse City, Michigan

This Gift Wasn't One To Sniff at

SANTA brought me a fancy little bottle of fragrance when I was 10. It was my first perfume! I put the bottle in its box atop our upright piano so that it wouldn't be broken.

Several days later, my aunt and uncle dropped by for a visit. My 4-year-old sister and I were naturally eager to show them our presents.

I retrieved my perfume from its spot of safekeeping and proudly opened the box. It was *empty*...and I was heartbroken.

Mother asked my sister if she knew what had happened to the perfume.

"Uh-huh," she replied. "It was *good*." She drank it!

My little sister didn't suffer any ill effects, but I could have hit her at the time!

This remains the Christmas I remember the most...that memory alone rates with the best Yuletide gifts I ever received.

—Dorothy Schoenthal
Davenport, Iowa

WHAT, NO REINDEER? No matter, dashing through the snow in a one-horse open sleigh was just as much fun. In some parts of the country, a sleigh was the only way to get around at Christmas in the good old days.

Neighbor Helped Santa Out of a Fix

THE CHRISTMAS of 1930 was approaching and I was 4 years old. We lived on an apple orchard in the Yakima Valley of Washington and Dad made very little money—it would be a meager Christmas.

Mother blew out eggshells to make tree ornaments, while my older sisters cut out colored pictures from old magazines to stick to the eggshells with flour-and-water paste.

Each child would receive a single orange for Christmas, and Mom had saved enough sugar to make one batch of candy.

On Christmas morning, though, we were surprised when Mom and Dad woke us up and told us to come see what had happened.

All sorts of colored packages were there under the tree, and sitting at the table was our old neighbor, George St. Denis.

He asked if we'd heard a racket the night before. Of course, we hadn't. He told us he went out to investigate and saw Santa Claus and his reindeer stuck in an apple tree!

The only way Santa could get untangled was to unload his sleigh, so Mr. St. Denis brought the presents into our house!

There was a toy grand piano and a doll with pink dress and bonnet for me. There was a truck for my brother, Warren, a green glass necklace for sister Virginia and a red glass necklace for sister Alice.

There was a bag of nuts and some wide ribbon candy. After breakfast, we each got a piece of that candy and tried to make it last as long as possible. Later on, we had a Christmas feast, and Mr. St. Denis stayed.

Years later, I learned that this little old gray-haired man had walked 7 miles to town and back again, carrying all those presents on his back.

An elderly bearded man who lived alone with his dog on a small railroad pension gave our family the best Christmas anyone could ever have.

—Audra Burris, Sequim, Washington

J.C. Allen and Son

***SANTA CAME!* Just like these two kids, Audra Burris had a wonderful Christmas in 1930.**

Excited Tyke Nearly Missed New Bike

MY NEPHEW, Jerry, was promised a bike if he brought up his grades. Jerry responded and was doing much better in school, but as Christmas approached, his parents didn't have enough money to purchase the bike.

Jerry's grandparents called all of us (his aunts and uncles) and asked if we'd chip in with them for a bike. Jerry's mother, Dorothy, knew nothing of this.

On Christmas Day, we had all opened our presents, then Jerry was told to open an envelope that was hanging on the tree. The message inside sent him upstairs to find another note.

He went running off with his mother following, so we brought the bike up from the basement. Running upstairs and downstairs, Jerry and Dorothy finally passed through the living room, where the rest of us were seated with that shiny new bike.

"I have to check for a note in the refrigerator!" Jerry shouted. In his excitement, he ran right past his new bike. But his mother saw it, and we snickered as we waved Dorothy on to follow her son.

When Jerry finally came back to the living room, the look on that little boy's face was truly a gift for all of us.

—Rosemary Rush
Yamhill, Oregon

Archive Photos/Statile

***WHAT ELSE* would a kid want for Christmas? Like this boy, it didn't matter what kind, just so it was a bike.**

Santa Must Have Been Mistaken

By Viola Smith, Port Richey, Florida

THE YEAR was 1929, I was 6 years old and *so* excited! Mother was taking me and my best friend, Marion, downtown to see Santa.

I was bundled in a hand-me-down coat and heavy shoes given to me by my teacher. They were old-fashioned and several sizes too large, but I didn't care—we were going to the five-and-dime to see Santa!

I told him my name, that I'd been a good girl and that I wanted a blond baby doll and buggy. I even remembered to give him my address. Marion asked for a doll and buggy, too—plus a tea set.

I could hardly wait for Christmas! When that wonderful morning arrived, I ran into the parlor, but there was no doll or buggy. There was just a checkers game and a small celluloid doll that looked like Betty Boop.

"I didn't realize my parents had done the best they could..."

I didn't realize that the Depression was on and my parents had done the best they could. Instead, I figured Santa must have brought my gifts to the wrong house.

I sneaked out the back way and went next door to Marion's house. The family wasn't home, so I boldly entered. Nobody locked their doors in those days.

There She Was!

Under their Christmas tree was *my* doll and buggy. I knew she was mine because she had the blond hair that I had asked for. I wheeled her back home to my room, hugged and kissed her and named her "Angel".

While we were eating Christmas dinner, the doorbell rang. A policeman was at the door. He asked Mother if we'd seen or heard anything, because there had been a break-in at the neighbor's house.

"How terrible," Mother said. "What was taken?"

"A doll and buggy that belonged to their little girl," the officer said.

I stood behind Mom and cried, "No, Angel is mine! Santa brought her to the wrong house!"

I told them the whole story, then cried my heart out when the policeman took the doll and buggy away.

About a hour later, the doorbell rang once more. There stood the same policeman, but this time he was holding a lovely doll wrapped in a pink blanket.

He said to me, "Santa was busy and asked me to drop this off."

I hugged the policeman and cried for joy, "I knew Santa wouldn't forget me!" He, too, was overcome, and had tears in his eyes.

That kind man then handed Mom a stocking filled with apples, oranges, nuts and candy canes, but I wasn't interested in those goodies. I ran upstairs with my new doll, and rocked her and sang songs to her. It was the best Christmas ever...and a lesson learned.

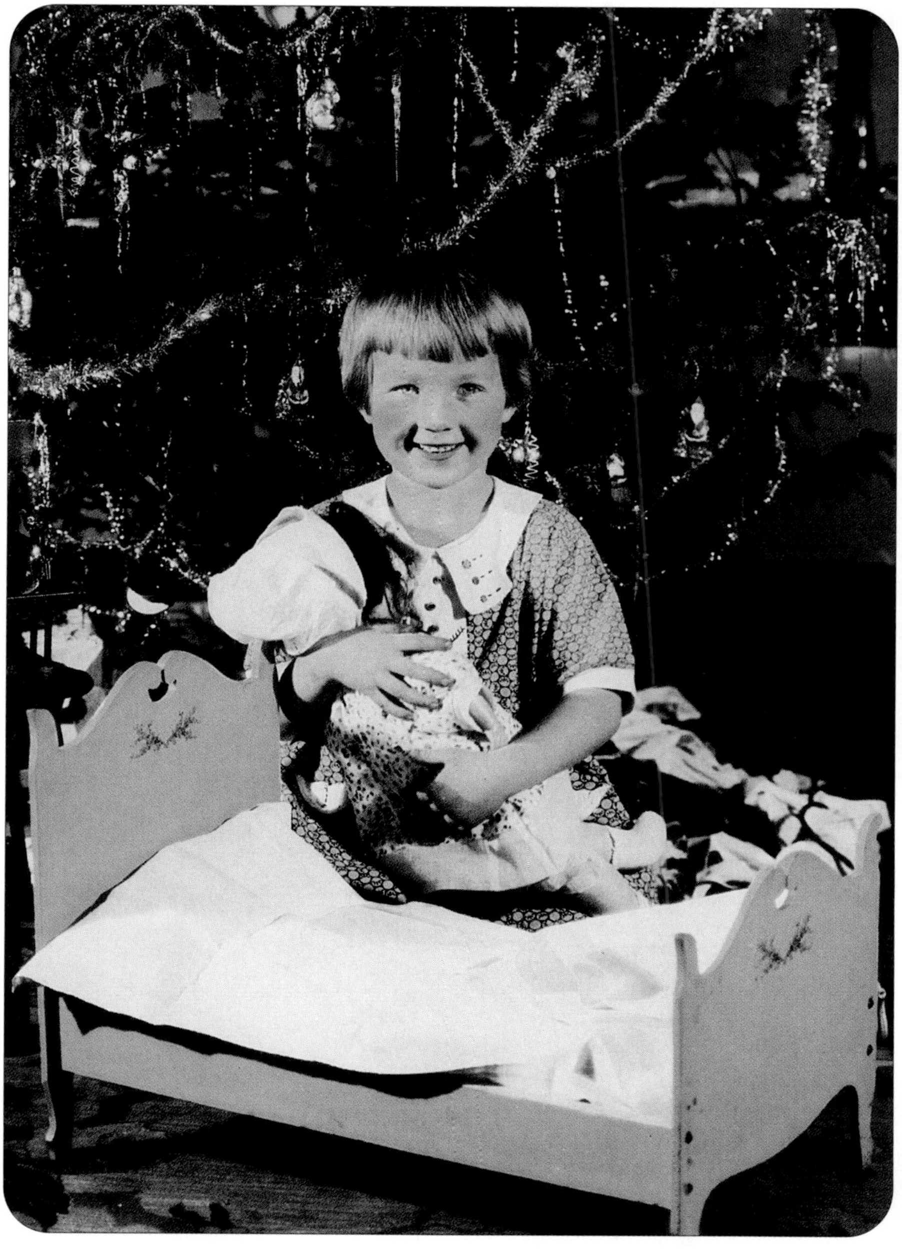

J.C. Allen and Son

GIRLS AND DOLLS. **If boys want bikes for Christmas, girls, like this one, want dolls. Sometimes, though, Santa gets the address wrong, as Viola Smith learned in 1929. But, because it's Christmas, miracles usually happen.**

Lesson in Love Was Mother's Gift

By Verla Mooth, Goodman, Missouri

DECEMBER of 1929 was bleak in the Ozark hills of southwest Missouri. Times had truly been tough that year, and it would be difficult for Mama to get our family through the winter without going hungry.

The austerity of our life in the hills had made Mama ingenious and resourceful. At the end of summer, she'd canned all the fruits and vegetables she could. And as Christmas approached, she was busy making plans. Even if there was no money to buy gifts for her children, she was going to make the holidays as nice as she could.

I had long forgotten the summer walk she and I had taken to pick watercress. We were exploring a deserted old house when Mama found a discarded doll with its arms off and its face chipped and dirty. I didn't notice that she had picked it up and brought it home.

As Christmas approached, I was sure that I wouldn't be receiving any gifts—and when the big morning finally arrived, even a fresh blanket of snow wasn't exciting enough to pull me from my warm bed.

Mama called for me to get up, and then, to my amazement, I heard the excited voices of my brothers and sisters and the tearing of wrapping paper. We had gifts after all!

Gathered for Gifts

Everyone had gathered in our front room, where a tiny tree had been decorated with strings of popcorn and red and white crepe paper.

I knelt beside the tree and saw the most beautiful doll bed with a handmade comforter, two chairs and a table with brightly colored tin dishes. Side by side on the little bed was my favorite old doll dressed in pretty new clothes plus a new black doll!

I grabbed the little black doll, pressed her to my heart and exclaimed, "Mama, she's beautiful! Where did she come from?"

"That's not important," Mama replied, then she told me this story:

"When God made this beautiful earth, He made his children all different colors like flowers. On the first Christmas, God sent His son as a tiny baby so His children could someday come and live with Him forever. He loves all His children the same, and we are supposed to love them, too. This is the true meaning of Christmas."

Mama needn't have worried. I loved my white doll and my new black doll just the same. I spent long hours playing with them. They would have tea parties seated in their chairs at the table. They rested side by side beneath the patchwork comforter.

Creativity Made Magic

Mama had created this magical Christmas with ingenuity. She used old strawberry crates to make the lovely toy furniture. And my treasured black doll was the one she'd found at the old abandoned house.

Later, Mama discovered a small can of black enamel in the attic of our farmhouse. She thinned it down with turpentine and painted the doll's chipped face and body a glossy black.

The lips were painted red with cake coloring, and new arms were improvised from black stockings stuffed with cotton. A crimson dress trimmed with scraps of white lace made her look beautiful.

I had been raised in a county where no blacks lived, so this was a new experience for me. A mother's love and resourcefulness and a recycled doll taught me to love all races the same.

It is said that necessity is the mother of invention. On that Christmas, necessity became the mother of truth. My gift that year was a lesson for which I am eternally grateful. ▲

CHRISTMAS ALL YEAR. Even when it was summer, little Verla Mooth (on the right above) played with her white and black dolls, sharing the fun with friends. Verla's mother (top photo, with her husband) had created a Christmas present that not only gave a little girl joy, but created lasting memories.

Surprising Star Appeared on Christmas Eve

I'LL NEVER FORGET Christmas Eve of 1936. All the relatives gathered on our Minnesota farm. About 7 p.m., we children were sent to the barn to help the hired man milk the cows and feed the cats. Just about the time the chores were finished, we heard sleigh bells and someone shout, "Merry Christmas, Santa!"

We rushed back to the house and, sure enough, there were sleigh tracks in the snow! Under the Christmas tree were beautiful packages of all kinds. I had asked for a pony, but changed my mind and said I wanted a bike. Obviously, neither was under the tree, so I was very disappointed.

But then came a knock at the kitchen door and Mother asked me to answer it. She said it was probably the neighbor boy (I had a big crush on him at the time). I didn't want to answer and reluctantly opened the door.

To my surprise, there stood a little buckskin colt! He had a white star on his forehead and a beautiful black mane and tail.

The little colt ran into the kitchen and nearly knocked me over, and that was how I met my best friend for many years. He was a Missouri trotter and I named him "Merrylegs Ginger Pepper Chase". (Chase was our family name, and the other names came from the horses in *Black Beauty.*) Merrylegs lived to a wonderful old age of 20, and my memories of him make the Christmas of 1936 one I'll always cherish.

—Rosemary Chase Clawson, North Port, Florida

***TROTTING GIFT!* Rosemary Clawson won't forget the year her present walked in.**

Little Lost Pup Made Christmas Bright

By Harriett Bump, Eldridge, Iowa

IT WAS a hot summer day in 1924 when Mama brought home a dog for the family. She'd been shopping in downtown Des Moines when the small black puppy whined at her feet, licked her hand and won her heart.

Mama felt sorry for the hot little pup, whose hair was matted and snarled with cockleburs. She brought him home to my brother, Leonard, who was 7, sister Kathryn, 11, and me, age 12.

We jumped right in and gave the puppy a bath and removed those awful burs. We fed him, watered him and, after a family vote, named him "Bozo".

***"BOZO" COMES HOME.* Not one to miss a holiday, Bozo surprised everyone by bumming a ride home with the family's Christmas tree.**

We discovered Bozo was a very good Catholic. Leonard was an altar boy, serving Mass each morning, and Bozo was always ready to go to St. Peter's Church with him.

All of the kids liked Bozo and somehow smuggled him into church each day. He had chosen a special niche beside the confessional. If Father Murphy or any of the nuns knew he was there, they never said a word.

When Mass was over, we went upstairs to our classrooms and Bozo headed home 'til noon. Then he would be back in front of school ready to walk home with us for lunch.

Alarm Went Out

One day in August, we went to the Iowa State Fair. When we returned home, Bozo wasn't there! By nightfall, the alarm went out. All the kids from the neighborhood and school went door-to-door searching for their little friend.

After a week of false leads, everyone glumly accepted the fact that something had happened to Bozo.

The months rolled by, and Christmas Eve day was a busy time for the entire family. I helped Mama fix our Christmas dinner, and Kathryn and Leonard had to clean the house thoroughly before going to buy the Christmas tree.

At nightfall, Kathryn and Leonard pulled the sled to the tree lot and chose a tree for 35¢. Tinsel was 10¢ extra. After those younger kids left to get our tree, I had a chance to wrap their gifts.

They had been gone about an hour when the noise started. Grandma and I ran to the door to see what all the laughing and screaming was about.

There was Bozo! He had just run up to my brother and sister and jumped on the sled with the new Christmas tree.

We never found out where that little dog had been all those months, but no one cared. Getting Bozo back was the best gift our family could have received. He made that Christmas the happiest one of my childhood. ▲

Look What

DOGS AND HEPCATS. You never knew what Santa was going to bring. Barry Brown (above) didn't get his dog, "Wiggy", for Christmas, but Wiggy sure enjoyed the holiday, says Barry's dad, Richard, of North St. Paul, Minnesota. Meantime, another Christmas in the '50s (below) promised to be musical, or at least loud, for this family.

Gail Denham

ROCKIN' BY THE BABY. On his third Christmas in 1914 (above), Richard Preusser of St. Louis, Missouri enjoyed his rocking horse, while his siblings joined in posing for their father, an amateur photographer.

Don Condon

ALL SMILES. Her children were thrilled when they opened their presents on Christmas morning in 1945, says Mrs. Charles Weusthoff of Jennings, Missouri. And why not? What girl didn't want a teddy bear, and what boy a truck and shovel?

Santa Brought!

GIFTS THAT LAST. **The toys John Leder of Mayville, Wisconsin is pictured with on Christmas 1931 (above) he still has. "Fluffy" the cat, however, has gone to catnip heaven. Patricia Goeke of Oak Park, Illinois at least has the photo of her third Christmas (below).**

CHRISTMAS CONCERT. **Shelly Patterson's recital this Christmas in the early '60s was a one-time thing, says her uncle, Gordon Preiser of Lancaster, Pennsylvania, who took the photo. Shelly gave up a musical "career" and became a physical therapist.**

SuperStock

SHE'S THE TOPS. **Debbie Schepker learned how to spin the big singing top all by herself on Christmas 1954. Mom Jane, of Midlothian, Virginia, shared the holiday photo. Looks like somebody else got a streamlined car to play with.**

Father's Dollhouse Gave Double Joy

By Eleanor Taylor, Westbrook, Maine

THE BEST Christmas present I ever received was given to me twice—with a lapse of 40 years in between!

Back in 1927, when I was 6, my father designed and built a special dollhouse for me. Since he worked a minimum of 74 hours a week as a grocery store clerk, it wasn't an easy undertaking.

Most produce was shipped in wooden crates then, so Dad had a good supply of lumber to build this two-story, six-room house. He designed the house with double walls, allowing it to be wired for electricity. He did so with an eight-bulb string of Christmas tree lights.

As the holiday approached, there was no way to keep this building project a secret. But knowing about it didn't diminish my joy at receiving that special dollhouse on Christmas morning. When we set it up in the living room window, the local power company in Garrettsville, Ohio was so impressed they tried to buy it!

I eventually outgrew my desire to play with the dollhouse. The last I recalled seeing it was when I was in my teens and it was being used as part of a Christmas display in the window of the grocery store where Dad worked.

> *"The local power company was so impressed they tried to buy it!"*

I eventually married and had three girls of my own, but I gave little thought to what had happened to the dollhouse. Then, in 1968, while reminiscing with friends, I shared my memories of that special dollhouse.

I assumed it was long gone, since the grocery store had moved to another location and the space had been taken over by a hardware store.

One night just before the holidays, a friend who'd heard my reminiscing asked me to go to a store with him. I assumed he wanted some advice on a Christmas gift for his wife, because I'd helped him in previous years. Instead, we went to the hardware store.

HOUSE IS HOME AGAIN. **The amazing dollhouse Eleanor Taylor's father built for her for Christmas 1927 was discovered 40 years later and brought home. Eleanor (above with the house) said the lights still worked! She then set out to redecorate her old house.**

He led me up some dusty stairs to the second floor and there, under piles of trash, sat my dollhouse! The men loaded it into a pickup truck and we brought it home. The little house was in poor shape, but amazingly, the lights still worked.

Since then, my father's thoughtfulness so long ago continues "giving" to me. I've spent many pleasant hours renovating my dollhouse.

I've redecorated the walls, upgraded the damaged fireplace and chimney with real miniature bricks, replaced broken windows and updated the wiring. I've even added to the electrical system, which is now controlled by 20 miniature switches.

I built kitchen appliances and other furniture and made linens for the beds. One of the most innovative items in the house is a lighted aquarium on a little wrought-iron base. Inside is real sand from Florida and bits of Maine sea glass.

I plan to finish the house, write its history and then donate it to the historical society in my hometown. That way, the best Christmas present I ever received will bring joy to others and honor the memory of my father, who gave me so much. ▲

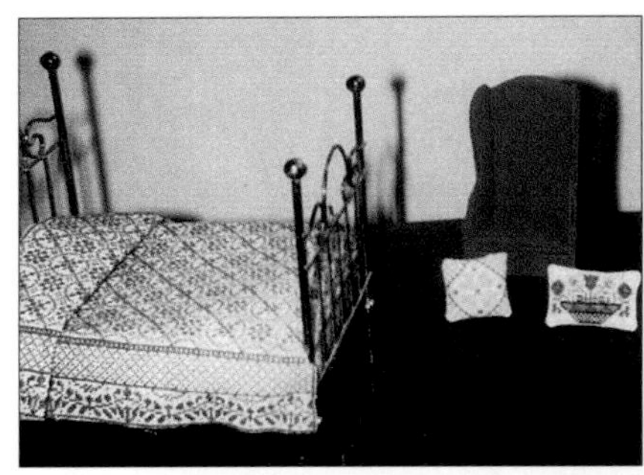

CUSTOM-MADE. **No store-bought furnishings in her house, says Eleanor. The kitchen (below) and a bedroom (above) contain furniture and fixtures she made. Eleanor will donate it to the local historical society.**

LIKE FATHER, LIKE SON. Not one to let a Christmas tradition end, Margaret Smith's "little" brother, Ted (above right), picked up where Dad (above left) left off.

Dad's Gifts Colored Christmas

By Margaret Linn Smith, Prescott, Arizona

MY DAD was an original. Each December, he'd mysteriously disappear for half a day. He'd arrive home later with small identical packages for every female over age 15 in our family.

He usually went alone on these trips, but when I was 6 years old, he told me, "Come on, Pidge. It's time to secret-shop."

I slipped my hand in his as we started down the walk. I moved closer to him and felt his strong hand and his rough tweed overcoat, which smelled faintly like Old Spice after-shave.

Soon we saw the neon sign blinking: "Horne's Department Store". In the window stood elves in green velvet suits with pointed hats. Their tiny hands moved up and down as they worked, and Santa stood in the middle of the bustle, smiling and humming *Deck the Halls*. Mrs. Claus cut out Christmas cookies in time to the music.

Favorite Ladies Listed

Dad squeezed my hand—I could see he was excited. Inside the store, he made a beeline for the cosmetics counter. At one end were perfumes and body lotions; at the other end were rouges and powders. In between were the lipsticks, and that's where he wanted to be.

Dad took a ragged piece of paper from his back pocket. It had been folded and unfolded many times from the looks of it. On it was a list of names of women in our family. My name would not appear for 9 more years.

Momma's name headed the list.

"Now, Mother doesn't wear too much makeup," Dad explained to the clerk. "She wears a little loose powder and a little rouge. On very special occasions, she wears a tiny bit of lipstick."

The salesgirl picked up the first tube and dabbed a bit of color on the back of her hand. Too red.

"The salesgirl dabbed a bit of color on the back of her hand..."

She reached for the next one. Too orange.

She brought out Classic Red, Victorian Mauve, Simply Scarlet, Morning Mist, One Perfect Rose, Coral Fire, Peach Blush, Red Velvet Silk, Tea Rose...

"Ohhhh," Dad and I crooned together. Soft Pink Silk was *perfect* for Momma.

Next on the list was my oldest sister.

"Now for Ruthie. She has big, dark, dancing eyes. She wears her hair short and curly. She works in an office and wears gray and navy suits with white or pink blouses," Dad said, before describing his daughter's sense of humor and love of practical jokes. Dad was in his glory when describing his children, all eight of us.

More Hues to Choose

We looked at more shades: Orchid, Blush Pink, Watermelon, Mauve, Natural Frost, Woodrose, Burnished Copper, Peach Champagne. And finally the one—Cherry Tart!

At last we found the perfect lipstick for each girl in the family. "Wasn't that fun?" Dad asked on our walk home.

It *was* fun. But the most fun came on my 15th Christmas, when I received my very own special lipstick! It was Cabernet.

For the next 24 Christmases, I received a tube of Cabernet from Dad. Then, in October of 1972, I knew Christmas would never be the same again. Dad passed away, and no special little package would be under the tree.

But early that December, I found a familiar-sized package in the mailbox. My hands began to shake as I slowly unwrapped the package. I pulled the top off the lipstick and there was my Cabernet! Tears fell on my hands as I slowly rolled the lipstick out.

Our little brother, Ted, had taken up Dad's tradition. He's now been at it for 23 years. ▲

***SQUEEZE BOX SERENADE.* Howard Batchelder (above with great-grandchildren) still gets a kick out of playing his accordion for them, or anyone, at Christmas. Great-grandson Sean will inherit the instrument.**

This Present Held the Key To Lifetime of Enjoyment

AT CHRISTMASTIME in 1948, I was 11 years old, and all the girls in my Scout troop were going caroling around town in Wilmington, Ohio.

I dressed as warmly as possible and went out to sing on that cold wintry night. When I returned home much later, everything seemed strangely dark.

I walked into the living room and noticed something big and unfamiliar. I turned on the lamp and there was an old upright piano.

I couldn't believe my eyes! A piano had been my dream for *years*. Immediately, I sat down just to run my fingers over the keys. I didn't know how to play but knew that I'd soon take piano lessons.

I was so excited I didn't even notice I wasn't sitting on a piano bench. A kitchen chair had been placed there for me.

That old piano came from a country church, and a group of my sister's friends had moved it to our home to surprise me.

What a wonderful Christmas gift! Today, as I play a more modern piano, I think about the one I learned to play on. It was truly a gift that provided me with a lifetime of enjoyment.

—Mary Lou Sprowle
Pagosa Springs, Colorado

Musical Gift Continues To Make Folks Merry

IN 1924, when I was 15, I went to a barn dance a few miles from home. When I arrived, I was mesmerized by the beautiful music of a gentleman playing an accordion. The sound completely absorbed me.

When I got home that evening, I told my mother I wanted an accordion someday. For nights afterward, I dreamed about being able to play.

When Christmas finally arrived, I dashed downstairs and looked under the tree. There among the packages was the small accordion I wanted.

It wasn't a fancy instrument with rows of buttons, but a simple box with one row of buttons and two spoon basses.

I took it in my hands and squeezed it until I began to hear a hint of a song. Soon I could play *Home Sweet Home*.

After 6 months, the musician from the barn dance bought a new instrument and offered me his old accordion for $5. I purchased it and practiced day and night.

Playing the music came easy to me, and I have been making music with my accordion ever since. Today, I volunteer my time, playing at senior centers and for my own lovely grandchildren.

Over 70 years after that barn dance, I haven't forgotten the gift of music—my best present ever.

—Howard Batchelder
Rathdrum, Idaho

They "Got a Leg Up" On Christmas Gift Search

WE LIVED in a small house, so Dad always hid our gifts in the attic. One Christmas, curiosity led my older sister and her friend to explore the attic to find our gifts.

My sister's friend wasn't experienced at walking on attic rafters and accidentally stepped off a beam onto the plasterboard below.

Down through the ceiling came her leg! That dangling leg punched through our living room ceiling was such a funny sight we never forgot it. There were no more gift searches in the attic after that.

—Tressie Sileven
Houston, Missouri

Ewing Galloway

***KEYS TO MEMORIES.* A Christmas piano, like the one this girl is playing, was Mary Lou Sprowle's dream. It came true and led her to a lifelong love of music.**

'Gift of Grace' Was Her Dream

By Dorthea Nordstrand, Seattle, Washington

THE CHRISTMAS that remains forever fresh in my mind happened during the 1930s, when I was nearly 6 years old. That was the year Grace became mine.

She was a beautiful bisque doll, with jointed arms and legs and the loveliest painted china face. Her shining brown eyes could close in sleep. Dark brown curling hair crowned her head, and slightly parted lips showed the tips of tiny perfect teeth.

Grace had first been a present to my youngest aunt, Anne. When Anne outgrew dolls, Grace was given to my older sister, Florence, to love and enjoy in her turn.

When Florence was about 13, her long chestnut hair was bobbed. Mother had the shorn locks made into a wig for Grace, making her even more a part of the family.

She was Florence's doll for several years, so I was well acquainted with Grace. But I wasn't allowed to touch things that belonged to anyone else without their permission, so I admired Grace from afar and dreamed of the day when she would be mine.

Responsibility Required

I was told that I would have to be "old enough to take care of her", and unknown to me, the big moment was near at hand.

In the gray of early dawn, we crept downstairs, hearts filled with anticipation. The first thing I saw was Grace sitting under the Christmas tree in my own little red rocking chair. That could only mean she was now mine!

Mother had made her a rose-pink organdy dress, and she was wearing new black patent-leather slippers and white socks. My big sister's beautiful hair in the new wig was curled to perfection, and the smile on Florence's face let me know that she was ready to pass Grace on to me.

After over 60 years, I can still feel the thrill of that morning and recall the reverence with which I held that beloved doll. She was even more spellbinding now that she was mine. Her eyes seemed to sparkle just for me, and now only my arms would rock her to sleep.

I'd yearned for this day with every ounce of my being, and it finally had come. Grace was mine! ▲

GRATEFUL FOR GRACE. Dorthea Nordstrand (above left with Grace and sister Florence) had the best Christmas ever when the bisque doll became hers.

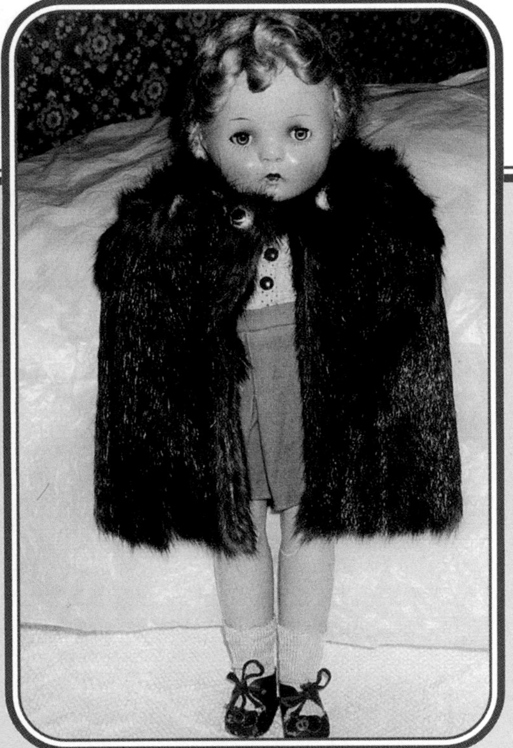

A Memorable Gift "Fur Sure"

MY MERRIEST MEMORY of Yuletides past is especially warm—I'll never forget the year Santa brought a real fur coat for my favorite doll!

Little girls of today might laugh at my Alden Company Catalog doll wearing her blue jumper dress, ankle socks and fur coat. But during the World War II era, that doll would have delighted any girl.

Mrs. Claus made that coat from a beautiful soft brown fur she'd worn when stepping out with Mr. Claus. Several years later, Mr. and Mrs. Claus brought me an encore gift. It was a deep brown mouton fur coat in *my* size! *—Janice Burnett, Reynoldsburg, Ohio*

ALL DOLLED UP. A fur coat for her doll (left) was the best present ever for Janice Burnett, until she got a matching one from Mr. and Mrs. Claus several years later. Janice says her Alden Company Catalog doll might not be stylish in a fur coat, jumper and socks, but she loved her.

***THREE FOR THREE.* When Sue Starnes (standing center above) was a girl, she and her two sisters got matching dolls they named after the sisters in *Little Women*. The dolls differed only in hair and eye color, and Jo and Amy (right) still provide joy when dressed in their finery.**

"Little Women" Still Make Memories

ONE MEMORY of a Christmas morning in the 1920s remains crystal-clear today. My two sisters and I awoke early to find three dolls in separate shoe boxes at the foot of our bed.

The dolls were alike in every respect except for hair and eye color. And, miracle of miracles, their eyes opened and closed!

My sisters and I named our dolls after the main characters in Louisa May Alcott's *Little Women*, Jo, Meg and Amy. Today, Jo and Amy stand proudly in display cases on a desk in my living room.

I doubt Santa Claus paid more than a dollar apiece in the 1920s for those dolls. Today they may be valued by collectors, but they are valued even more highly by me. *—Sue Starnes*
Tyler, Texas

Doctor Takes Gamble on Giving a Special Gift

WHEN I GRADUATED from nursing school in 1931, work was very scarce. Even if someone needed a private duty nurse, they usually had no money to pay.

When the phone rang on December 15, 1935, the voice on the other end said, "This is Dr. Gamble!" It was the head surgeon at the local hospital, a man of respected ability, but one whose gruff manner frightened most nurses. My heart pounded. I couldn't imagine what I had done or didn't do that would prompt him to call.

"I have a Christmas present for you," he said. I breathed a sigh of relief. I had been taking care of a close friend of his and thought perhaps he wanted to give me some fruit or a card.

"I have a job for you. If you want it, meet me tomorrow at Talon and we'll discuss the details," he said. Talon was a factory in town, and I could scarcely breathe a "thank you".

I remained at Talon for 10 years as the nurse on duty for the night shift until my son was born. I'll never forget that Christmas when the world finally seemed filled with possibilities and hope, thanks to the generosity of my own Santa Claus—Dr. Gamble.
—Frances Logue
Meadville, Pennsylvania

Tyke Found Trike An Exciting Gift

BACK IN 1946, metal and rubber items were still scarce because of the war. So when I saw an ad a month before Christmas for an auction that included a steel tricycle with rubber tires, my husband and I scratched together $25 from our monthly milk check. I wanted badly to buy the trike for Franzie, our 4-year-old son.

It was a cold November day, so buyers huddled inside the house until the auctioneer announced, "Now to the garage for lawn equipment and the tricycle!"

Bidding started cautiously...$10 ...$12.50...$15. Slowly the price inched up to *$20, $20, $20...*

"Twenty-five!" I yelled, and the tricycle was mine.

I drove home with it hidden in the car trunk. When Franzie was asleep that night, my husband stashed the bike in the attic to await Christmas.

The next day, Franzie came running from the house, shouting, "Santa Claus brought me a tricycle!" For some reason, he went rummaging in the attic and found the trike. Christmas had come a month early.

Franzie rode that tricycle for years. A floor scraper was put on the front, which made it into a bulldozer. With much *vrooommming*, he cleaned up the barn floor while we milked.
—Sylvia Messerschmidt
Myerstown, Pennsylvania

Would Christmas Prayer Be Answered?

By Molly Ehrlich, Sunrise, Florida

THE STREET where I grew up in New York City was a grand mixture of people representing different nationalities and religions.

My family was Jewish, and we lived on the third floor of a five-story tenement. We had so many Irish and Italian neighbors that we were well aware of their Catholic holidays, which were especially obvious during the Christmas season.

One floor below us lived the Massi family, with two daughters about my age. One December, I listened wide-eyed to Martha and Catherine talk about Christmas and visits from that jolly gift-bearing fellow named Santa Claus. In our family, we seldom saw gifts for any occasion, because it was such a struggle to make ends meet. Just the same, I couldn't help longing for a new doll.

H. Armstrong Roberts

"How do you ask Santa Claus for a doll?" I inquired of Martha and Catherine. "Is there a special prayer?"

"You have to listen to your mama and papa," said Catherine.

"And you have to be a good girl and say your prayers," added Martha.

"Then show me how to pray," I said. They pointed toward their bed. On the wall was a cross and a framed picture of a pretty lady and an infant.

Martha knelt at the foot of the bed, folded her hands and began to move her lips silently. "Say your prayers every night," Catherine explained, "and then Santa Claus will bring you a doll."

For me to pray to the Christian God would be a sin—but I believed in God and had faith that He would listen to my prayers. So December passed, and on Christmas Eve, I went to bed with a prayer and anticipation in my heart. Surely, God wouldn't forget me.

***PUPPY LOVE.* Molly Ehrlich (above right with sister Lillian) might have been in love with this puppy in 1927, but there was no Christmas like the one when her prayers were answered with a new doll from a wonderful neighbor.**

About 4 a.m., we were suddenly awakened by a banging on our hallway door. From their bedroom, Papa appeared in his long underwear, followed by Mama in a robe over her flannel nightgown. They ran through our darkened bedroom and through the dining room.

> "How do I ask Santa for a doll?"

"Who's there?" called Papa. He opened the door and we heard hurried, hushed voices. Then the door closed quietly and Papa went back to his bedroom, but Mama didn't return with him. Soon we drifted back to sleep.

When I opened my eyes, Christmas morning was about to dawn. I shared a bed with my little sister, so I was careful not to wake her when I crawled out and tiptoed in the dark to the dining room. Had Santa Claus left my doll?

I peeked into the room and saw that nothing was on the table. *Nothing!*

Tears filled my eyes. Hadn't I been a good girl? Hadn't I listened to Mama and Papa? Why hadn't my prayers been answered? I crept back to bed.

A Christmas Baby

Later that morning, Martha and Catherine came upstairs with exciting news. They had a new baby sister, they said—a Christmas baby!

During the night, while their father ran for the doctor, my mama had brought their baby sister into the world.

I didn't really understand what this meant. But everyone was so happy and proud of Mama that I was happy, too, and almost forgot about the doll.

Later that morning, Mr. Massi brought gifts to our family. He handed me a long package tied with string. Inside was the most beautiful doll in the whole world!

She had long brown curls, brown eyes that opened and closed and tiny rubber fingers that felt and looked real. Above all, she was dressed like a princess, right down to her lacy underwear and tiny boots.

Trembling, I thanked Mr. Massi and named the doll Antoinette after the new baby.

That night, with the doll cuddled next to me in bed, I thanked God for my present. Although Martha and Catherine and I prayed to a different God, I knew that all of our prayers were heard. ▲

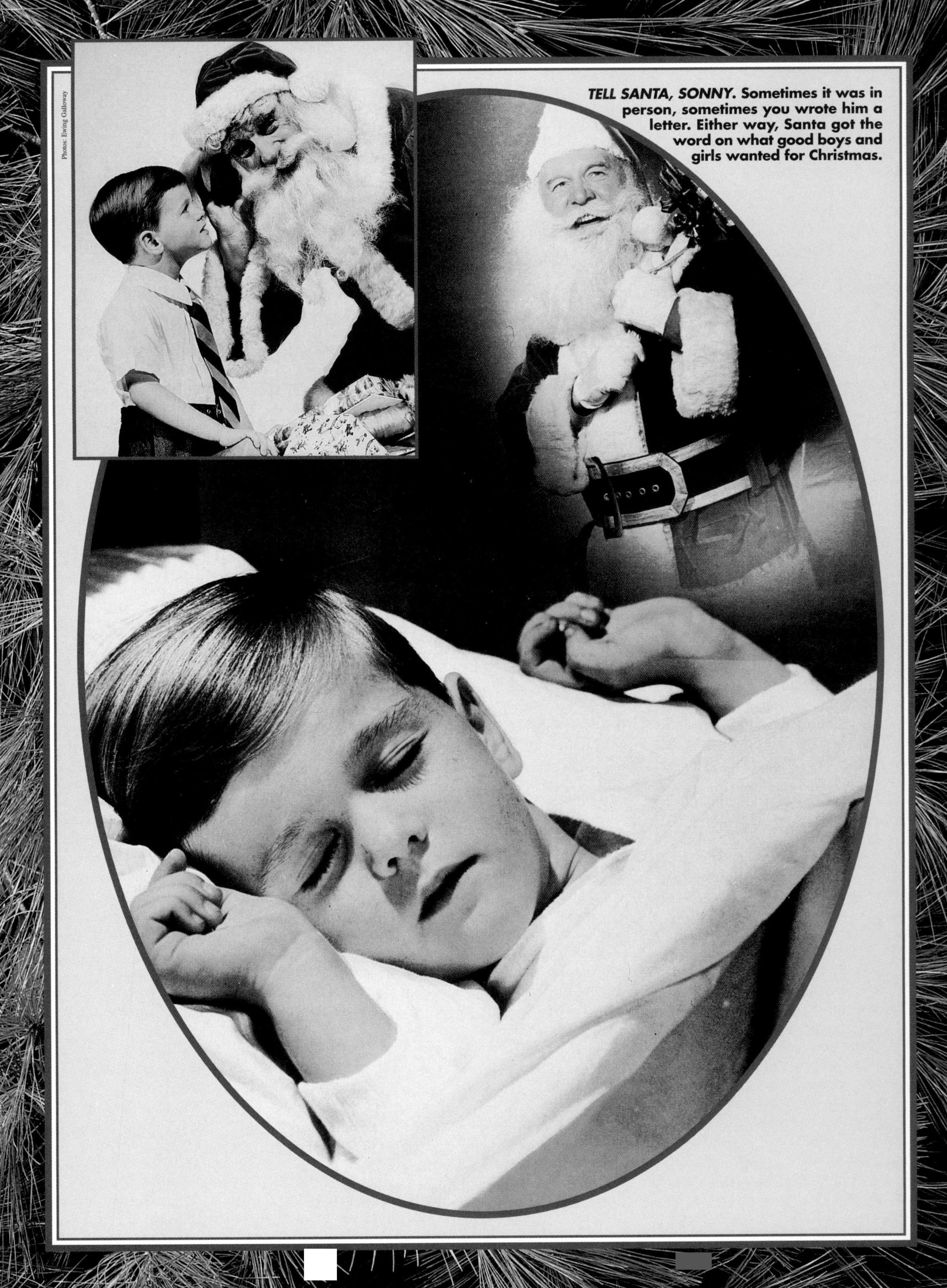

Photos: Ewing Galloway

TELL SANTA, SONNY. **Sometimes it was in person, sometimes you wrote him a letter. Either way, Santa got the word on what good boys and girls wanted for Christmas.**

Chapter Eight

'Santa's Coming!'

Whoever came up with the idea of Santa Claus was a genius.

A plump, jolly white-bearded fellow in a fire-engine-red suit who brought Christmas presents to good little boys and girls? Yes, *pure* genius!

First and foremost, Old Santa took a lot of pressure off us parents. "Don't whine to me about that Betsy-Wetsy doll you want. Tell Santa Claus...sit down and write him a letter. His elves are probably busy in the workshop making Betsy-Wetsies right now."

Almost equally helpful to parents is the benign blackmail that Santa made possible. Remember, the old gentleman only brings gifts to *good* little girls and boys.

"You better be good, you better not cry, you better not pout..." as the old song goes. Shape up, Jimmy, or else Santa Claus won't be coming to town!

I know it works. At least up to the age of 6 or thereabouts. After the older kids wise up, they're sworn to secrecy and enlisted to help keep the younger ones convinced. You need all the help you can get when coping with a 4-year-old.

Go to Bed or Santa Won't Stop

Unfortunately, even invoking the wrath of Santa doesn't do a whit of good when it comes to getting the kids into bed and asleep on Christmas Eve. How well I remember when I was a kid!

I'd lie there in bed, eyes wide open. I'd review all the things I'd put on my Christmas wish list and told Santa about, calculating my chances to actually receive any of them.

The electric train? Fat chance! Only rich kids got electric trains. The Daisy BB gun? No way. Mom would nix that for sure. Well, how about the Lincoln Logs? Please, just so everything isn't *clothes*!

There I lay, balancing hopes against reality. It wasn't much different from wondering these days if you'll win the lottery.

The reality was that the Depression was on, and we were living hand-to-mouth at the time. I'd be lucky if Mom and Dad could even leave a pair of socks under the tree. But then again, maybe Santa would come through after all. Had the North Pole been hit by the Depression, too?

Those were long nights.

In later years, my dad, like many retired men, took on the role of playing Santa Claus. He did it for the neighborhood kids, making surprise appearances on Christmas Eve. His own grandchildren lived in other states, so he "adopted" those who lived nearby. He just couldn't give up seeing the awestruck, hopeful little faces.

Christmas Eve Visits Were Reassuring

Most of the kids already had perched on the lap of the local department store Santa a few weeks before. But that was long ago. What if he'd forgotten? He saw hundreds of kids every day. How could he remember them all?

So for Santa to come right into the living room on Christmas Eve gave kids renewed hope during the nervous night ahead. Dad enjoyed the evening as much as the kids did.

These days, any weather forecaster worth his salt shows "radar sightings" of Santa on Christmas Eve. There he is with his reindeer team leaving the North Pole. Rudolph's red nose is blinking nicely. Finally comes the good news that Santa has crossed the Canadian border, on a heading that should bring him near your home sometime after midnight.

Hey, if anyone should know, it's the weatherman, right? Look, Heather, there he is on the radar. Now get into bed and stay there!

"He only brought gifts to good little girls and boys..."

My own kids happily went along with the Santa Claus legend for so long that I began to wonder just how bright they were. Then one Christmas night after a happy and tumultuous day, I tucked the exhausted urchins into bed.

"Thanks for all the presents, Daddy," murmured the eldest.

"Santa was good to all of you this year, wasn't he?" I said, hoping to duck the issue.

"Daddy, you're our Santa Claus," she answered.

"How long have you known?"

"Oh, for years and years."

She was 6 then. *—Clancy Strock*

This Santa Loved His Job... And His Granddaughter

By Donna Swedberg, Alamo, Texas

AS Christmas Eve approached each year, long knit stockings filled with walnuts, tangerines and candy canes were hung from the mantel in my grandparents' home. Excitement filled my heart as I wrote Santa a letter, asking for a visit from him and a special gift.

As the holiday drew closer, cookies were prepared for his arrival. I was bundled to bed early on Christmas Eve and instructed *never* to raise the window shade or look out onto the back porch. As I listened, I'd shiver with anticipation because I knew what was about to happen.

Around midnight, the sound of distant sleigh bells rang through the crisp winter night. Soon, Santa's heavy footsteps were heard crunching through the snow on the back porch. As I pulled the blankets up closer around me, I heard a loud banging at the back door.

My grandmother always hurried to see who was there. Every year, Santa's loud voice asked the same questions, "Had I been a good girl and what did I want for Christmas."

Behavior Was Exemplary

As always, my grandmother assured him that I had indeed been good and that I had written him a letter. Santa announced he was hungry, mentioned how tired his reindeer were and allowed that he had time for some of my cookies. I was thrilled!

Then came the big announcement. He had a special package for me, right from his workshop at the North Pole! Huddled in my bed, I listened with pure delight and never made a sound.

After lots of munching sounds and whispering from the kitchen, Santa said he'd have to leave. I heard him stomping back through the snow while the sleigh bells faded into the night.

Then I'd leap out of bed and race into the kitchen, always to find the food gone and a lovely present sitting right in the middle of the kitchen table. Grandmother cleverly dodged all my questions.

> *"No wonder that voice always seemed so familiar..."*

How did Santa eat all that food? How did he know what I wanted for Christmas? Grandma assured me that Santa knew everything—and that he loved cookies.

Memories Remain

My grandfather passed away when I was 9 years old. Santa never made his annual midnight visit after that, and Christmas was never quite the same. Much of the fun, the fantasy and the excitement were gone—but I still have the memories.

Years later, my grandmother told me how Grandfather always wanted to give me a happy Christmas by posing as Santa. He'd read my letter with great pleasure, then go out to shop for that special gift.

Grandfather lovingly wrapped it himself and placed it on the table. Then he'd take all my cookies and eat them later. Grandmother told me he even came back to the kitchen window silently while I was opening my present so he could see the happiness on my face.

If I had ever raised the window shade in my room, I would have seen Grandfather stomping through the snow. No wonder that voice always seemed so familiar!

For me, the "real" Santa Claus will always be my beloved grandfather. With his giving and caring ways, he represented the true spirit of Christmas. Yes, I *still* believe in Santa Claus. ▲

H. Armstrong Roberts

SANTA SWEETS. As every child knows, Santa loves cookies and milk. While sugarplums danced in the head of the little girl above, Santa would come to her house, eat the treats and leave a present, just as he did for Donna Swedberg.

Ewing Calloway

BIG BROADCAST. All the way from his home at the North Pole, Santa said hello boys and girls over the radio, a real Christmas miracle for one boy.

Static Didn't Stop Santa's Broadcast

By Wayne Knapp, Seattle, Washington

I WAS the youngest child of a poor family living in the backwoods of northern Wisconsin in the early 1920s. Our home was a one-room log house without running water.

In winter, snow would often pile up to the eaves of our cabin, leaving us snowbound for weeks. One of my most vivid memories of such times is a Christmas Eve when our nearest neighbor (2 miles away) invited us smaller boys to come to his cabin for a special treat.

He'd recently acquired something called a "radio" and asked if we'd like to come over to hear Santa Claus speaking from the North Pole. I'd never even heard of a radio and was most eager to see this strange instrument.

"Hello, boys and girls, this is Santa Claus..."

Mother dressed my brother and me in our warmest clothing and accompanied us to our neighbor's house. As I recall, the night was crystal clear and bitter cold. I can still hear the dry snow squeaking underfoot as we made our way down an old wagon road under a full moon.

When we arrived, we were shown the most complicated apparatus we could have imagined. It was an early Atwater-Kent powered by wet cell batteries.

We sat down and were instructed to be very still while our neighbor carefully synchronized the dials and fine-tuned the radio. Strange squeaks, squawks, whistles and groans were pouring from the large speaker.

Each sound was a thrill for my brother and me—we'd never heard anything like it before. Finally, we were able to discern some faint strains of music interspersed with static and background noise.

Then it happened! A high-pitched male voice broke through the static to announce that the broadcast was coming from WLS in Chicago and we were about to hear Santa Claus "speaking from the North Pole".

The announcer asked us to stand by and listen very carefully. We could hardly believe our ears!

Our hearts were nearly exploding with anticipation when another, deeper voice came through the speaker saying, "Hello, boys and girls, this is Santa Claus speaking to you from the North Pole"...then the voice faded away completely and was replaced by more static.

Our neighbor immediately shut off the radio to preserve his batteries, but we were satisfied: We'd heard a miracle that night—Santa Claus speaking to us from the North Pole!

Santa's Sister Feared a Hot Holiday Time

ONE SNOWY CHRISTMAS in the 1920s, our family eagerly awaited Santa's visit.

Our tree was trimmed with ornaments carefully saved over the years, and we had exchanged our gifts.

We kept an ear out for the *thump, thump, thump* on the porch that would herald his arrival. A plate of cookies and a glass of milk were ready.

Soon there was a commotion on the porch. Santa had arrived! We quickly opened the door and in he came, laden with two huge sacks of toys and goodies. After he questioned each of us kids about being good, he handed out the gifts.

He ate the cookies and drank his milk, which he obviously enjoyed, then he pulled out a long curved pipe and struck a match to light it.

At that moment, a friend of the family who was visiting, cried out, "Everett!"

Our guest, who was "Santa's" sister, feared his long whiskers would catch on fire. In the excitement and joy of the moment, this went unnoticed by us kids.

But Santa did give our guest a rather piercing look!

—Grace Olejniczak
Wausau, Wisconsin

EVERETT CLAUS? Grace Olejniczak didn't care that a guest seem to know Santa real well.

Dad Playing Santa Was A Moo-ving Experience

By Marlys White, Marshalltown, Iowa

AT OUR HOUSE, we weren't expecting Santa—we were always helping him on his way!

For 38 years, my father played Santa to our town of 900 residents, and he loved it!

On a December Saturday afternoon before Christmas, Santa would arrive on the Main Street square and hand out sacks of goodies. Apples, oranges, candy and peanuts were donated by area businessmen, which were then given to children from town and the surrounding countryside.

There was always a Mrs. Santa and a costumed driver accompanying Dad. Each year, the three of them arrived in a different rig that Dad had constructed and decorated.

One of his best rigs was a sleigh pulled by a cow disguised as a reindeer (see the photo above). Dad had spent many weeks working with our milk cow to get her used to the harness and sleigh. To give the cow real reindeer authenticity, he fastened a pair of antlers to her head!

Before and after his appearance on Main Street, Dad and Mrs. Santa called on the elderly and sick of the community in their homes. It was a day-long job.

I'll never forget the bustle in our house on those "Santa Saturdays". My mother, two brothers and I were the "backup crew", helping Santa in whatever ways we could. Mother kept a big kettle of soup on the stove so we could grab a quick bite whenever we had time to eat.

Those Saturdays were grueling for Dad, but he came home happy that he could give a little bit of happiness to others. ▲

Would Santa Make It Through the Storm?

THERE WAS a terrific snowstorm on Christmas Eve in New York in 1946. I was 9, my sister and cousin were 5, and we kids thought it would be impossible for Santa to come.

We were visiting my grandma's house, along with our parents and aunts and uncles. Grandma was short, jolly and in her early 70s at the time. Her kitchen was filled with the aromas of Italian cooking, and she adored her grandchildren.

At 11 p.m. on Christmas Eve, we kids were seated on the sofa, wondering if Santa could make it through the storm. But then he did! Our parents helped poor tired Santa inside the house amid lots of laughter.

Santa gave out the presents, shook our hands and asked if we had all been good. After hearing us declare we were indeed good, Santa was about to leave via the kitchen door. Someone said Santa probably needed some refreshment for his trip, so he was given a cup of coffee.

I peeked through the kitchen door and saw that Santa's beard was lifted as he sipped the coffee. His boots looked a little crooked, too.

But then I recognized Santa. He was Grandma! *—Arlene Spadaro*
Lake Ronkonkoma, New York

Daddy's Story "Rang Some Bells"

I ALWAYS believed in Santa Claus, but my two younger sisters had their doubts. They wanted to believe but just couldn't. They needed proof.

On Christmas Eve in 1957, we were in bed when we heard sleigh bells. I knew it was Santa, but my sisters thought they knew better.

My sisters figured Daddy was outside our window ringing the bells, but when they looked out the window, they didn't see him. They ran to our parents' bedside, but both Mama and Daddy were sound asleep. My sisters scurried back to our room—believers.

Many years later, we discovered what happened that Christmas Eve. Daddy had mounted a set of bells on the roof over our window and ran a long string down the side of the house, through the window to his bed. Then he simply pulled the string!

—Carolyn Milazzo
Baton Rouge, Louisiana

Santa Claus Wore Dad's Parka

By Henry Tietjen, West Haven, Connecticut

MY FATHER was a Lutheran minister, and between 1916 and 1918, he served a circuit of seven mission congregations in Alberta, Canada. His Indian friends there gave him a parka made out of deer hide and coyote fur trimmed in red fox fur.

After moving back to the States, my parents settled on the East Coast to raise their family of four boys. We had a large home, and Dad's office was on the second floor.

Two weeks before Christmas, my parents closed off the parlor's sliding door, pulled the shades and locked the doors. Every night after my brothers and I went to bed, they spent a little time in there wrapping presents, trimming the tree and setting up the electric train.

When my brothers and I found traces of pine needles on the stairs, we were told that the *Heinzelmannchen* (Christmas elves) had been there, starting to get things ready for Santa's arrival in a few days.

One week before Christmas, my mother's uncle always arrived to spend the holiday with us. He was a big man with snow-white hair and mustache. On Christmas Eve, we heard Santa's bells jingling coming from the third floor (that meant his sleigh and reindeer were on the roof).

"We read our Christmas pieces for him..."

Mother and her uncle would then gather us together in the living room to wait for Santa to come down the stairs.

At last, he arrived with a "Ho! Ho! Ho!" and his bells jingling. He wore Dad's fur parka and deerskin boots and carried a big burlap sack of presents on his back.

He was really something to see! In fact, he was so real to all of us that one of our dogs, "Spotty", once bit his leg. I can still see Santa trying to shake Spotty off!

We read our Christmas pieces for him, the ones that we'd be reciting at the children's program at church later that night. Santa always seemed to know whether we were good or bad and how we were doing in school.

Finally, he would go through the dining room to the parlor, turn on the Christmas tree, start the trains and open the sliding doors to the living room, where we waited.

He then emptied his bag of gifts on the living room floor and was gone, back up the stairs to the third floor and his waiting sleigh and reindeer.

Father Was Forgotten

We were so overjoyed to see our presents that we completely forgot about our father not being around. We knew that he was upstairs in his study getting ready for the children's Christmas Eve service.

After church, we hung our long white stockings over the end of the bed because we didn't have a fireplace, much less a mantel. When we awoke on Christmas morning, we'd find them filled with nuts, apples, oranges, candy and a small gift.

These are the Christmases I will always remember—no matter how old I get. My twin brother still has Dad's parka, deerskin boots and bells—and to this day, we continue the tradition of a parka-clad Santa appearing on Christmas Eve. ▲

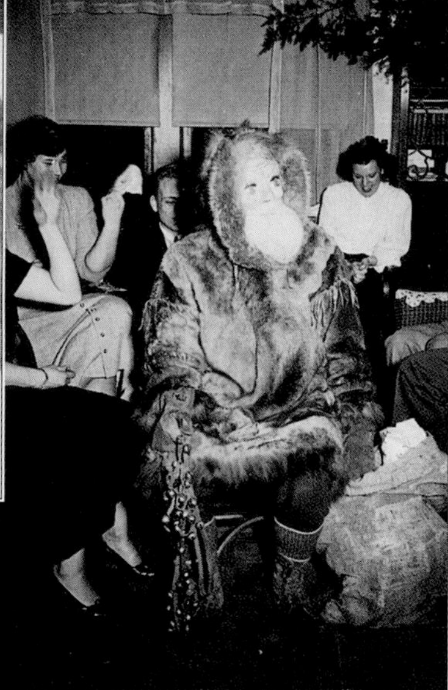

PASSING THE PARKA. **Santa (Dad), Mom, Henry and twin brother Max pose in the snow in 1933 (above). In 1949, Henry suited up (right) in the old parka to the delight of friends and family. The family's tree in 1927 was BIG (far right).**

Woolworth Santa Had an Accent

MY DAD loved to play Santa Claus for all the youngsters in College Point, New York. He never missed a Christmas party if he could help it. He was a stocky jovial man who didn't need any extra stuffing to play the part.

In December 1960, the local Woolworth's asked him to play Santa for a week before Christmas. He accepted the opportunity with great joy.

When Santa arrived at the store, there was already a long line of children waiting to see him. I stood somewhere in the middle of the line with my fidgety 3-year-old son, Billy.

Santa walked along the line, wishing everyone a merry Christmas. He then spotted Billy and led him into the store and onto his huge lap. "What would you like me to bring you for Christmas, little boy?" Santa asked.

Billy listed everything he could think of...and then some. When he was done, Santa asked, "Un den is there anything else you would like?" Billy looked at Santa quizzically and said, "No."

On the way out of the store, Billy turned to me and said, "Santa sounds just like Pop Pop. They must have come from the same town."

My dad had never lost his Danish accent!

—Patricia Michaels, New Hyde Park, New York

***GRANDPA'S NEIGHBOR?* When little Billy Michaels sat on Santa's lap in 1960 (above), he told his mom he sounded just like Grandpa. Well, Denmark is pretty far north.**

***SECRET'S OUT.* Mary Jane Brown (on the right in both photos) and her sister, Dale, enjoyed reading with Mom...and sharing a secret on Christmas 1958.**

Those Cookies Were for Santa!

IT WAS Christmas Eve 1958, and all was right with the world. Visions of a cowboy outfit danced in my head. Visions of girlie stuff were uppermost in my sister's mind. All we had to do was survive *one more night*.

After our bath, we settled into the living room for the reading of the story of Jesus' birth. It seemed like we were right there along with the characters. Then it was time to put out the cookies we'd made, along with a glass of milk for Santa.

We had always wanted to stay awake to see Santa but never quite made it. This time, my sister was determined. We heard something in the living room, so we got up and peeked our heads around the corner. It wasn't Santa at all!

Instead, it was Daddy in his boxers and T-shirt sitting on the edge of the fireplace, eating Santa Claus' cookies and slurping his milk!

Just when I was about to tell him not to eat the cookies or Santa wouldn't come, my sister clamped her hand over my mouth and backed us out of the doorway.

Once under the covers in our room, she explained that parents were actually Santa's helpers. If they stayed up so late, they must love us and Santa an awful lot. We never told our parents about our discovery and shared impish glances whenever the subject of Santa came up.

As an adult, I finally figured out why they never made a big deal out of us not making those doughy cookies anymore after my sister hit high school!

—Mary Jane Brown
Statesville, North Carolina

"YES, SANTA, WE'VE BEEN REAL GOOD." **So claimed Larry Magura and his brother when they visited Santa at the Marshall Fields store toyland in downtown Chicago in 1938. The visit to Santa to tell him what they wanted for Christmas was the highlight of a trip to the city to see all the store windows decorated for the holidays, says Larry, who now lives in La Grange Park, Illinois. Well, at least the brothers were good on this day.**

Santa's Arrival Drew Country Folks to Town

SANTA always came to town the Saturday before Christmas, and we kids waited all year for him.

Folks would come to town from all over the countryside in hayracks, sleighs, stone boats and on horseback. If it was cold, our father heated bricks or gunnysacks full of oats to warm our feet.

Santa always appeared from nowhere with a large sack of goodies he passed out to all us kids.

It was such a thrill to get a little brown bag of candy from Santa. Inside were peanuts, an apple and sometimes a piece of ribbon candy.

Oh, how we waited for that moment when Santa arrived! To us youngsters, it was just about the best thing that happened all year. *—Dorothy Behringer*
North Branch, Minnesota

Santa Had Big Boots to Fill

By Mary Meckley, Elyria, Ohio

AS A CHILD in the late 1920s, I still believed in Santa Claus. One year, my mother and father were having a Christmas Eve party for my father's co-workers and their wives. My three brothers and I had been put to bed upstairs, but who could sleep with all the piano playing, singing and laughter downstairs?

After a while, Mother came to get us out of bed. She took us down to the landing of the stairway, where we could see through the banister. She told us to be quiet and stay there.

Suddenly, we heard the jingle-jangle of sleigh bells outdoors and stomping feet on the front porch. The door opened and Santa Claus came in! My brothers and I were mesmerized with wonder, and Santa didn't seem to notice us there on the landing.

With many "ho-ho-ho's," he stomped his way to the Christmas tree and put packages from his sack under the tree. Then he was out the front door and we heard the bells jingling again.

We were too stunned to move! So we were still on the landing when my father's boss came in the front door wearing his business suit. But he had forgotten to change from Santa's shiny, black patent-leather boots!

My oldest brother and I looked at each other and covered our mouths so we wouldn't reveal our newly discovered secret to our two younger brothers.

Bob Lynch/Chronicle-Telegram, Elyria, Ohio

COVER STORY. **When Mary Meckley's story of the surprise visit from Santa made the local paper, the paper's artist drew a color rendering of the big event. Good thing, says Mary, no one took a photo then.**

Trail of Goodies Led to Stronger Belief in Santa

IN MANY WAYS, Mama was a kid again at Christmas. We lived on a farm and had lots of chores to do, but Mama always made sure her four children had a special holiday, including gifts and a long stocking filled with an apple, an orange, nuts and candy.

One year, I was really doubting if there was a Santa. After chores and supper on Christmas Eve, Mama sent us outside to close the doors on the chicken house. We were almost back to the house when we noticed a big orange on the ground. As we reached down to pick it up, we saw nuts scattered along.

Such excitement! We knew these meant Santa had come, because Christmas was the only time we ever got such treats.

We followed the trail into the house, where we found the Christmas tree lighted with tiny candles and packages all around. The big stockings were full of gifts, too.

So there really was a Santa after all! Hadn't we just seen his trail of spilled goodies? *—Anna Carman*
Anson, Texas

MESSY SANTA. **A trail of goodies leading to the house was all Anna Carman (front left with Viola, Margie and John) needed as proof that Santa was not only real, but had come to their house.**

SANTA DADDY. **Rick Gladu (with daughters Cassandra and Samantha) played Santa twice.**

Return Visit Made an Impression

EVERY YEAR at Christmas, our family gathers at our house. We have three married children and seven grandchildren.

One holiday, we asked our son Rick to dress up as Santa Claus and give his nieces and nephews their gifts. Since he didn't have any children of his own at the time, he was happy to borrow a Santa suit and make the appearance.

On Christmas morning, we heard a snowmobile in the front yard. Santa came in the patio door with his bag of goodies and toys. He stayed for a while while we took pictures and then he left, roaring off on his machine.

Dean, our 3-year-old grandson, missed Santa's visit because he had a fever and was asleep at the time. When he got up, he was disappointed.

After supper, Dean was feeling better and was sitting with his mother while the other kids were playing with their toys.

Rick took action again. He put the Santa suit back on and came to the patio door near where we were sitting. When Dean saw Santa, his eyes became as big as saucers. "Santa came back to see me!" he cried.

It brought a tear to my eye to see such a small gesture make a little boy so happy. *—Noella Gladu*
Lavigne, Ontario

Smoke Signals Got Messages Through to Santa

HUDDLED under blankets in our unheated bedrooms, my sister and I wrote our secret letters to Santa.

After they were carefully printed, they were painstakingly folded into small squares. We carried them out to the warm farmhouse kitchen and put them in Mama's apron pocket. The next step in the process was entrusted to her.

She opened the wood stove door and consigned our precious hopes to the fire, where the smoke delivered the messages to Santa. We were never sure how Santa got the words out of the smoke, but Mama said that was the way it worked, and we never doubted her.

And with good reason. Each Christmas morning, we received the dolls we'd asked for. And the coats, dresses, bonnets and nighties with them were made from fabric exactly like the prints and calicoes that Mama had used to sew for us throughout the year.

Our admiration for Santa's wisdom in making such perfect choices was shared by Mama and Papa over our breakfast of hot chocolate and toast.

In later years, we came to realize the fantasy and special spirit of Santa, starting, I think, with the news that Mama could still "mail" our letters even though we then had an oil stove.
—Molly Parks, Huachuca City, Arizona

SPECIAL VISIT. **When her grandson Dean (seated in front) was ill one Christmas, Santa made a return visit just to see him, says Noella Gladu.**

Surprise Santa Saved Family's Christmas

By Delbert Graham, Port Townsend, Washington

TIMES WERE pretty bad in my old hometown in central Washington in December of 1932. The Great Depression was deepening and grinding poverty was everywhere.

My dad's taxi business wasn't doing well, since only salesmen and wealthy people could afford to hire a cab. Christmas was looking pretty bleak for my two sisters and me.

But we had a tree, and it was decorated with traditional ornaments of German origin saved from my mother's childhood. My sisters and I also brought home paper decorations we'd made in school.

By Christmas Eve, no presents had appeared under our tree. Earlier in the week, we'd overheard our parents talking in low voices about how hard times were and how meager our Christmas was going to be. Those conversations now began to take on added meaning.

Would There Be Any Gifts?

Later that evening, we were gathered around the wood stove in the parlor when we heard the unmistakable sound of sleigh bells. Turning off the parlor light, we raised the window shade and peered through the frosty windowpane toward the street.

It had snowed on and off for a week, so the snow was packed hard by the automobile traffic. Now, up the street came a horse-drawn sleigh driven by —no, it couldn't be...but it was! Santa Claus himself was driving that sleigh (the thought that Santa's sleigh should rightly be pulled by reindeer didn't occur to us).

"Up the street came a horse-drawn sleigh..."

The sleigh stopped right in front of our house! Santa bounded out of the sleigh, strode across our snow-covered lawn and climbed the steps to our porch. Pounding on the door, he shouted, "Is this the Graham residence?"

My mother, just as wide-eyed as we were, quickly opened the door and assured him that it was. He then presented her with a huge sack bulging with colorfully wrapped packages and returned to his sleigh, leaving almost as rapidly as he'd come.

No Unwrapping Yet!

We could see our names on the tags affixed to the packages. As Mother placed them under the tree, she cautioned us (as she always did) not to peek, pinch or rattle them until Christmas morning.

It was a long night of waiting! But when morning finally came, we opened our presents and found all sorts of delightful toys.

It wasn't until years later that my parents found out who had sent those gifts. They were former employers of my father, partners in a hardware store. Years before, Father had saved their store from a fire by carrying a flaming lantern out into the street. Father had suffered burns, but he'd eventually recovered from them.

Knowing how hard times were for my dad, and remembering his heroism, his former employers decided to provide our family with a truly merry Christmas. It was the best Christmas ever.

FATHER CHRISTMAS FIGURE of clay depicts Santa wearing a flowing robe and a hat decked with holly.

Shiny Black Boots Meant Santa Claus!

WE WERE living in Great Falls, Montana in 1951 where my dad was stationed at an Air Force base.

On Christmas Eve, my two sisters, brother and I were bathed, pajamaed and put to bed to await the morning's festivities.

With all the excitement and anticipation running through my 5-year-old mind, I couldn't sleep. The house turned dark and quiet, and everyone else drifted off into a sound slumber.

But not me! That's how, in the very early hours of Christmas morning, I saw light under my bedroom door.

I knew who was in our living room and what he was doing. I could hardly breathe as I got out of bed and crept over to the door.

Trying hard not to make a sound, I laid down on the floor and looked under the door. I saw him! Well, I saw his black boots. They were polished so brightly that the lights of the Christmas tree were reflected in their tops!

I watched as the boots walked here, there and all around the Christmas tree. What a glorious Christmas morning this was going to be! What a tale I had to tell—I had witnessed the arrival and departure of Santa Claus!

I was in my late 30s before I could admit to myself that what I'd really seen that night were my dad's shiny Air Force boots, and him busily preparing for a flight after being called to duty earlier that morning.

—Marty Kennedy, Tempe, Arizona

Rooftop Toys Convinced "Non-Believers" That Santa Had Visited

BACK IN 1915, when I was a girl of 5, I was a true believer in Santa Claus.

There were many children in our neighborhood then—some believed in Santa and some didn't. In a vacant lot near our homes, we often gathered for a tug-of-war in which the "believers" and "non-believers" pulled against each other. As a strong believer, I always gave it my best for Santa.

As usual on Christmas Eve, I was tucked in early so Mama and Daddy could be ready to help Santa.

My parents had just built a new house, and over my bed was a flue that was never used. On Christmas morning, I discovered that Santa had lost a Christmas stocking full of toys. It was hanging from the flue over my bed.

I ran to tell Mama and Daddy to come and see what I had found. They immediately suggested going outside in case Santa had lost anything else.

Sure enough, all across the roof were toys. Daddy got a ladder and began gathering them up. He had an audience because I had time to get all my friends together to show them what Santa had dropped on our roof.

It made believers out of the non-believers and made me the envy of them all. *—Margie McAdams Maher*
Minco, Oklahoma

Santa's Visit Sent Her Scurrying

ONE OF OUR neighbors always played Santa for our Christmases in the 1920s. The parents gave this man the toys for their children ahead of time. He dressed as Santa and drove his horse-drawn sleigh from farm to farm. Of course, there were plenty of sleigh bells!

The Christmas when I was 3 years old, I heard Santa's bells getting closer and closer—and I got more and more scared!

Before he stopped at our house, I dove under the bed. There was no way anyone could get me out! Santa came inside, "ho-ho-ho-ing" with the gifts. He called out all our names, but I stayed hidden.

Finally, Santa knelt down, holding a doll for me to see. I grabbed the doll and remained under the bed. When he left and I heard the bells ringing way down the road, I came out from under the bed...holding my new doll and smiling happily. *—Audrey Brimbery*
Fort Mitchell, Kentucky

This Santa Was Put on Ice

MY HUSBAND, Augie, had a special Christmas planned for us in 1958. Back then, we were living in Anchorage, Alaska, and our two children were ages 3 and 1. We invited another young couple and their children over on Christmas Eve.

As we played cards in the kitchen, Augie slipped out of the room. He planned to sneak out the front door, go around to the garage, don his rented Santa suit and return with a sack of presents for the children. We seldom locked our doors, so he didn't think to check if he had his key.

He went outside without coat or boots and found the garage door locked. He retraced his steps over the slippery path and found the house was locked as well! Shivering in the subzero cold, he had no choice but to ring the doorbell.

We were surprised to see him on the porch and asked what he was doing. "It was such a beautiful night, I stepped outside for a minute to see if I could see Santa and his reindeer in the moonlight. I didn't see them, and when I tried to get back in, the door was locked," he explained.

After wrapping him in a blanket and warming him up with a cup of hot tea, I went back to the kitchen to continue the card game. In a few minutes, Augie again slipped out the door (this time with his key). He let himself into the garage and put on his Santa suit, then burst into the kitchen with a pillowcase of presents over his shoulder.

"Ho, ho, ho! Merry Christmas!" he shouted.

It was one of the merriest I can remember. *—Mary Trimble*
Berryville, Arkansas

WHO'S THAT? **Mary Trimble's children, Holly, 3, and Tony, 1, were decorating the tree in 1958 (photo 1) when Dad got locked out after he went to look for Santa. Later, who should come into the kitchen but Santa himself! (2). The kids were surprised (3) but sorry that Dad, who went to the garage, missed the event.**

Finding Footprints Meant Santa Had Come

ON Christmas morning, my two brothers and I were not allowed to go downstairs until both our parents were awake. We sat eagerly at the top of the stairs making noise so Mom and Dad would get up. Then we ran downstairs in our bathrobes to see if Santa had come. He did every year, filling our stockings and leaving presents.

Santa's footprints were always in the fireplace, proving he had been down the chimney! It was a thrill to look for his prints. We then opened the presents from our stockings. After breakfast, we opened our other gifts.

Years later, we learned Mom put the footprints in the fireplace ashes late at night. This is my fondest Christmas memory, and my husband and I continue the footprint tradition to this day.

—Julie Higdon
Edgartown, Massachusetts

GRANDMA SANTA. **For 32 years, her grandmother, Myrtle Friel, played Santa, first for her daughter, then for her grandchildren, remembers Lisa Otto of Drexel, Missouri (at left with her sister, Kimberly, opening the door for Grandma Santa in 1966). Santa would come down the street, ringing his bells, calling to all the neighbors that Santa was near, Lisa says. Then he'd visit the house, drop off the presents and continue down the block until he was out of sight. Shortly after, Grandma would appear to "ooh" and "ahh" over all the treasures that Santa had just left.**

Santa's Second Visit Surprised Mama

ONE CHRISTMAS, Mama wanted to make things extra-special. So she asked our next-door neighbor, who played Santa every year at our school, if he'd make an appearance at our house on Christmas Eve.

Mama even told him what time to arrive. Well, the appointed hour on Christmas Eve came and we six kids were upstairs. But Santa didn't show.

Fearing he'd forgotten, Mama pretended he had arrived. She went to the front door and said, in a loud voice, "Bye, Santa! Thank you for coming!"

At that, she beckoned us to come downstairs so we could open our gifts. Imagine our surprise, and Mama's, too, when Santa walked in the front door.

"Why, Santa. What are you doing here?" asked Mama, hoping desperately he'd pick up her cue.

"Well, I just came back to see how the kids like their gifts!" he explained.

I knew of no other home where Santa came *twice*, and that made my Christmas extra-special. And I'll never forget the look of surprise on Mama's face when she saw him walk into the house!

—Louise Brewer, Melbourne, Florida

Mom Made Sure All Kids Were Visited by Santa

ALTHOUGH we were poor, Santa Claus *always* came to our house and brought me nice toys. But he never seemed to make it around to a lot of the other families in our community. That's where my mother took up the slack.

I don't know how it ever got started, but months before Christmas, people would bring boxes and bags of used toys and clothes to our house. Mother would sort through the clothes and decide which ones she could use. Mom then used the irreparable clothing to sew new outfits for the dolls. My job was to wash the baby dolls.

The week before Christmas, local merchants delivered oranges, apples, nuts and candy to our home. We'd fill bags for every needy child on her list.

Late on Christmas Eve, one of my brothers would take Mom around town. On Christmas morning, every poor child in town had a gift from Santa.

I never went on the deliveries. I went to bed early to wait for the real Santa Claus…to return. *—Ivelee Dick*
Bigelow, Arkansas

CHRISTMAS CARD KIDS. **When Ferne Vance of Delavan, Wisconsin got this cardboard Santa in 1951, she saw a photo opportunity. All the kids posed, and the photo went on to become the family's Christmas card.**

Santa's Puppy Made This Boy a Believer

By W. Ray Skiles, Weirton, West Virginia

ALL I WANTED for Christmas was a puppy. But it was 1932, and our coal-mining town was feeling the effects of the Depression.

Mom and Dad told me we couldn't afford a puppy, but, at 7 years old, I knew Santa Claus would bring me one. I was informed that Santa didn't bring puppies. This argument went on until Christmas Eve, when I finally told everyone that I didn't like Santa and he was a big fake. Then I went to bed.

Sometime during the night, I awoke from a deep sleep. I saw a red coat covered with snow, and two gloved hands putting a puppy in my arms. I remembered cuddling him in my arms, then falling right back to sleep.

Archive Photos/Lambert

PUPPY LOVE. **When a child gets his first puppy, like the boy above, it's a magical time, as W. Ray Skiles found out when his dream of a puppy came true.**

But when I woke up in the morning, there was no puppy. I ran downstairs where my sisters had already been at the Christmas tree and were opening their presents.

I went all through the house looking for my puppy. When my parents asked what I was doing, I told them about the midnight visit from Santa.

They informed me that since I didn't believe in Santa, the whole thing had been a dream, and there was no puppy.

But I continued my search for about an hour, when my dad suggested I also try the cellar. If I didn't find a puppy there, I'd have to admit it had been a dream, he said.

Was It a Dream?

Dad took me outside and opened the door to the dirt cellar. I looked everywhere and was starting to believe it had been a dream when I heard a couple of whimpers coming from behind the base of the brick chimney.

There, in a rag-lined basket, was the cutest beagle puppy I'd ever seen! I picked him up and ran back into the house to bask in the gaze of smiling adult faces, and the amazed glances of my sisters.

I learned years later that my Uncle Ray, who lived with us, had walked to his dad's house, about 7 miles away, to pick up the puppy. Then he walked back in a snowstorm with the pup tucked under his red Mackinaw.

It was Uncle Ray's snow-covered red coat I'd seen that night when he woke me to give me my puppy. But I hadn't seen his face.

I've thought of that Christmas every holiday season since. And I still believe there's magic in Christmas. There was for me! ▲

Water, Water, Everywhere...

CHRISTMAS was always a most special time in our home in Nashville, Tennessee. Anticipation was keen.

It seemed like weeks passed between December 24 and 25. My brother and I concluded that Christmas Eve was the longest night of the year. The anticipation kept us awake, but there was something else that interfered with our sleep.

Before retiring, he and I would drink lots of water. Of course, that meant we'd have to get up several times throughout the night to visit the bathroom.

This strategy allowed us to peek into the front room to see whether Santa had come yet.

Somehow, we always fell sound asleep before he arrived. *—John Tresch*
Bluefield, West Virginia

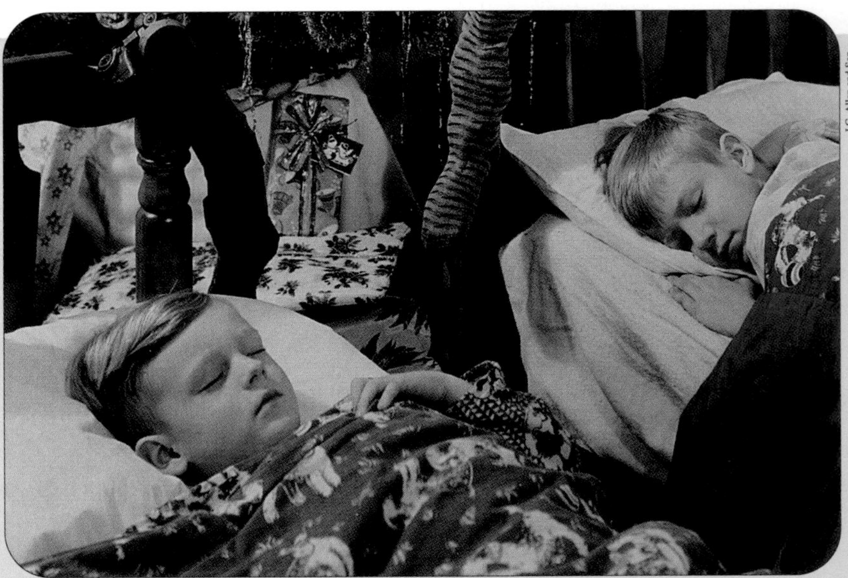

J.C. Allen and Son

GOOD BOYZZZZ. **No matter how hard we tried to stay awake Christmas Eve, the next thing we knew, it was morning. Like the two tykes above, John Tresch and brother succumbed to sleep, in spite of the water scheme.**

***NOEL NERVES.* Little Donna Campbell wasn't quite sure what to make of Santa in 1960, says her mother, Betty-Lee Campbell, Whittier, California.**

Tracks in the Snow Couldn't Lie...Could They?

THE WINTER of 1931 was tough for our family, who was living in South Carolina at the time.

My father had lost his business the previous year, and the approach of Christmas brought little cheer for Mom and Dad.

With seven children to feed and clothe, there was little money for gifts. We did have a tree—Mom saw to that, and to its being decorated with homemade trinkets and popcorn strings.

I'd turned 7 the week before Christmas, and some of the older children at school told me Santa was just made up by parents trying to make their children be good.

I hoped it wasn't true, but doubts lingered as we were hustled off to bed Christmas Eve.

It was snowing that Christmas Eve, a rare and special treat in our part of the South.

On Christmas morning, there were a few presents under the tree, along with a meager supply of oranges and nuts. I tried to relish the joy of the moment, and suppress the thought that maybe Mom and Dad had put that stuff under the tree. But my spirits were dampened.

Then someone called from a window, "Hey, everybody, look outside! You can see Santa's tracks in the snow!"

"Where? Where?" I cried, looking wildly in all directions but seeing only the glistening white landscape.

"Down there," my brother said, lifting me in his arms and pointing down, beneath the window. "See his tracks?"

I saw them! Jagged rows of reindeer tracks, followed by the unmistakable marks of sleigh runners, deeply inscribed in a snowbank.

The tracks looped through our front yard, paused by the chimney, then went around the house and into the woods. My joy was complete. There was a Santa Claus after all!

How was I to know that while I slept, my wonderful 13-year-old brother fashioned a crude sled from scrap lumber, then quietly towed it behind our sleepy milk cow across our yard, inscribing forever upon my heart the childhood magic of Christmas.

—Howard Alley, Roswell, Georgia

Firehouse Santa Put Christmas on Another Level

PLAYING SANTA during the annual Christmas parade in our small New York community was an opportunity coveted by each member of our volunteer fire department.

One year after I'd been elected mayor, I decided to "pull rank". I warned the crew they better let me ride on top of the fire truck as Santa that year, or there wouldn't be any new boots or hoses for them the following year!

It was a bitterly cold night, with snow falling. Dressed as Santa, I was strapped in tightly atop the fire truck and we set off to spread holiday cheer around the village.

With Christmas music pouring from the truck's loudspeaker and pure white snow falling, I felt as if I were moving through a Norman Rockwell painting.

We turned down one narrow street, and the height of the truck was almost on line with the second floor of the homes along the block. I don't think I was more than 15 feet away from the upstairs windows on these houses.

As we passed one house, a mother was putting her young son to bed. She was holding him when he suddenly turned his head to look out the window. He saw Santa Claus!

I'll never forget the look of astonishment, wonder and amazement in his eyes as they locked on me and followed me along.

Through the years, I've often wondered how great it would be to meet that young boy of so many years ago. I'll bet the memory of that moment is as clear to him today as it remains for me.

—James Reese, Holiday, Florida

Photographic Design

***SANTA CLAUS CAME TO TOWN...*in this case, to Peoria, Illinois in 1947. James Reese, as mayor of his village, got to play Santa one year and it was the thrill of his life.**

LITTLE BIT OF HOME. **For the soldier far from home, a letter or card at Christmas could be the only thing he'd get for the holiday, and that might come in March! Just being gone from home at Christmas, be it in the service or elsewhere, wasn't fun. But it made coming home so nice.**

SuperStock

Chapter Nine

Christmas Far from Home

There I sat on the windowsill in my hotel room, lights turned off, looking out the window as a steady rain fell on downtown Houston.

It was Christmas Eve 1942, and I was a thousand miles away from home in northern Illinois. My captain at nearby Ellington Field Air Force base hadn't come through with the 10-day furlough I'd requested. He pointed out that every man and woman at Ellington had applied for a Christmas furlough. We couldn't all leave. "There's a war on, son."

The best I could get was an overnight pass, so I went into town. Anything to get off the post and out of the barracks.

I had spent the early part of the evening at the USO, which had a nicely decorated tree plus eggnog and cookies. Someone tried to lead our little group of soldiers and sailors in Christmas carols.

But finally, the USO closed down so the people who staffed it could get home for their own Christmas Eve. Everything was closed, in fact. Downtown Houston was empty and there was no place to go but back to my economy-rate room.

Suddenly I heard explosions. Up in the sky I saw fireworks. Fireworks on Christmas Eve? What sort of pagan land was the state of Texas, anyhow?

Self-pity sat on my shoulders, heavy as the Rock of Gibraltar. It was the gloomiest, loneliest Christmas of my life.

Could Have Been Worse

A sad tale? Yes, but a familiar one to anyone who served in the military. At least I didn't spend Christmas in a frigid foxhole during the Battle of the Bulge. Nor in a bunker in Korea. Nor in the jungles of Vietnam. Nor on a submarine in the Atlantic.

I'll give the military credit, though. No matter where you were, they tried to make a bad situation as tolerable as possible. Okay, so the Christmas tree was a bunch of palm fronds and the ornaments were spent shell casings—it was better than nothing.

The mess sergeants and their crew labored long and hard to come up with home-style Christmas dinners. There was turkey, ham, stuffing, sweet potatoes, creamed corn, cranberry sauce, mince pie. Sometimes there was even a cigar to go with your coffee. At least you had a taste of home that day.

On the downside was the matter of Christmas presents. No matter how carefully the folks stateside heeded the post office warnings to ship early, the likelihood was your gifts would show up weeks and even months late.

There also was the puzzlement back home over what to give someone in the service. I received at least five money belts in 4 years. So did everyone else I knew. None of us wore them. Nor did we have a lot of need for sewing kits, diaries, stationery and shoe trees.

Special Delivery?

When I was in the Philippines, my packages arrived in mid-March. Somewhere during the trip, it appeared they had been driven over by at least one tank and then left to ripen in a swamp for a month or two. Everything was ruined beyond description. Except the money belt. Oh well, it was the thought that counted.

Regardless of where you are on this planet, Christmas is the one day of the year when you desperately want to be home.

It's the day when you crave the nearness of family and the comfort of family traditions.

Nowadays we live in a time when children leave home, marry, produce grandchildren...then usually move far, far away. Peg and I have kids who live in five different states. More than anything else, we dream of Christmas with all of them under our roof again. The chances are remote indeed.

> *"Christmas is the one day of the year you desperately want to be home..."*

"Over the river and through the woods, to Grandmother's house we go," was what we sang when I was a kid. Today, "Down the turnpike and through the Atlanta airport" is more like it.

But I take comfort in the words of a wise old Greek, who observed, "Home is where the heart is."

He's right. Even though we may be far from St. Louis and Minneapolis and Houston and Milwaukee, our hearts have many homes at Christmas.

—Clancy Strock

Donald L. Jeffrey/Laatsch-Hupp Photo

Tense Voyagers Felt Christmas Magic

By Estrella Montgomery, Inverness, Florida

IT WAS Christmas Eve and we were coming home!

The year was 1914, and our little ship, crowded with refugees from the early days of World War I, plowed courageously through the stormy North Atlantic.

I was 4 years old and my brother was 6. Though we'd been born in the United States, our parents were Russian-born. Mother, my brother and I had been visiting our grandparents' in the part of Russia that would later become Finland when war broke out and we had to flee.

During the voyage, our beloved mother languished on the bunk we shared. She was seasick and terrified about prowling German U-boats. Food was brought to her, but she could not eat.

Then, much to our surprise late one afternoon, Mother got up and dressed us in our Sunday best. Holding our hands, she led us through the crush of passengers to the dining salon.

Santa on a Ship!

There, as if by magic, stood the most beautiful tree I had ever seen. It held lighted candles, popcorn garlands, cranberry strings, brightly colored ornaments and candy canes.

Nearby, a smiling old gentleman with long white whiskers and a bright red suit opened a big sack and handed an orange to each little boy and girl. I clutched this precious gift in my small hands, overwhelmed with joy.

Music and singing began, and we stood dazed with the wonder of it. Then Mother whispered, "Tomorrow is Christmas and you will receive the greatest gift of all!"

I could scarcely sleep that night, wondering about my gift.

Early the next morning, Mother dressed us in our warmest clothes. Carrying the orange in my mittened hands, I followed Mother to the deck.

There we joined a milling, noisy throng. Suddenly, out of the harbor mist, I saw the Statue of Liberty. I stared at that great lady holding her torch, then back at Mother, her face radiant with joy.

"Mother! Mother!" I cried. "Is this America? Are we home?"

She was too overcome to answer me. Her head was bowed and I heard her giving a prayer of thanks.

***HOME FOR CHRISTMAS.* Estrella Montgomery, her mother and brother, Bill, were photographed just before they left Europe to come home in 1914. That Christmas was doubly magic, as it was also a homecoming after a trying Atlantic voyage.**

Gift Surprised Whole Family

THE DAY before Christmas, we received a phone call from our son Lynn, who had been at National Guard training camp for 6 months and was due to come home.

He hadn't been able to get a flight home for Christmas and wouldn't be coming after all. His father and I and his eight brothers and sisters were devastated. More than a few tears were shed.

Then, about 6 p.m. on Christmas Eve, the phone rang again. I answered and heard Lynn's voice. "Mom, I'm on my way home," he said. "The plane arrives at 2 a.m. on Christmas morning. Can you meet me and bring me home? And don't tell anyone else I'm coming!"

I met his plane, then quietly got him back in the house. We put his sleeping bag (with him in it!) under the Christmas tree with the rest of the gifts and then I went back to bed.

Early on Christmas morning, the family gathered in our big bedroom before going to see what Santa had left for us. Imagine the joy, the tears, hugs and kisses when our children found their brother under the tree!

It was a Christmas I shall always treasure. *—Elizabeth Morgan*
Salmon, Idaho

Ewing Galloway

***BEST GIFT EVER.* A soldier home for Christmas is the best present.**

SANTA'S V-8 SLEIGH. **The 8-hour drive to Grandpa's house didn't seem like a very good way to spend Christmas. But Dad found a way to make the trip fun...and it's a Christmas that is still a fond family memory.**

Our Great Christmas on Wheels

By Sherrie Murphree, Odessa, Texas

IN OUR FAMILY, 1952 will always be remembered as the year we didn't have Christmas around the tree at home. Instead, we celebrated Christmas in a different way.

We were leaving our Amarillo, Texas home early on Christmas Day to visit our grandparents in Cleburne. It would be an 8-hour drive.

Since Mother and Daddy were always adamant that we four girls should open our gifts on Christmas Day, it looked like we'd have to wait until the *evening* of the 25th to open our presents. We were four miserable youngsters!

One night at the supper table, my two older sisters wondered what would be wrong with opening our gifts on the 24th.

"I've got a better idea," Daddy suggested. "Why don't we just celebrate Christmas on wheels?"

"Christmas on wheels?" Beverly asked. "What are you talking about?"

"I'm not kidding," Daddy replied. "Why don't we open our packages in the car while traveling? The Magi took gifts on their camels, so we can take ours in the car. It'll make the trip shorter, too."

No Driving for Sis

"But, Daddy, how can you open presents and still drive?" teenage Janice questioned (hoping she'd get to drive part of the trip).

"You girls can take turns opening my presents," Daddy explained. He knew his gifts would be the proverbial Old Spice, a tie and a shirt. He didn't mind not opening presents —to him, the fun was watching us.

We wouldn't have to wait until Christmas evening to open our presents! To my 10-year-old mind, this "on wheels" thing sounded like fun.

Early on Christmas morning, our parents nestled our gifts in the car with us. We didn't mind being a little crowded—there was lots of room in our new blue Hudson. Gifts for our relatives went in its spacious trunk.

We girls usually slept, snacked and played games while traveling. Each of us had an assigned post. Three-year-old Suzie sat in front between Mom and Dad. I dozed on the backseat floor while Janice and Beverly napped leaning against a door.

That day, though, everyone was wide-eyed. Even my usual car sickness took leave.

Harmonized in a Hudson

"I pray that God will give us a safe trip," said Daddy as we pulled out of the driveway. For a while, we sang Christmas carols.

Then Mother read the Christmas story to us from the Gospel of Luke.

Finally, it was time to open our presents. Daddy monitored the mileage carefully. Every 10 miles, someone opened a present and passed it around so all could see.

I got a ring with a chartreuse stone. And I still remember the bottle of Evening in Paris I bought for Mother at Woolworth's.

For those cold Panhandle nights, Mother had made each of us a flannel nightgown, and she'd bought sweaters at last year's winter sales.

"Every 10 miles, someone opened a present and passed it around for all to see..."

Whenever we went through a town, we stopped opening gifts to admire the decorations. And at noon, we ate the lunch Mom had prepared earlier—our 1952 version of "meals on wheels"!

The last few miles of the trip, we were quiet. I reflected that it had been a good Christmas, maybe even better than others since we all felt so close.

The world hadn't expected to find the Baby Jesus in a manger...and I certainly hadn't expected to celebrate His birth in the back of a Hudson. Still, our "Christmas on wheels" was memorable because it put Christmas in our hearts. ▲

Sneaky Santa Caught in the Act

By John Forrest, Orillia, Ontario

"HOLD IT RIGHT THERE!"

I froze in mid-step, pinned to the wall by a brilliant beam of light. The voice behind the flashlight echoed hollowly in the emptiness of the dimly lit hospital hallway.

"Where do you think you're going?" the voice demanded.

"Well, you see, nurse...," I stammered, "my wife is on this floor and..."

It was Christmas Eve 1957, and here I was, caught in the corridor of Soldier's Memorial Hospital dressed as Santa. I was sneaking in to visit my wife, Carol, in the surgical ward. How could I make this stranger understand the importance of my mission?

Carol and I were newlyweds and this was to have been our first Christmas together. Not only that, her birthday was on December 25, which would have made our celebration all the more special.

The holiday season had begun well enough. Baking, mailing, shopping and wrapping had all gone smoothly. The tree was a thing of beauty—so tall it brushed the ceiling in our walk-up apartment.

Our preparations were nearly complete when, late on December 22, disaster struck! Carol woke me complaining of severe stomach pain. Her ashen complexion and the beads of sweat on her forehead made it clear her condition was serious.

Christmas to Be Canceled?

We rushed to the hospital, where the doctor in the emergency room confirmed my suspicions. Acute appendicitis was the diagnosis...immediate surgery was the treatment...Christmas in the hospital was the prognosis.

The surgery was successful, but I worried that having to spend Christmas Day in the hospital would break Carol's heart.

Shortly after 6 a.m. on the morning of December 23, Carol was wheeled into her room in the surgical ward. She was still groggy but alert enough to recognize my voice and squeeze my hand.

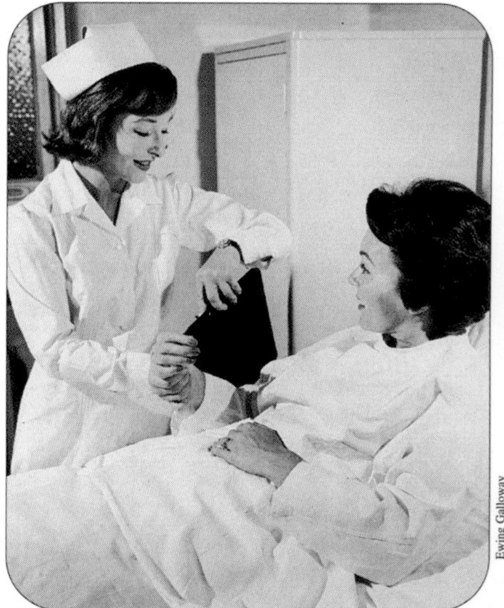

Ewing Galloway

***YUCKY YULETIDE.* Being away from home at Christmas is bad enough. But spending it in the hospital, like the woman above, was the worst.**

My stay with her, however, was brief. The ward supervisor, Nurse Krause, arrived to settle in the new patient. In those days, visiting hours were strictly enforced and I quickly discovered that Nurse Krause wasn't one to bend the rules.

After exchanging greetings, she advised me her patient needed rest, informed me that my visit was over and dismissed me from the room.

I spent the next 2 days creeping about the hospital's hallways, dodging Nurse Krause and trying to extend my visits. Unfortunately, she seemed to have a sixth sense about such things and invariably thwarted my efforts.

Nabbed by Night Nurse

So, when my Christmas Eve visit was terminated promptly at 9 p.m., I had a backup plan. Three hours later, dressed in a Santa suit, I snuck back into the hospital.

I almost made it to Carol's room but was apprehended in the corridor by the night nurse just short of my goal.

Ignoring pleas for clemency, she dutifully delivered me to the nursing station—and into the clutches of Supervisor Krause.

Despite my disguise, she recognized me immediately. When her colleague

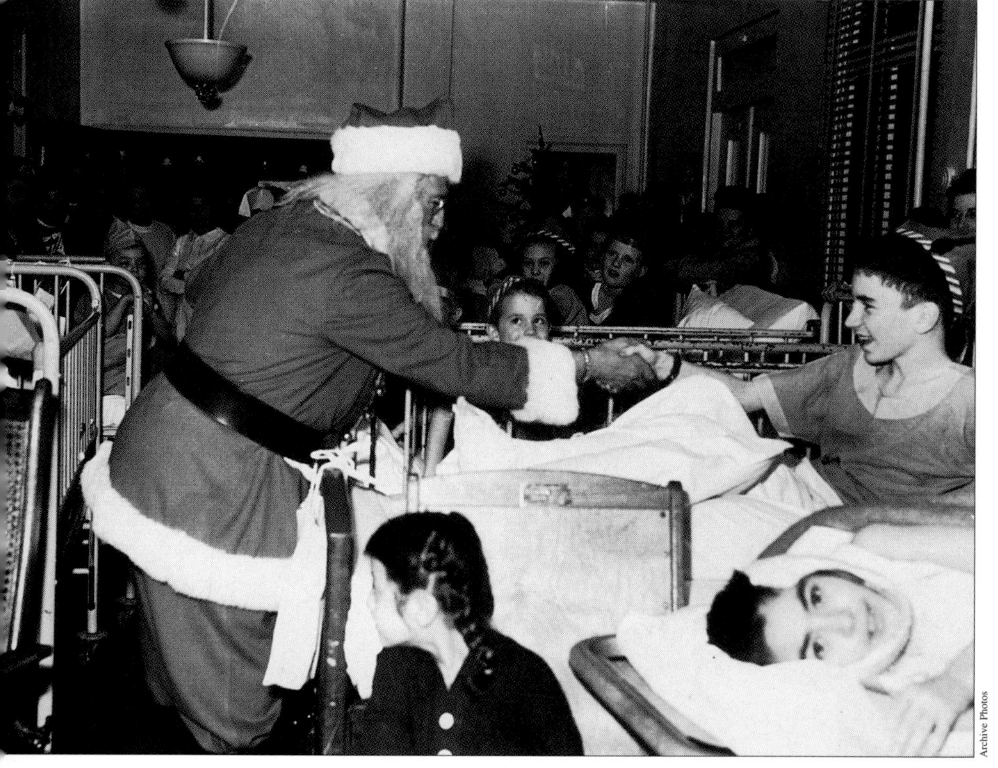

Archive Photos

***JOLLY BEDSIDE MANNER.* When John Forrest tried to sneak into the hospital as Santa to see his wife, the ever-vigilant Nurse Krause put him to work doing what Santa did—making kids happy, like those pictured above.**

departed to continue her rounds, Nurse Krause and I were left alone, facing each other over the counter.

She stared at me for a moment, then, after ordering me to stay put, she set off down the hallway. I stood rooted to the spot, awaiting my fate.

Would *He* Need a Nurse?

Then a Christmas miracle occurred. Nurse Krause returned pushing a wheelchair. My heart leapt with joy when I recognized its smiling passenger. Nurse Krause parked the chair beside me without a word, then disappeared around the corner.

Leaning forward, I was about to give Carol a Christmas kiss when I was interrupted.

"Okay you two, that's enough of that!" Nurse Krause barked. "We've got work to do!" She swept back into the corridor pushing a laundry cart filled to overflowing with wrapped presents and assorted stuffed toys.

Santa's Special Delivery

Nurse Krause had a special mission of her own that Christmas Eve. Just down the hall was the children's ward. The parents of kids who couldn't be home for Christmas had left their gifts with her for delivery.

She'd taken one look at my outfit and decided to recruit me! With Carol accompanying us in her wheelchair,

"Despite my disguise, she recognized me..."

we spent the next hour visiting every bed in the children's ward.

Carol and Nurse Krause checked the tags, selected the appropriate present and then passed it to me. I tiptoed from bed to bed, placing gifts inside the rails with their occupants.

By the time we'd finished, we'd left more than one sleepy-eyed young believer in our wake.

As far as Carol was concerned, that late-night mission must have had a remarkable healing effect. On Christmas Day, we received the best gift of all—her early release from the hospital.

Carol and I have celebrated nearly 40 Christmases together, and we have fond memories of each. But none hold as many cherished memories as our first Christmas Eve—when a special nurse gave us the precious gift of togetherness. ▲

Robin Rudd/Unicorn Stock Photos

***CHRISTMAS SURPRISE* awaited GI at his quarters in war-torn Yokohama.**

Former Enemies Showed True Christmas Spirit

THE WAR was over by Christmas 1945, and those of us on occupation duty in Yokohama wanted to be back home celebrating the holidays with our loved ones. Apart from having Christmas Day off, and a change in the menu, there was little to look forward to. That is, until a roommate said he knew where he could get a small evergreen for our already crowded room.

That afternoon, I walked the streets of Yokohama looking for Christmas tree ornaments—or something that could be used for them. I found nothing. Leg weary and dejected, I trudged back to our quarters to report my failure.

Entering our room, I saw the tree already in place—and imagine my surprise to also see four Japanese women busily making decorations from colored paper they had obtained from who knows where.

These young women, employed to help with kitchen and cleaning duties, had voluntarily undertaken to decorate our little tree. They seemed surprised and a little embarrassed to be caught at it, and they disappeared before I could thank them.

A few months earlier, their city had been heavily bombed. But these women, completely on their own, were trying to help us foreigners celebrate the birth of Christ. I've never witnessed a more tangible expression of peace on earth and goodwill toward men as I did on that December afternoon.

—Preston McGrain, Lexington, Kentucky

***NOT SO MERRY.* Fred McMullen (on right in photo with buddy Hugh James) of Hillsdale, Michigan "celebrated" Christmas 1944 fighting the Battle of the Bulge. All soldiers in the First Infantry Division were issued these cards (below) to send home to loved ones, Fred recalls. Fred was glad to follow the card home after the war.**

Orphanage Was Home Away from Home

By Betty Stover, Mishawaka, Indiana

WHEN Dad died in 1929, Mother was unable to support four children—but she was determined to keep us together.

She was able to because Daddy had been a Freemason, and the organization provided a self-supporting home for members or their children.

That's how my brother, two sisters and I were placed in the Masonic Home in Franklin, Indiana. I was there from age 7 through my high school years.

The institution had a large complex for the aged, plus eight cottages that housed 30 children each.

We knew Christmas was coming when the Sears catalog was passed around for each of us to pick a $5 "wish" item. Holiday preparations moved right along—but not fast enough for a cottage full of eager curious children!

Followed Paper Trail

We had work assignments, and when the little ones emptied the wastebaskets, we'd catch up with them to search through our governess' basket.

Sometimes we'd find return addresses on brown wrapping paper. Then we knew who had received a package that day—and got an idea of how big the package had been.

Just before Christmas, a huge tree was delivered to each cottage. The oldest girls fetched boxes of ornaments from the attic and decorated the tree while the little ones watched.

Our study room was made festive with red and green twisted streamers. Paper fan bells hung in the center and the stairway posts were intertwined with red and green crepe paper.

> *"What happy holidays we shared with our substitute family..."*

Gathering around the piano, we sang Christmas carols and ate cookies made by those of us who had kitchen detail for the month.

What delightfully happy holidays we shared with our substitute family!

On Christmas Eve, we went to the main chapel, where the superintendent greeted us. Then the lights went out and the high school girls came down the aisles in pairs. Holding candles and singing *Silent Night*, they looked like angels.

They entertained us with Christmas songs, and the children in the audience joined in. As the girls went back to their seats, we heard a bell ringing from the fire escape and a loud "Ho, ho, ho".

Pass the Parcels!

As Santa Claus bounded in a side door, a curtain onstage was opened to reveal a huge Christmas tree with piles of packages (our Sears orders!). As we children clapped and squealed, Santa, along with teachers and employees of the Home, handed out the packages.

Later, the older girls sang for the elderly residents in the main building. They then joined friends from other cottages for more caroling outside.

On Christmas morning, after breakfast and chores, we'd gather around the tree. In addition to gifts from his or her family, each child received a sack of mixed nuts, colorful hard Christmas candies and a huge orange. The dinner we shared later that day was delicious.

We missed our own families, of course. Yet, at reunions still held every year, we fondly recall those wonderful holidays at the Masonic Home.

MERRY MEMORIES. **Although unable to spend Christmas at home for several years, Betty Stover and her sisters had some wonderful holidays at the Masonic Home in Franklin, Indiana. Her sister Lillian (peeking above the piano-playing governess' head in photo above) enjoyed singing carols in 1939. Betty (standing second from right below) and sister Polly (kneeling just left of tree) posed at the home that year. They missed their family, but they enjoyed their Christmases and recall them fondly.**

HEALED FOR THE HOLIDAY. **When she was a nurse (left above), I. Wynne tried hard to work her way into the heart of a gruff patient she thought was beyond caring. Would the Christmas spirit help her succeed?**

A Christmas Surprise To Always Remember

By I. Wynne, Honolulu, Hawaii

I LEFT HAWAII during the Depression to complete my studies at St. Mary's Hospital School of Nursing in St. Louis. I sailed from my home with great apprehension.

After 5 days at sea (and 3 more on a Greyhound bus), I arrived at the nurse's quarters on a warm June day.

My studies and work on the pediatric floor kept me busy and helped overcome my homesickness. Before I knew it, November had arrived.

Early on Thanksgiving morning, I glimpsed my first snowfall. While everyone else slept, I ventured outside.

The immense whiteness left me breathless—it was just like the Christmas cards I'd sent home! Excitedly, I scooped up snow with my bare hands. Only someone from a land far away could be so thrilled by a simple snowfall.

Met New Patients

The next week, I was transferred to Mount St. Rose, a sanitarium for tuberculosis patients. My first day there, Miss Hale, my supervisor, introduced me to the patients.

"Good morning, Mr. Martini," Miss Hale said. "How are you?"

"Why do you ask?" grunted the 53-year-old man.

Ignoring his gruffness, Miss Hale continued, "Miss Yayo is from Hawaii. She'll be with us for a month."

Mr. Martini wouldn't look at me. A few days later, I took a pitcher of fresh water to his room.

"Who sent you here?" he glared.

"Why...nobody," I stammered. "I was just bringing you fresh water."

"What nationality are you?" he snapped.

I explained that I was a Japanese-American citizen.

"Your folks come from Japan?" he asked. Japan is making trouble for China." Somehow, he made me feel personally responsible for everything going on over there.

Suddenly, he was seized by a fit of coughs. "Enough talking," I said. "Lie quietly while I get Miss Hale."

"Get out of here!" he whispered between painful coughs.

Put Resentment Aside

Although I ran to get help, my day had turned miserable. Considering Mr. Martini's serious illness, I tried to put away my resentment. Still, I resolved to stay away from his room if possible.

A week or so later, it snowed again. Knowing I'd get a better view of the surrounding hills from Mr. Martini's floor, I went up there. As I passed his room, I heard commotion.

It was obvious he was having a problem, so I ran to help him. Mr. Martini grabbed my arm tightly and begged for assistance. This was a real emergency, so I sounded the bell and summoned help. An emergency crew arrived and took him to the operating room. I later learned the crisis was averted.

Just before Christmas, I returned to St. Mary's. I'd completed my studies and was preparing to leave for home, but I was bothered by the feeling I'd left something undone.

I was packing my suitcase when it hit me—for some reason, I needed to say good-bye to Mr. Martini.

For one last time, I trudged through the snow to Mount St. Rose. But when I arrived, I learned he was spending the holidays with his family.

"For some reason, I needed to say good-bye..."

Glad that he'd recovered enough to do that, I thanked the clerk and turned to leave. Just then, Sister Maureen hurried toward me.

"Oh, just a second, Miss Yayo," she called. "A gift was left here for you."

Sister handed me a box wrapped with Christmas ribbon.

Opening it carefully, I found a card on top of some white tissue paper. The card read: "To my young friend from Hawaya, Miss Yayo." Inside the box, I found two pairs of white nylon hosiery and a lovely lavender handkerchief.

My eyes welled with tears. Holding the gift close to my heart, I ran outside and faced the distant snowy hills. "Mele Kalikimaka, Mr. Martini! I wish you well!" I shouted into the icy air.

He had given me a very special Christmas...and a beautiful memory to take back home to Hawaii. ▲

GI CAROLERS. **Eileen Stein (center right) and her GI chorus did what they could to bring a little bit of Christmas to the soldiers near the Battle of the Bulge. She'll never forget that Christmas, as they sang for the medics headed for the battlefield.**

Red Cross Volunteer Entertained Through Tears

I WAS very far from home on Christmas 1944—attached to Third Corps Headquarters in Longwy, France on the French-Belgium border.

I was a Red Cross volunteer, as lonesome and homesick as all the soldiers. Being in the same boat, we became sort of a family.

So on Christmas morning, we all helped clear the mess hall for church services. Then my partner, Effie Hazlett, and I scrounged around town for decorations for the tree. We also cut up a silk German parachute and made scarves for the men.

We had our Christmas turkey dinner in that big cold mess hall at noon. The meal was shared by newsman Eric Severeid and his driver. They were on their way to Bastogne to cover the Battle of the Bulge.

Effie and I had organized a little GI chorus, and after the dinner, we all loaded into Jeeps and trucks and headed out to entertain the troops in the forward area at Arlon, Belgium.

Arlon was very close to the battle. The Germans were going to allow a 1-hour truce at 3 p.m. to let the Allies onto the battlefield to rescue some of the wounded.

As our medical officers and men left to join the convoy of 133 ambulances going to the battlefield, we sang *I'll Be Home for Christmas* with tears rolling down our faces.

How could I ever forget?

—Eileen O'Leary Stein
Oak Creek, Wisconsin

Christmas Carol in Korea Gave Guard Joy

NOT ONLY was Christmas 1951 my first away from home, it was my first as a married man. I'd had only 13 days with my young bride before I shipped out to Korea.

I was a company armorer in the Chemical Corps but was getting plenty of guard duty, 2 hours on, 4 hours off. In fact, I drew guard duty Christmas Eve.

My first 2 hours on were from 6 to 8 p.m., so I got to sleep until midnight, when I'd pull another lonely 2 hours on.

About 15 minutes after I relieved the guard at the motor pool and started my tour, I heard something in the distance. As the sound came closer, I could tell it was a bunch of Koreans, which caused me some concern.

When they emerged from the darkness, I could see a smiling, jostling crowd of children, accompanied by a few adults. They formed a line in front of the motor pool gate, where I was standing with my rifle, and sang *Silent Night* to me.

I've attended many Christmas Eve services since, and even conducted some. But never have I experienced a more meaningful *Silent Night, Holy Night.* *—John Thorsness*
Durango, Colorado

Italian Children Enjoyed A Bountiful Christmas

CHRISTMAS 1945 was coming up, and most of my friends in the 15th Air Force had left for home. The war was long over, but not for those of us on occupational duty in Italy.

Moping around, waiting for our discharge numbers to come up, we had little ambition ...until the chaplain came up with an idea that mobilized us.

He'd found a small church in Foggia and decided to give its children a real Christmas party. We began loading up on items from the PX, and two trucks were obtained from the motor pool.

The mess hall was alerted, and the cooks went all-out for the feast. The hall was decorated and they even managed to get some ice cream.

Christmas Day arrived cold and rainy. There was a crowd of people at the church, where a man started reading off a list of names. As each name was read, a small child would work his or her way through the crowd to be lifted into a truck.

It was at this point we realized we'd made one mistake. We said we'd take children aged 1 to 12. We didn't know that in Italy, a child is considered a year old at birth. So we had some very small children on our hands.

But that turned out to be no problem. Back at the base, the GIs who had children of their own took care of the "1-year-olds".

We realized our efforts were successful when the children came into the mess hall and saw all that food. Most of them couldn't eat everything on their plates because it had been so long since they'd had that much to eat. We wrapped up the leftovers so they could take the food home.

After the meal, each child was given a bag containing a toothbrush, toothpaste, soap and candy. It was something to see the way their eyes lit up and their grins radiated across their faces.

The event was something everyone in the squadron would remember, and I'm sure the children of Foggia learned about the love that comes from Christ to all mankind.

—Evan Towne, Huntington, Indiana

Gail Denham

***CHRISTMAS TREATS.* Goodies like these brought Christmas to children in war-torn cities, and tears to the eyes of tough GIs.**

First Real Christmas For British Kids

THE SMALL village of Glastonbury, England had a large population of children for a time during World War II. They were sent there from other cities to escape the bombing.

I was stationed in Glastonbury, and as Christmas 1943 approached, we GIs were told we could have 1 pound of chocolate or hard candy per man for Christmas, along with an apple and an orange.

Captain Crooks, our commander, suggested we combine all our candy and fruit and make up Christmas bags for the children. Many of the kids were from 3 to 5 years old and had never known a real Christmas because of the war.

Captain Crooks contacted the lord mayor of the village, who was able to assemble all the children in the town square on Christmas morning. One of the cooks made a Santa suit and handed out the bags.

Anyone seeing the joy in those little kids' eyes that day would have known the true meaning of Christmas.

And anyone seeing the eyes of those in our troop would have had trouble finding a dry one.

—William Kuester
Bakersfield, California

❄

Church Built in Time for Christmas

CHRISTMAS 1943 was only 2 weeks away. My buddy, Frank Humphries, and I were in the Philippines, an awful long way from home.

We casually mentioned to a 14-year-old Filipino boy we knew how much we'd like to find a church where we could worship on Christmas Day.

Imagine our surprise when, the very next day, a multitude of Filipinos arrived in our area with water buffalo carts loaded with bamboo. The men began building a church, while children scampered up the palms to gather fronds, which the women weaved into squares for the sides and roof.

In 2 days, the building was finished, complete with altar and pews, also made of bamboo. The pews were two bamboo poles, side by side, anchored into the ground with shorter pieces.

The pews were quite uncomfortable, especially with no backs. But they worked.

Although we found it awkward having to carry our weapons to church, I guess it wasn't much different than carrying them to the mess hall, shower stalls or latrines!

—Albert McGraw, Anderson, Alabama

***CHRISTIAN SOLDIERS.* Although Albert McGraw (left above) and Frank Humphries had to carry their weapons on Christmas, at least they had a church.**

Ewing Galloway

***DERAILED CHRISTMAS.* A troop train was no place to spend Christmas. But some lucky soldiers and sailors, like Wally Windscheffel, got sidetracked in a friendly city where the folks temporarily "adopted" a serviceman for the holiday. Wally recalls the hot bath as fondly as the friendship.**

Sailors Given Home For Christmas Present

IT WAS SO cold, the thin layer of new snow squeaked under our feet outside the Minneapolis-St. Paul train station. Finding ourselves in an urban area on this late December night in 1944 was quite a surprise for my mates and me.

We'd been riding a slow-moving troop train for days, going from boot camp in Farragut, Idaho to a school in St. Louis. Most of the time when the train stopped, it was on a little-used siding to allow faster trains to pass.

We were cold, hungry and covered with soot. The cars were heated with coal stoves and had only the bare necessities. We were sure that cattle cars were more luxurious...and had rounder wheels.

We carried our food from the train kitchen, across the open spaces between cars, using flimsy paper plates and paper cups for the scalding-hot coffee. It was a life-threatening adventure in dining—if you had anything left to eat when you got to your car.

But things were about to change. Families from the Twin Cities arrived to take us to their homes until the train pulled out. A friend and I left with a man in a '36 Ford, just like my dad's.

We were met at the house by the man's wife and two children. It was an ordinary home in an ordinary neighborhood, but it seemed like Heaven to me.

We jumped at the chance to take a hot bath. The ring we left around the tub more than likely had to be removed with a chisel.

While we bathed, our clothes were washed, and we wore borrowed robes while our things dried.

Then we enjoyed dinner with the happy, gracious family, and even received a wrapped present from under the tree. That family's act of kindness on my first Christmas away from home has had a lasting effect on me. Their spirit of Christmas gave me memories that will live forever.

—Wally Windscheffel
Grand Junction, Colorado

WACs Dig into Stores For Christmas Gifts

MACARTHUR'S ARMY had moved forward, and my WAC unit was now stationed on Leyte Island in the Philippines in December 1944.

Our quarters were in a grove of coconut trees just off the beach. One day we were surprised to see a white woman holding a child. She wore a sack dress and tattered sandals.

We crowded around and discovered Mrs. Johnston and her missionary husband had been hiding in the mountains since the war broke out. They were often inches from the enemy, and their baby was born in the bush, under primitive conditions. Their two Filipino servants remained loyal and sometimes risked their lives sneaking into Japanese camps to steal food. But now all were safe. Mr. Johnston and the servants were in a men's camp, and Mrs. Johnston was with us.

It would be months before we would receive our Christmas packages, so every WAC jealously guarded any treasures she had. But when it came time to outfit Mrs. Johnston for her flight back to the U.S., out came the perfume, lingerie, a WAC uniform and boots. We found out Mr. Johnston was being helped in similar fashion by the GIs.

We also had a great meal, complete with ice cream, filched by the cook from the officers' mess, and bid the family good-bye with this unusual and unexpected Christmas. Later that night, they were put aboard a plane for the trip home.

WACs were brave young women, not given to tears. But when Mrs. Johnston opened that pillowcase of precious, feminine goodies, she cried, and so did we.

—J.G. Anderson
Sun City, California

National Achives/Jeff Ethell

***IN THE PINK.* These WACs in their new dress "pinks", were a lot more stylish than J.G. Anderson and her unit in the Philippines when they helped clothe the missionary's wife.**

For One Shining Moment, War's Misery Was Forgotten

By Robert Schwerdt, Poughkeepsie, New York

DURING CHRISTMAS week of 1944, my first holiday ever away from home, I was a private in an infantry regiment in Belgium.

I was trying to return to my company after having spent some time in an English hospital.

But the Battle of the Bulge, the last-ditch effort by the Germans to penetrate our lines and recapture Antwerp, had just begun. My fellow replacements and I were not yet in the actual battle, but we were close enough to the fighting.

Things were confused because word had spread that German soldiers dressed in American uniforms had infiltrated our lines. No one was sure who was friend or foe.

To make matters worse, there weren't any familiar faces among the men who had accompanied me the past several days.

So there we were, a dozen or so GIs uncertain of each other, uncertain of where we were, and all trying to return to our own outfits near the front. Now the German surprise attack had left us stranded in a small Belgian town on Christmas Eve.

I stood guard duty that night from 10 p.m. until midnight. I don't recall much about that shift, except that I was cold, lonely and frightened—and that the password was changed hourly.

What I do remember—and vividly—happened after my shift ended. I was returning to my makeshift sleeping quarters when the door of one of the darkened houses opened slightly and a hand beckoned me inside. I hesitated for a moment, then entered.

> *"I was cold, lonely and frightened..."*

Inside, I found a candlelit table spread with a meager array of food and wine. A man, his wife and small daughter had apparently decided to celebrate their Christmas by sharing their limited means with a lonely American soldier.

Words Not Needed

No words were spoken, but with nods and smiles, the four of us, for a brief time, forgot the war, the misery and the hatred by honoring a birthday and enjoying the goodwill of men everywhere.

To this day, I regret not having had anything to offer those kind people except a handshake. Perhaps the presence of even a few American soldiers gave them a measure of security. I certainly hope so.

I've celebrated more than 50 Christmases since that night, but none have held quite the same emotional impact as that one so briefly spent with a wonderful Belgian family, when no words were ever spoken.

Healing Helped by Christmas Party

I WAS serving in the Air Force in October 1943 near Gela Sicily. I became ill and was sent to a series of hospitals for testing.

I was eventually transferred to the 33rd General Hospital in Charleston, South Carolina, where I got the immediate attention of a caring, compassionate staff.

I was diagnosed with poliomyelitis, and because treatment was now available, my recovery began rapidly. By the time Christmas 1944 came, I was up and—almost—around.

The day before Christmas, one of the nurses mentioned they were having a party the next afternoon in the nurses' quarters. "If you feel up to it," she invited, "why not stop by for a while?"

My two previous Christmases far from home had been pretty bleak, so this was too much to resist.

At the appointed hour, decked out in my GI pajamas, robe and slippers and with my hair slicked back, I shuffled off to the nurses' quarters.

The room looked festive, and all the officers and off-duty nurses were in their dress uniforms. Here I was, the lone sergeant, dressed in pajamas!

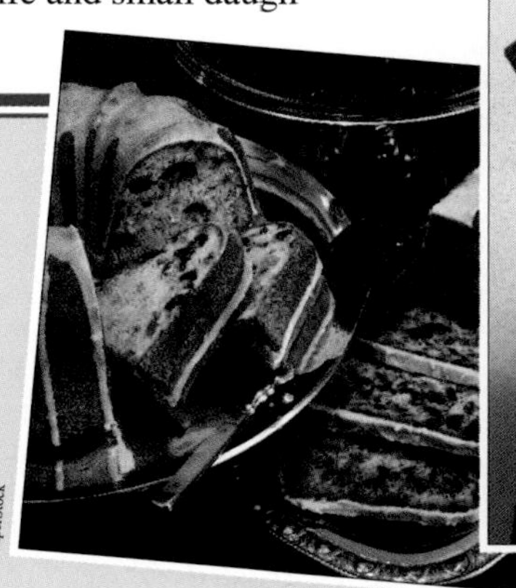

SuperStock

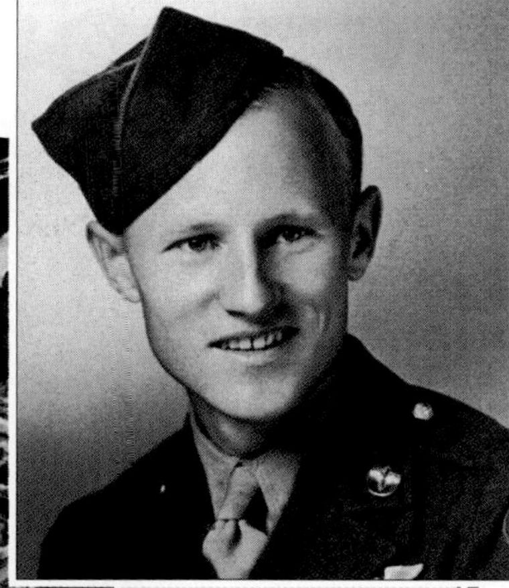

LASTING MEMORIES. **The only thing that lasts longer than fruitcake are James Cowan's happy memories of Christmas 1944.**

But I enjoyed this party more than I thought I would. I got my first taste of Coca-Cola in 2 years, and, as I was trying to slip away, Lieutenant Morrison gave me a large fruitcake to share with the other fellows in my ward.

That gesture was the finishing touch to an unforgettable Christmas far from home.

Though my appetite for fruitcake decreases as my years increase, I believe that had to be the best fruitcake ever eaten by anyone, anyplace. *—James Cowan, Sedalia, Missouri*

Ewing Galloway

CHRISTMAS AT SEA. **Even when there was a war on, soldiers and sailors were often able to get something a little special for chow at Christmas. These sailors are about to enjoy a turkey on a destroyer escorting convoys across the Atlantic. Of course, many were lucky if they were able to heat up their C rations for a Christmas dinner in a foxhole.**

Silent Pacific Night Set Scene for Carol

WE HAD spent all of Christmas Day 1943 loading the Fifth Regiment of the First Marine Division for the initial assault on Cape Gloucester, on the South Pacific island of New Britain.

Now it was Christmas night, and our convoy of 300 vessels of all kinds was moving slowly in the dark in order to time the landing for 0630 the next day. It was warm, and the sea was like glass.

The Marines were all on deck, lying around their equipment. Since it was our first beachhead, we were scared and tight-lipped.

I went on watch at midnight to my station on the flying bridge. The only sound to be heard was the steady churn of the ship's propeller. I mentioned the silence to the officer of the deck. He just nodded.

Even though I knew there were over 1,500 people aboard, it was spooky and lonesome. We were over 10,000 miles from home on Christmas, and many of us were thinking this could be our last.

About 0200 hours, a small group started singing *Silent Night*. As the others heard, they joined in. In a short time, the whole ship was singing. When we finished, we could hear the singing from the other ships.

That was what we needed, and our spirits brightened. *—Bill Wright*
Ortonville, Michigan

Gift of a Call Home Makes GI's Christmas

THE WEATHER in Aroostook County, Maine the Christmas of 1957 was as brisk as ever—between 15° and 20° below zero.

This was my second year as director of the USO club in Caribou, where we served military personnel and their families stationed at the nearby air base.

We had a traditional Christmas dinner the Sunday before the holiday, with area churches taking turns providing the meal.

As each serviceman entered the USO club, he was given a number. After dinner, the numbers were pulled out of a box, and everyone received a gift from under the huge Maine fir tree in the middle of the dance floor.

The highlight of the evening was the awarding of free phone calls to anywhere in the U.S.

During the festivities, one of the lady volunteers said she'd spoken to a particularly homesick airman who was a native of Ireland. (In those days you could be awarded citizenship upon completion of military service.) This would be his first Christmas away from home.

The lady wondered if there was something we could do for the airman, but I didn't have any ideas. She then began whispering with one of the other hostesses. The two went into the cloakroom where their purses were kept.

Soon, the hostess made an announcement that this year, a special award would be given—a free phone call to the serviceman who was farthest from home.

Of course, the winner was Airman Second Class Dennis Markey from Swords, Ireland. He was jubilant.

The call was made from the club the next day, and placing an overseas call was no easy thing back then. But Dennis returned to the base happy...and I went into my office to count the coins and bills that had been collected in a paper bag to pay for the call.

—Will Kennedy, Erie, Pennsylvania

Air Force Santa Conquered Loneliness

By Pat Stoltenberg, Angleton, Texas

THE YEAR was 1954, and it was going to be a warm Christmas Eve in Riverside, California. My front kitchen window was open and I could hear children playing up and down the street.

As I picked up my baby son and headed to the front door, I found it hard to believe that this was the night before Christmas—and I was 1,500 miles away from my hometown of Angleton, Texas.

Although the stars were bright in a beautiful December sky and I could see snowcapped mountains in the distance, all I really wanted to see was the flat expanse of the Texas Gulf Coast. My eyes filled with tears as I thought of the distance between me and all that was familiar.

My husband was a first lieutenant in the Strategic Air Command and a navigator on a B-47 bomber. We were stationed at March Air Force Base and although each day was exciting as we rubbed elbows with famous people and did new things, the fact remained that this was Christmas Eve and I was alone.

The Strategic Air Command was well known for its alerts. If a siren sounded, men and planes had to be airborne within 30 minutes. In order to keep the crews sharp, this exercise was practiced many times a year, always when it was least expected.

Gone for How Long?

A few hours earlier, my husband had left on just such a mission. I had no idea how long he would be gone. It could be another hour, another day—even a week. Anything was possible in the Air Force.

Loneliness engulfed me as I edged a little farther out onto the porch with my son. This wasn't how I'd wanted to spend my first Christmas Eve away from home.

The dark sky seemed to stretch forever over my head and I began to realize that, whatever kind of Christmas my son and I were going to have, I alone would be responsible for it. I wasn't sure I was up to that responsibility.

As I stood there contemplating my sorry lot, I noticed something moving in the street. Coming up the road toward me, was a jolly little man with a white beard and a red suit.

He was surrounded by children and, as he came closer, I saw he was pushing a wheelbarrow laden with packages. At each house, he'd pause for a moment and dole out some of those packages. I could hear him laughing and calling out, "Ho, ho, ho...Merry Christmas!"

Each time he stopped, mothers came out to greet him, bringing whatever children were still awake. Miraculously, a transformation was taking place in our neighborhood.

"I could hear him laughing and calling out, 'Ho, ho, ho!'"

People began to appear from nowhere. In the blink of an eye and the nod of a head, we suddenly had a gigantic block party going on! I met neighbors I'd never seen before and was invited into one of their homes for punch. Strangers who'd come from hometowns all over the United States melded together and became one big happy family.

Because of one man's actions and one man's caring, I was no longer lonely. I felt as if I had a new family gathered around me...the family of mankind.

The next morning when I awoke, I discovered that Santa had brought me the greatest gift of all. There, sitting near the Christmas tree and drinking his morning coffee, was my husband.

Tragically, less than a year later, our wonderful neighborhood Santa, better known as Captain Edward O'Brien, was killed in a plane crash within sight of our street of homes. He became a hero in death, and that crash made national headlines.

Still, I'm sure he would have been pleased to know that a part of him lives forever in my heart. Because on that lonely Christmas Eve over 40 years ago, he taught me the true meaning of the words "Merry Christmas".

Archive Photos/Express

SANTA'S EVERYWHERE! **This Santa slowing traffic in Bethlehem is a long way from California. But Pat Stoltenberg remembers a Christmas when the man in red cured her homesickness.**

UNFORGETTABLE. **With a mop for a tree, good friends and gifts from family and loved ones, these sailors will likely never forget this shipboard Christmas celebration. No matter where you are, home or thousands of miles away, Christmas is the best time for making memories.**

H. Armstrong Roberts

Chapter Ten

The Christmas I'll Never Forget

This will be my 72nd Christmas. That's a lot of Christmases for anyone to think back upon, especially when you pause to ask yourself which is the *one* you'll never forget.

To begin with, I can't recall but two or three really bad Christmases. Those were the times when it was impossible to get home—a proper Christmas should be spent with family.

Another Christmas celebrated far from home stands out in my mind, but it was enjoyed with family. Peg and I and three of our children lived for a few months in Madrid, Spain, and that Christmas comes very close to being our most unforgettable holiday.

There was the excitement of shopping in a foreign land and trying to do our best in an unfamiliar language. Even the lights for our Christmas tree were unlike anything we'd seen before—not really lights, but intricate ornaments that glowed.

As Christmas approached, there were no signs of street decorations at all. But then, a few days before December 25, *WHAM!*, millions of lights all came on the same night.

Made Spirits Bright

Lights festooned every pole, and thousands more hung on tall pine trees that had been brought down from the mountains and stood in the median strips of wide boulevards. There were lights in office building windows and storefronts. Lights, lights, lights!

It's astonishing that every circuit breaker in the city didn't trip when all those lights surged on at once. I've never seen anything half as grand anywhere, and I never expect to again.

Not literally as bright, but warm beyond measure, are my childhood Christmases. How could I ever forget those we spent at my grandparents', with aunts, uncles and cousins filling the house with hugs, kisses and happy chatter?

Joyous as those gatherings were, how can I call them better than the years when I was a parent and privileged to help light up excited little faces on Christmas morning?

I have dozens of pictures shot during the years when I was a young parent. Since I was designated photographer, I appear in nearly none of them. Still, they let me once again revisit all those Christmases past.

Remember "Easy Assembly"?

Here's the year we stayed up Christmas Eve—nearly until dawn—assembling those fiendishly designed toys that came with 20-page "easy assembly instructions".

Here we are spending Christmas in my eldest daughter's home with our first two grandchildren. Forget it? Never!

Oh, and here's the Christmas when six of the kids, along with spouses and their own children, all were able to get together at another daughter's home for Christmas. It was the closest we ever came to having the whole tribe together. I know for sure it was Mom's most memorable. Just look at the smile on her face, sitting there surrounded by children, grandchildren and three great-grandchildren.

I don't want to forget a single one of these holidays. Each was special in its own way.

Another memory I'll never forget is a sort of odd

> *"I don't want to forget a single one of these holidays..."*

sidelight that proves even dogs have unforgettable Christmases. A large German shepherd named "Victor" was part of our family for a dozen years. While he was still a youngster, one of the kids wrapped up two of those large, crunchy, bone-shaped doggie treats and put the package under the tree.

The dog was a curious bystander as gifts were opened. When most of them had been distributed, our daughter said, "Hey, here's one for Victor!"

He sniffed the package and, with fang and claw, ripped it open.

It was the Christmas Victor never forgot. For the rest of his life, he crowded in among the rest of the family on Christmas morning, ears on full point, waiting for someone to pass him his present. I sometimes pondered whether he, too, stayed awake on Christmas Eve in happy anticipation.

In recent years, Peg and I have had a handful of Christmases alone, just the two of us. But the house is as beautifully decorated as it would be if the whole family were coming home. We put up the tree together a week before Christmas, grittily resist opening our presents until Christmas morning, have a scrumptious mid-morning brunch, and walk around the neighborhood to inspect the outdoor decorations on Christmas night.

Yes, it would be better with the kids and grandchildren around, but together we happily recall all those unforgettable Christmases that so enriched our lives.

—*Clancy Strock*

It Was No Fair Peeking

By Lorenz Frankfurth, Oconomowoc, Wisconsin

I WAS the youngest child in our large German family, and we had certain strict Yuletide traditions.

On St. Nicholas Eve, December 5, my brother, three sisters and I hung Dad's wool hunting socks on our bedposts. The next morning, they would be filled with nuts, oranges, apples and candy, all from good St. Nick. There were no chocolate candies, because St. Nick didn't think they were good for children.

The next great event was December 18, when Santa Claus visited our home to set up and trim the tree in our breakfast room.

Each year, a sheet was hung over the glass door that separated the breakfast room from the dining room. Father always insisted no one was to peek once Santa had visited and set up the tree. But we could sniff under the sliding door just to be sure there was that telltale pine scent of Christmas.

On the morning of December 19, 1922, sure enough, a sheet covered the breakfast room door! I dropped to my knees and took a good long sniff. There was no mistaking that northwoods perfume. Our tree was up and trimmed!

Or was it? Did Santa have time to hang all the ornaments? We always had an abundance of candy and decorations, and I had nagging doubts. So I devised a plan to check if Santa had finished his task. I'd take a ladder from the garage and look in the window. It wouldn't be a *look* really, just a *glance*. And no one would know because the ground was frozen and no marks from the ladder feet would show!

I got home from kindergarten before Dad returned from his office. Mother was busy in the kitchen baking Christmas cookies.

I sneaked to the garage, lifted the stepladder off its hook and went to the breakfast room window. With unbridled delight, I saw that Santa had done his usual professional job. In fact, this year, he'd outdone himself!

> *"I guess we'll have to wait a year for Santa to come back..."*

All the German lights and ornaments were properly placed, the feathery angel was perfectly positioned on top of the tree and...

My reverie was broken by the sound of a Hudson Super Six coming up the drive. Dad had come home early! I scrambled down the ladder and dashed for the back door. It was close, but he hadn't seen me.

Dad opened the garage doors and parked the car. He was walking to the house when he noticed the telltale ladder. One of his children had obviously peeked and he probably had a good idea who the culprit was.

Supper was very quiet that evening, and Father just wasn't his jovial self.

Something Was Wrong

When I came down for breakfast the next morning, something was very wrong. The door to the breakfast room was wide open and the tree was gone. My brother and sisters were glumly sitting around the table.

"What happened to the tree?" I croaked.

"Someone peeked, that's what," said my brother, Willie.

"There won't be any Christmas this year!" Elsa offered sadly.

"I'd like to get my hands on the one who did it," warned Paula, the oldest.

"Well, I know it wasn't me," chirped Helena.

"I didn't do it," I lied unconvincingly. But after a few minutes, I couldn't stand it any longer. I looked my father in the eye and blurted out the truth. "Dad, I peeked. It's all my fault—I ruined Christmas for everybody."

"At least we know who peeked, for all the good it will do," Dad said. "I guess we'll have to wait a year for Santa to come back...if he ever does."

My appetite vanished and I asked to be excused. I went to my room feeling dreadful because I stole Christmas from the whole family. My remorse was complete, and I suffered through the next few days.

On the morning of the 24th, I came down for breakfast. The sheet was back over the door! Santa had returned!

"Santa, I love you!" I cried. "I'll never peek again!"

Dad walked into the dining room and said, "Well, what do you know. Santa came back after all."

Then he looked wearily over to Mother and said in a very low voice, "Paula, I believe we made our point."

"I sure hope we did," Mother replied. "Santa was put to a lot of extra work this year."

HE SPOILED CHRISTMAS! **When little Lorenz Frankfurth disobeyed the long-established rule about checking Santa's work, he learned a lesson he never forgot. Lorenz posed for a photo (inset) in 1925 at age 8. His parents (above in 1910) knew how to make a point with misbehaving children.**

SANDY CHRISTMAS. Newlyweds George and Karen Eddy were strolling along a California beach on their honeymoon in 1942 when a roving photographer snapped this striking photo. Karen's handsome Marine Corps pilot was bound for the Pacific Theater, but their first Christmas together would make a lifelong impression on Karen.

Newlywed Felt Childlike Wonder of Christmas

By Karen Eddy, Westborough, Massachusetts

I WAS BORN in Alabama, the daughter of a tenant farmer, and grew up during the depths of the Depression. It was a very difficult time, and for my family, Christmas was pretty much just another day. I never saw a Christmas tree, never received a toy nor hung a stocking.

I began working at age 12 and continued until I was 20. In 1942, I met a handsome well-to-do Marine pilot from New York. We were married in July of that year and were immediately transferred to California. My husband was about to be sent to the Pacific war zone.

Since there were many service families in the area, we were blessed to find a lovely room in the private home of a Navy widow. When December came, I was overjoyed to find that a beautifully decorated Christmas tree appeared in the large living room. I'd never seen anything so magnificent, and I was breathless with excitement.

Each day as we passed through the house, I couldn't take my eyes off that tree. To add to my excitement, colorfully wrapped presents began to appear beneath it.

Celebration Would Be Private

I asked my husband if he thought we could watch while the family opened their gifts. Our landlady had two sons in the Navy, and I assumed they were coming home with their wives for the holiday.

But my husband didn't think that was likely to happen and thought we'd best not interfere with whatever celebration our landlady was planning. Of course, I was disappointed.

"Could we watch the family open their gifts?"

Christmas morning came, and my husband woke me with a surprise—we had, indeed, been invited to the "present opening"!

Even now, over 50 years later, it's difficult to describe my joy at the thought of being present at my first Christmas celebration.

We walked into the living room, and I was surprised to see only our landlady sitting there, smiling broadly.

We also sat down and, after a moment, my husband said to me, "Open them. They are all yours."

When I could get my tears under control, I opened each brightly colored box. They were from my husband, except for a couple from our wonderful landlady.

Is it any wonder that to this day, more than 50 years later, Christmas of 1942 remains my most memorable holiday ever?

Quarantine Meant Christmas Togetherness

By Albert Zabel, Huntington, West Virginia

CLOSE QUARTERS. Albert (above left with brothers Jonathan and Michael in 1942) had fun cooped up with Dad.

AS THE holiday season approached in 1943, I was a third grader in a small city in northwest Washington state. Mother was a homemaker and my father worked long hours as a salesman.

Dad was often on his way before I got out of bed in the morning and returned in the evening long after I was asleep.

Dad kept his same busy schedule as Christmas neared, but this year, things would be different. Early in December, a case of diphtheria was diagnosed at my school and all the children were tested. I don't remember my parents being unduly alarmed, and I didn't think much about it after the brief discomfort of having a throat culture taken.

Ten days later, less than a week before Christmas, a health officer nailed a notice on our front porch. "Quarantined 2 Weeks for Diphtheria," read the sign. "No Admittance."

The throat culture had shown I was carrying the disease. There was only a small chance I'd come down with diphtheria, but there was a danger I could spread it to others.

Mother was in a tizzy! According to health department rules, no one could leave the house. When Father arrived home that night, she met him at the door.

"If you come in, you're here for 2 weeks," she said.

Father must have hesitated, because his job demanded he call on his customers daily. But spending Christmas away from us was unthinkable. He marched right in and phoned his boss. They agreed he'd make his rounds by telephone for the next 14 days.

> "If you come in, you're here for 2 weeks..."

There we were, locked in together for 2 weeks! This much togetherness was unknown in our family—Father had never taken much more than Christmas Day away from his work. Even his summer vacations had a way of shrinking into a couple of long weekends.

Mother must have wondered how we'd cope, but she needn't have worried. Dad was acting like a kid himself. All of us finished the holiday decorating together. Then we played games and had a wonderful time.

As word of our situation spread, there were the expected expressions of care and concern. Soon gifts of food arrived from well-wishers. It was fun to peek out the front window and watch the furtive deliveries.

A car would stop, someone would jump out, run up the walk to the porch, set down a casserole, quickly ring the bell, then dash away at top speed.

Getting groceries was no problem, either. In those days, Mother always phoned the grocery store and read off her long shopping list. A few hours later, the delivery truck would arrive with her order. During our quarantine, the boy would leave the bags on the front porch and beat a hasty retreat.

For those 2 weeks, our family celebrated Christmas as we never had before. Father spent a few hours each morning on the phone with his customers, then the rest of the day was devoted to family fun. I never showed any signs of diphtheria and, after a few days, no one seemed to give that possibility much thought.

The special joy and closeness was the best part of that unforgettable Christmas season, but I do recall one added bonus. Our uncles and aunts didn't want their children to have any of the "infected" gifts from our house. That meant Mother turned over to us all the presents she'd purchased for our dozen or so cousins!

J.C. Allen and Son

CANE-EATING CANINE. This pooch enjoyed a Christmas snack, just like Eileen Marguet's did one year.

Holiday Dog Barked Up Wrong Tree

MY FRIEND AND I bought a cookie press and made our Christmas cookies in all sorts of shapes. A string was put in each cookie before it was baked. We added sparkles, frosting and green and red icing to them. The colorful cookie "ornaments" turned out great!

On Christmas Eve, my husband and I put the tree up as soon as the children were asleep. The cookies looked gorgeous when the tree lights were on.

We were awakened a short time later by a strange noise. We went to the living room and found our big Airedale, "Andy", with the tree on the floor. He was happily munching the cookies!

We banished him to the garage and stood up the tree. When we did, we scratched the ceiling, but *finally*, between the two of us, we managed to decorate the tree all over again.

Though we later sanded and repainted the ceiling, I could still see the scratches. We lived in that house 30 more years and I couldn't look at the ceiling without seeing Andy, staring up at me with a mouthful of cookies. It was indeed a Christmas I'll never forget. —*Eileen Marguet, West Halifax, Vermont*

***CHRISTMAS WITH DAD.* Little Wardie (on her dad's lap in November 1944) would remember the last Christmas with her father years later in a touching essay she wrote in school. The memories of that Christmas live on in the essay and in one of the dolls Wardie received as a present that year (below).**

Child's Memory Was Moving for Mother

By Virginia Bean, Liberty, Texas

DURING the 1950s when ruffled petticoats were all the rage, I was busy sewing countless yards of ruffles for my girls' Christmas outfits.

My oldest daughter, Wardie Virginia, came into my sewing room and asked me, "Mom, how old was I when my daddy died in the war?"

"Oh, about 4," I answered, without looking up or missing a stitch. My ninth grader had brought up the year 1944, a painful part of our past. As she turned to leave the room, I wondered why she'd asked such a question.

A week or so later, I learned why. She came home from school and handed me a handwritten paper. On top of the assignment, Wardie's teacher had inscribed a big red "A" and the comment, "Very beautifully written". Here is what Wardie wrote:

"Christmas is always such a wonderful time of year, a time when all of us look forward to being with our families and waking up to find what Santa has left under the tree for us.

"Usually, this is the happiest time of the year, but the year of my fourth Christmas was a little different.

"My daddy had been in California in the Navy, and we had not seen him for several months. Then he came home in November, only to stay a few days. These were the happiest days for my mother and father and my little sister and me.

"My parents were busy shopping and making plans for our Christmas. They would come home from shopping, loaded with packages that went into the closet to await the day of days, December 25.

"With all the shopping done, and all the visits made to see the relatives, my daddy had to return to California. This left my mother, little sister and me to await Christmas alone, but it was a wonderful Christmas with all the gifts and especially the lovely dolls.

"The dolls are not so lovely today as they were then. They are worn and the paint is cracked and an arm is off. But they hold a fond memory because they are the last dolls my daddy gave to me. For you see, he died in the Pacific soon after my fourth Christmas."

When I read this, I was overjoyed to realize my little girl could turn such a tragedy into a beautifully written memory of her most unforgettable Christmas.

Grown-ups often don't pay attention to the inner workings of children—their fears, anxieties and emotions. Nor do we realize the depth of their understanding. Christmas has a way of bringing out the best in us—no matter what our age. And we have a wonderful reminder of our unforgettable Christmas.

Big Brother's Trek Saved Christmas

IT WAS December of 1925, I was 8 years old and all the roads to our Michigan farmhouse were impassable due to more than 4 feet of accumulated snow.

Mother had already explained to us children that there would be no Christmas presents this year—she knew no one could make it to town to buy gifts.

My older brother, Bill, was attending a teacher's college in Ionia, Michigan. Mother had sent him $20 to purchase Christmas presents in the hope that, after the weather cleared, we could enjoy a late Christmas. But Bill knew how important these gifts would be to his younger brothers and sisters, so he planned to find a way home for Christmas. After purchasing enough gifts to fill two gunnysacks, he took the train from Ionia.

BIG BROTHER. **Hank Cusack's brother Bill (seated left of tree) showed real Christmas spirit when he battled the snowdrifts to make it home.**

In the afternoon, the train let him off at a town about 11 miles from home. Because of the snowdrifts, there was no car travel, so Bill began walking. It was about 4 p.m. and severely cold.

The snow was so deep that sometimes even the fences bordering the road were buried. Bill wasn't always sure he was following the road, but the light of a full moon guided him through the night. Finally, after lugging those gunnysacks on foot for 11 hours, he arrived home at 2 a.m. on Christmas Eve. Bill had accomplished his task...to make Christmas special for his family.

Because of my brother's love and unselfishness, this was the most memorable Christmas I ever had. *—Hank Cusack*
Tulsa, Oklahoma

Sacrifice Smoothed Over a Rocky Christmas

GROWING UP in the mountains of East Tennessee was tough in the 1950s and 1960s. It was all Mom could do to take care of me and my three brothers, but we did the best we could. We were together and healthy, and life was good as far as we were concerned.

The year I turned 12, we decorated a tree and strung up our lights. Mom told us money was so tight we wouldn't receive any presents. I can still see the hurt and sadness in her eyes as she told us this.

But we would enjoy a nice dinner with Granny and Grandpa, as well as my sister and her new husband. My older brother, who worked at a plant in town, said everything would be all right—that sounded like a good Christmas to him.

My younger brother and I were embarrassed that we had a tree with no gifts. We wanted to make a good impression on our sister's husband, so we put rocks in different sized boxes and wrapped them in colorful holiday paper before the guests arrived.

We enjoyed Mom's great meal, and after dinner, we reminisced about past Christmases. As we did, my older brother got up and went outside. He came back in toting a big sack over his shoulder, saying, "Ho! Ho! Ho! Merry Christmas!"

I'll never forget that day as long as I live...he had gifts for all of us! He said later that it broke his heart to see my brother and I wrapping those boxes. I'm sure that there were plenty of other things on which this young man could have spent his hard-earned money.

But he sacrificed so we could have a good Christmas. And thank heavens we didn't have to open those rock-filled boxes! *—Barb Snyder*
Vandalia, Ohio

Immigrants Faced Lonely Christmas

IT WAS December 1919, and we New Zealanders were standing on deck for our first sighting of the Golden Gate Bridge in San Francisco. Our Pacific crossing aboard the old *S.S. Tofua* had taken nearly a month.

We children were excited, but our parents had plenty of anxiety. Left behind were relatives, lifelong friends and most of our worldly possessions. Every soul in this new land would be a stranger. What would these Americans be like?

Our family settled out in the countryside, many miles south of San Francisco. Telephone lines didn't reach the area, and the closest neighbors were a mile off.

Christmas Eve soon came, and it was sad and lonely. We children went to bed early, thinking of our friends and relatives back at home in New Zealand. Maybe our family had made a mistake in coming here.

But then we heard Christmas carols! A group of neighbors were walking up the long dirt trail, swinging lanterns.

One man wore a Santa beard and carried a sack of toys over his shoulder. Others had a Christmas tree, ornaments and candles. The wives carried mince pies and other goodies. They set up the tree and handed out presents as we watched, wide-eyed with excitement.

After warm handshakes all around, our new friends left. It was time for us kids to settle down and head back to bed. Meantime, our parents added some logs to the fire and sat quietly, looking into the flames.

I finally heard my mother speak up and say, "Now we know that we made no mistake in coming to this great and wonderful land." *—Lloyd Brown*
Shingle Springs, California

Mom Kept Christmas on Hold Just for Sick Kids

JUST A FEW DAYS before Christmas in 1938, my younger brother and I were hospitalized with scarlet fever. We spent almost 3 months in quarantine!

When we arrived home in March, we were both thrilled to see the nearly needle-less tree still standing in front of our living room window with all our presents waiting to be opened.

My mother said that a lot of passers-by did double takes when they saw that tree in the window months after Christmas!

That belated Christmas is one I'll always remember. *—Lois Moss Castro Valley, California*

Child's "First Secret" Made Mom's Christmas Bright

FOR OUR CHRISTMAS of 1928, Dad and my sister Viola decided to surprise Mother by giving her a seven-bulb electric light set. Our Christmas trees had always been lighted with candles, so this surprise was special enough that Dad and Viola let me and my two brothers in on the secret.

We were told that if Mother asked us to pick up candles in town, we were to say "We forgot" or "They were sold out". Finally, Mother became so concerned that she made a special trip to town for them. But it was late on Christmas Eve and the stores were completely sold out of candles by that time.

When she returned, we all pretended to put on sad faces because we didn't have any candles. But then Dad presented the gifts, giving the first one to Mother. We all were so excited when she opened that box of seven electric lights.

Being the youngest, I was probably the most excited—after all, it was my first secret, the most unforgettable of all. *—Edna Grape, Ione, Washington*

Church's Holiday Spirit Brought Basketful of Joy

THE DEPRESSION was in full swing and our parents were unable to purchase a Christmas tree or gifts for our family.

On Christmas Eve, no doubt feeling very depressed, my father went for a walk to ease his heartache. About 4 blocks from our home in the inner city of Chicago, he heard Christmas music coming from a church.

He impulsively walked up the stairs and entered. The lights were dimmed and a stereopticon slide show of the Christmas story was flashing on a big screen.

After the program was over, Father got up to leave the church. He felt someone tap him on the shoulder and ask if he could use a Christmas basket. The gentlemen who spoke with him must have sensed Father's discouragement.

The man drove Father home with a heavily laden basket. Mother, my two brothers and I gathered 'round and thanked the kind gentleman for sharing with us.

The basket contained a plump roasting chicken plus all the other foods needed to prepare a festive holiday dinner. As Mom made the meal, one of my brothers went out and found an evergreen branch one of our neighbors had cut from his Christmas tree.

We stuck the branch in an oversized wooden spool from my father's tailor shop, then put candles on the tree, using old-fashioned holders. We had so much fun dripping the melted tallow over our fingers to meld the candles.

I don't recall feeling sad that we received no gifts that year. The Christmas basket was such a wonderful surprise. It filled us with the Christmas spirit, and a true appreciation for the caring and sharing of our neighborhood church congregation. *—Myrtle Amundson Carol Stream, Illinois*

LIVING DOLL. **Little Roberta was 1 when she and brother Ray, 8, played "Santa's Helper" and "Toy Doll" in 1954. Their dad, Mike Costley of Modesto, California, says his wife, Betty, played peekaboo with Roberta all afternoon to get their living doll to go in and out of the box!**

"Peace on Earth" Held Special Meaning in 1945

THE MOST memorable Christmas I experienced was in 1945. My 3 years of wartime service were over and I was back home, not just for the holidays, but for good. As if ordered, it began snowing lightly on Christmas Eve.

I couldn't help but think of my past three Christmases in North Africa, Italy and France as we sang carols and decorated the tree. I went to midnight Mass with my mother and dad and the rest of our large family, and I think we all shed a quiet tear or two.

After the service, old friends and neighbors gathered at our house. There was good cheer among our small group on this gentle night when there was no more war. Later, after everyone had gone to bed, I decided to go for a walk.

As I traversed familiar streets that many times I'd never expected to see again, I recalled places half a world away and absent buddies who would never see their loved ones anymore.

And, I remember thinking to myself that this is what the Good Lord must have meant when He spoke of peace on earth and goodwill toward men.

—Allen Merrill
Madiera Beach, Florida

***FRIGID IN FRANCE.* Timothy McEvoy (above in 1944) attended church in a war-torn village with no heat or lights. But he remembers a warm and glowing Christmas nonetheless.**

Long Wartime Walk Brought Christmas Home

IN 1944, I was an aircraft mechanic with the First Tactical Air Force in eastern France. We were living in tents on a snow-covered ridge, and it was obvious I'd be spending my third consecutive Christmas away from home.

On Christmas Eve, two mechanics and I decided to walk to the nearest village to attend midnight Mass. We had to hike 3 miles across snowy, windswept fields to get to the village. A full moon illuminated our walk.

The area was only recently liberated, so there was no electrical power. When we finally arrived, the only lighting in the church was candles, so the moonlit night outside the church was as bright as it was inside.

The little church overflowed with people and I can still hear the choir singing *Silent Night* in French. When the service was over, we were greeted warmly again and again by the townspeople.

The next day, there were crystal blue skies and sunshine as we ate our Christmas dinner. We didn't have a tree or decorations, and the only music was the sound of *White Christmas* and *I'll Be Home for Christmas* being played over and over on a small record player we received from Special Services.

I'll always remember spending Christmas on that frigid ridge, and the midnight service that warmed me.

—Timothy McEvoy
Missouri Valley, Iowa

There Was No Stopping Mail Call

I'LL NEVER FORGET the Christmas of 1944. I was aboard a troop ship enroute to Tinian Island in the Marianas.

Sometime after midnight, I heard the exciting news about mail call, our first since we'd left the States 31 days earlier. I heard my name called time and again, as I received more than 20 letters from my beloved wife of 11 months, and several from other family members.

I sat against a bulkhead and first arranged my letters by date. I read for hours, during which time the song *White Christmas* was played over and over again.

Just about the time I was finishing all the letters, we were greeted with an air raid by the Japanese. All the same, I continued reading until I had finished them all.

—Raymond Cours
Pearland, Texas

Ewing Galloway

***MAIL CALL!* Letters and packages from home were especially welcome when Christmas approached, as these sailors would agree. When Raymond Cours got a stack of Christmas mail in 1944, not even an air raid could stop him from reading his letters from home.**

Servicemen Found Holiday Home Away from Home

By Dolores DeMott, Downey, California

ON CHRISTMAS EVE in 1943, our family had planned to invite two servicemen to share the holiday with us.

When we arrived at the local USO on that cold snowy night, however, there were five lonely young servicemen who had no place to go for Christmas. They were far from home and unable to be with their families.

So we piled everyone into our old car and started for home. Once we arrived, we hurried from the cold into a warm, fragrant, happy house filled with Christmas decorations.

We had baked cookies and breads, Christmas music was playing in the background and we tried to make everybody feel welcome. Soon each guest was very much at home.

What a Tree!

A bit later, three of the fellows and my dad left to get the "biggest, fullest and best" tree they could find. While they were gone, Mother made a huge pot of hot chocolate. After about an hour, Dad and the men returned with the most beautiful tree I'd ever seen. It almost filled the room!

Mugs of steaming cocoa and plates of cookies were passed around. Then we trimmed the tree. Boxes of ornaments were opened and everyone pitched in to help. A sense of peace and quiet filled our home as the visitors shared happy memories of their past Christmases.

"It was their first Christmas away from their families..."

For most of them, it was their first Christmas away from home. I'm sure my brother, Johnnie, who was stationed in the Pacific with the Navy, was wishing he was home, too.

One of the servicemen in particular seemed lost in thought on this evening. Aaron, who was only 18 years old and seemed even younger, asked if he might call his family in Denver. Of course, it was no problem and he felt much better after talking with his folks. Then each of the other servicemen took turns calling their homes.

Mass Exodus

Soon, it was nearly midnight. My parents, sister and I, with several of our guests, left for St. Leo's Catholic Church to attend Mass. Snow was falling softly and it was so cold you could see your breath. The service was quietly beautiful, with glowing candles and traditional carols.

When we got home, sleeping bags, pillows and blankets were passed around and everyone settled down for the night. The lights on the tree cast a lovely glow on the sleeping servicemen. It was a night to remember, and I think about it every year as Christmas comes once again. ▲

Ken Dequaine

A WARM WELCOME. Servicemen far from home at Christmas were welcomed by Dolores DeMott's family in 1943. A warm house, like this one, on a chilly December night was made all the cozier by the friendship shown to the men.

'Lineup' a Christmas Tradition

By Mary Guelker, St. Peters, Missouri

I GREW UP in a family of 11 children in the '30s and '40s, and there never was quite enough money. Still, we were a close and loving family.

Mom was a dedicated homemaker, we kids had our chores to do and Dad made sure there was food on the table. He had to work 12-hour days to do that and we didn't get many extras.

But things were different at Christmas when Dad got his bonus check from work. The day before Christmas, he'd come home early with a big box of chocolates for Mom. Then the two of them would do all the Christmas shopping in about 4 hours.

There was never any time for wrapping presents because Mom and Dad always decorated the tree in secret *after* we'd gone to bed on Christmas Eve. That way, they could surprise us on Christmas.

When the big morning came, we all had to line up (youngest first). Then Mom and Dad took down the blanket they'd tacked up across the living room door the night before. The first thing to catch our eyes was a big beautiful Christmas tree, all lit up.

We'd rush to find our individual "stacks". There was usually much-needed clothing for each of us, but mostly it was toys. In the center of the room would be the larger "shared" toys.

It was wonderful, and I'll never forget Mom and Dad standing on the sidelines, looking on with tired but happy smiles on their faces. They had made Christmas something special. ▲

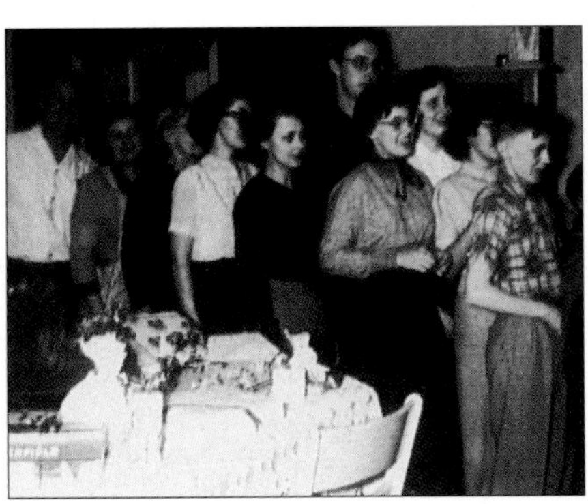

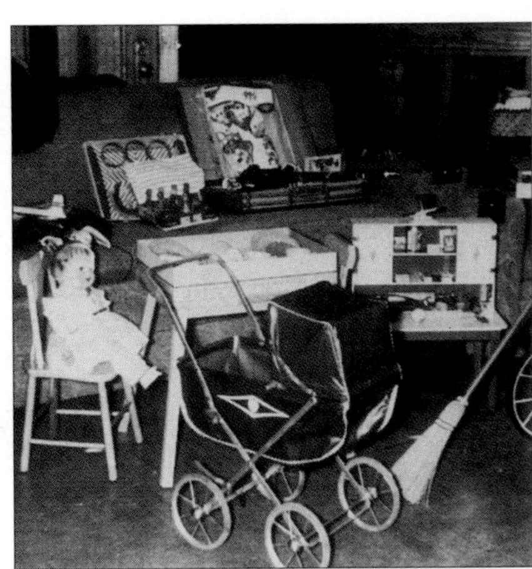

YOUNGEST FIRST! **When Christmas morning finally arrived, Mary Guelker and her 10 siblings had to get in line before they charged into the living room for their presents. The little ones were lucky and got to go first.**

Non-Traditional Holiday Remains Her Most Memorable

MY FATHER was a chief boatswain's mate in the Coast Guard in December of 1942. He was stationed in Benton Harbor, Michigan and was staying in a hotel that was being used by the Coast Guard.

My mother and I thought we'd be spending the holidays alone at our home in Takoma Park, Maryland. But when we received a call from Father inviting us to Michigan for Christmas, we hurriedly packed.

Staying at the hotel and eating our meals in the same dining room with all the men was so exciting for a 14-year-old girl. They taught me to shoot pool in the recreation room and would often take me out for a hamburger and milk shake.

One evening, my father asked one of his men to take me to the skating rink. While we were there, the man ran into his girlfriend. Naturally, she wasn't too happy—until I explained the situation.

There was also a telephone operator named Sophie who worked at the hotel. She taught me how to operate the switchboard and let me make a few calls. Making so many new friends and enjoying such novel experiences might not be a traditional holiday, but the Christmas of 1942 remains my most memorable. *—Patricia Estep*
Spring Hill, Florida

GUARDED BY COAST GUARD. **When Patricia Estep spent Christmas 1942 with her Coast Guardsman father, she had no trouble finding escorts among his men.**

***PUPPY LOVE.* A winter storm caused young Dale Brown some concern that Santa wouldn't be able to find their house. But Santa got there in time for cookies and milk, and to leave Dale exactly what he wanted. But this Christmas would be better than ever...there was a surprise in the cellar.**

Unexpected Gift Beat Santa's Best

By Dale Brown, St. Petersburg, Florida

THE HOUSE CREAKED and groaned as a Maine blizzard blew in from the northeast on Christmas Eve 1939. As I tried to sleep, bundled warmly under an eiderdown quilt, I feared that Santa Claus would never be able to find us.

Laying there listening to the wind, I could faintly hear my older sister and brothers laughing downstairs and wished they would go to bed. Dutifully, I had left cookies and milk on the kitchen table for Santa. But I was afraid that, even if he found our house in the storm, he might not stop if anyone was still up.

Finally all was quiet and I knew the coast was clear. I thought I heard sleigh bells a couple of times but then slowly drifted off to sleep.

Christmas morning dawned bright and clear, the sun a golden globe on the horizon. I leaped out of bed and padded to the window to see if there was any evidence of Santa's visit. The snow was unbroken, but I remembered that his sleigh could fly.

> *"The scene was magic...like Santa's North Pole workshop!"*

Smelling the aroma of frying bacon, I knew Mom was already up. So I went to the kitchen to see if the milk and cookies were gone.

After wishing me a Merry Christmas, she gave me a hug and a kiss and showed me the empty plate and glass. Santa had found our house!

Then the waiting began. No one could go to see what Santa had left until everyone finished breakfast. At last, the moment arrived. Dad made a big production of leading the way to the parlor, pausing at the door to listen, then finally throwing it open.

The scene was magic, looking like Santa's North Pole workshop. One look told me Santa had gotten my letter, just as Mom said he would! In all its glory, a green and white toy police car sat alone in front of the davenport.

"Cops and Robbers" Put on Hold

It was *just* what I wanted, with real headlights, taillights and a siren that worked, all on batteries. It was the most wonderful gift I'd ever seen, and I couldn't wait to play with it! Mom convinced me to join the others at the tree and open the rest of my gifts, but I kept straying back to that wonderful police car.

After we'd unwrapped and admired the other presents, including a shiny new sled, I was ready to start playing cops and robbers with that new car. Then my sister said, "Just a minute, there's something you have to do for me before you can play with your car."

Pouting, I followed her down to the cellar, but my disappointment at the play delay disappeared when I saw what awaited me there. In a box by the furnace was a wiggling, whimpering ball of fur. It was a tiny puppy named "Snooky", and he was my very own!

My sister had brought him home from Bangor and somehow managed to hide him from me for 3 whole days. Snooky made me forget about the police car, at least for the moment. I was the luckiest boy in the world! ▲

Uncle Harry Boomed Out Santa's Arrival

I'LL NEVER FORGET Christmas Eve in 1946, when I was 6 years old. I was bundled in my pajamas and sitting in our living room enjoying the warmth of a family celebration.

Suddenly, I heard a hullabaloo coming from the kitchen. My Uncle Harry was shouting for me to hurry.

"Santa Claus is here!" he cheered. (Uncle Harry was always the loudest in our family.)

I ran to the porch, anxious to see Santa and his reindeer in all their glory. But, of course, I was too late.

"You *just* missed him," Uncle Harry said. "But he left something for you." On the table was a phonograph the color of a Christmas tree.

I had so much fun playing the little red records on that bright green phonograph through the years. I can still hear *She'll Be Coming 'Round the Mountain* and *Peter and the Wolf*. But most of all, I can still hear Uncle Harry's loud, happy voice and I remember how he made the Christmas Eve of 1946 magic for me.

—Karen Hanninen
Minneapolis, Minnesota

Not-So-Silent Night Left Bright Christmas Memories

IN DECEMBER 1940, I spent the holidays as a patient at Sutter Maternity Hospital in Sacramento, California. My new son, David, had been due to arrive on Christmas Eve, but he put in a week-early appearance.

There was a major flu epidemic that year, so the hospital was in quarantine. Fathers were allowed to visit only 15 minutes each night, so my 2-week stay seemed like 2 years.

There was a bumper crop of babies that year, and I was the fifth new mother wheeled into the four-bed ward. We mothers had each other for company and enjoyed talking about our newborns.

But even though I had plenty of company, I felt alone when my husband left after his brief visit on Christmas Eve. The thought of spending Christmas away from my family made me feel so lonely I couldn't sleep.

At 11 p.m. when the nursing shifts changed, a nurse came through the corridors and opened our doors. The corridor lights went out, and in the darkness, I heard the faint sound of song.

As I watched from my bed, I saw dim light begin to flicker in the hallway. The light gradually brightened, and the nurses of both shifts slowly passed, carrying candles and softly singing *Silent Night.*

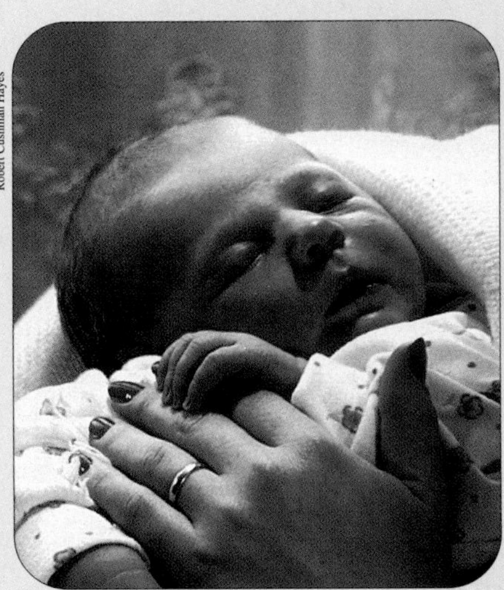

Robert Cushman Hayes

CHRISTMAS BIRTH. **A newborn, like this one, and singing nurses made for her most memorable Christmas back in 1940, says Frances Bond.**

When the lights came on again, the night-shift nurses brought us our babies and wished us a Merry Christmas. I'll never forget this experience, so in keeping with the spirit of Christmas.

Of all the memories I've collected in more than 50 years since then, this remains my brightest and best.

—Frances Bond
Long Beach, California

Homemade Gifts Brightened Depression Christmas

AT CHRISTMAS in 1929, we had very little, like many other people during the Depression. So we weren't sure Santa would visit us that year.

But on Christmas Day, we awoke to a beautiful surprise. We had sliding doors to the living room, and for our holiday ritual, we would patiently wait until Dad opened those doors.

When he did, what a beautiful sight! An 8-foot-high tree with lighted candles greeted us. There beneath the tree were some wonderful toys that Dad had secretly made.

I got a tiny table and chair, kitchen cabinet, twin doll beds and a little dresser. All were painted ivory and green. My mother had made a rag doll and bedclothes for the twin beds.

For my brother, Dad had made a wooden sled and wagon and painted them bright green and red.

These handmade toys made our Christmas more beautiful than any.

—Jeri Bornemann, Middletown, Ohio

J. C. Allen and Son

ROCKIN' BY BABY. **This tot is having a great Christmas playing with her cradle. Homemade gifts are the best, says Jeri Bornemann.**

Greeting Troops Was a Community Project

By Lucille Hendrickson, Mandan, North Dakota

MANDAN, North Dakota was far from the bustle of wartime activity during the 1943 holidays. But as a terminal on one of the major railroad lines, its station swarmed with people several times a day. Many servicemen stopped for a brief respite from the monotony of long journeys on crowded trains.

In the days before Christmas, the women in town baked 37,560 cookies and made thousands of sandwiches. These they sacked in an assembly line set up at the community building. Each sack contained a dozen homemade cookies, a sandwich, an apple, some candy and a postcard.

On the 3 days before Christmas, the ladies armed themselves with wash baskets piled high with the sacks. Then they trooped to the station, where they met every passenger train and distributed the goodies to servicemen.

Santa Greeted the Boys

The genial city auditor helped out, too. Dressed as Santa Claus, he passed out peanuts to the troops. During those 3 days, some 2,500 servicemen received a cheery greeting and a gift packet from our town.

After meeting the last train on Christmas Eve, the women turned their attention to their own holiday preparations. But within a couple of hours, they received word that one more troop train would make a short stop at the station.

All over town, phones rang as the word spread. The women went back to their assembly line. Choir leaders of every church in town were called to assemble their singers. Everyone hurried to the railroad station.

"The station looked like a Christmas card that night..."

The station looked like a Christmas card that night—the red brick building with its white facade, the tall evergreens heavy with snow, lights strung across Main Street, sparkling stars and a swarm of people bundled warmly. Their breath curled before them in the crisp, clear air.

We stood there expectantly. All was ready as we heard the shrill note of the train whistle. Then we started singing.

I'll never forget those faces pressed against the frosty glass of the train windows. The soldiers poured joyfully from the train and joined in the singing.

They swept the young girls off their feet and kissed them. They furiously pumped the hands and clapped the backs of the men who greeted them.

Most touching of all was the exchange of greetings between men and mothers whose own sons were far away. They gently hugged, whispered "Merry Christmas" and furtively wiped a tear away.

It wasn't long before the train had to pull out. For a few moments, no one moved or spoke, reluctant to break the spell.

The postcards tucked into the sacks had been intended for the troops to write notes to their own loved ones. Instead, for weeks, they came flooding back to our town, all bearing messages of thanks.

The one most cherished by the project chairman came months later from the mother of an Army captain. She wrote, "I shall never be able to express my thanks for the bit of Christmas happiness you brought my son. It was his last Christmas."

FRIENDLY STOP. The Mandan depot, shown here in an oil painting by Gary Miller, was a welcome sight for traveling servicemen in the '40s.

FAMILY TIME. **There's nothing like Christmas to draw families together. Relatives who haven't seen each other for months enjoy getting acquainted all over again. Kids have the most fun, getting together with cousins to play.**

Chapter Eleven

Christmas Is Togetherness

Offhand I can't think of any family who doesn't, from time to time, have little misunderstandings and disagreements. Especially the big tribes.

Brother Jim never returned the chain saw he borrowed. Sister Ethel wore exactly the same dress to Sally's wedding, while cousin Bob's family didn't even show up or send a gift. Why didn't Millie's family replace the vase their overly active 5-year-old Joshua broke? It always seems to be little stuff like that.

Then comes Christmas and the annual family get-together. All those trivial slights and imagined offenses are washed away, and an outbreak of love and goodwill occurs right before your eyes. It's magic!

Everyone shows up bearing gifts and food for dinner. There are happy shouts of greeting as each family comes through the front door. Kisses and warm handshakes are exchanged. Even little Joshua gets wary hugs.

When I was growing up, Mom's family always gathered at Gramma and Grampa Stevens' home in Dixon, Illinois. They had a big house (although it somehow gets smaller every time I drive by) that comfortably accommodated the four married children's families, six grandchildren and an elderly aunt.

The week before Christmas, everyone paid close attention to the weather reports. A blizzard would mean at least two of the families might not be able to make it. They only lived 40 miles away, but roads didn't get plowed clear very quickly back then. Many snowplows were horse-drawn road graders that couldn't begin to keep up with a serious blizzard.

Could Everyone Make It?

There would be last-minute calls Christmas morning. "We think we can make it," Aunt Bea would say. "Don't even start out if the roads are dangerous," Gramma would caution. "Call the state police before you leave. They'll have the latest road reports." One way or another, everyone would show up.

During World War II, I was lucky enough to get one Christmas furlough. I took a train from Houston to St. Louis to Chicago to home.

Every train station was packed wall-to-wall. Half the crowd was trying to get *to* their train, and the other half was trying just as hard to get out of the depot or make a connection at another gate. The result was a giant exercise in frantic pushing and shoving.

The train out of Houston was so full that I stood in the aisle for the 10 hours it took to get from Houston to Texarkana. Some of the more fortunate ones climbed up and slept in the overhead luggage racks. The conductors finally gave up trying to check tickets.

When we reached St. Louis, I tried to make my connection and felt like a salmon fighting my way upstream at spawning time. But it turned out to be a piece of cake compared with Chicago's Northwestern Depot, where most of the armed forces seemingly had come together.

Things aren't much different nowadays. Christmas is the strongest magnet ever invented. Crowded train stations have been replaced with equally crowded airport terminals.

Too often, winter weather turns schedules to a shambles, and impatient homeward-bound travelers find themselves sleeping on hard floors as they wait for the weather to clear.

The interstate highways look like rush hour in downtown Los Angeles. Every car is packed with luggage and brightly wrapped presents. And in every car with kids, someone is asking yet again, "Are we almost to Gramma's house?"

"We've got to get home for Christmas..."

We've *got* to get home for Christmas. On the pages that follow are stories that illustrate just how important family togetherness is on this most sentimental holiday of the year. I'm sure they'll bring back memories of all those times when you, too, headed home for Christmas regardless of convenience or cost.

Nothing else brings families together like an old-fashioned Yule celebration. We at *Reminisce* wish you and your family many more to enjoy in the years ahead. Merry Christmas! *—Clancy Strock*

Sister's Sacrifice Gave Renewed Hope

By Vern Berry, Bettendorf, Iowa

I'LL NEVER FORGET 1933, when my sister invited us to spend Christmas Eve at her house. She knew my husband and I were having a tough time then.

How tough? I couldn't afford a 3¢ stamp!

Our dreams of the good life had blown away with the tumbleweeds. Our business failed, so we took our two little daughters and moved in with relatives in Iowa. They had two boys. We pooled our resources to survive the winter until both men could find work. Thank goodness their basement was stocked with canned foods from their garden.

But Christmas was coming, and the little ones had stars in their eyes. They wouldn't understand that Santa would need more than his reindeer to make Christmas dreams come true.

Quietly, I did whatever I could to help old Santa. I raided the scrap bag and made new clothes for old dolls. I kept the sewing machine humming until I broke the last needle.

Then a card came from my sister across the river in Illinois, inviting us for Christmas Eve. She and her husband had no children, and both had jobs. She walked a good mile across the Mississippi River to run an elevator in a department store for $7 a week.

When the big night came, my sister greeted us at the front door. What a wonderful sight!

There stood a huge tree, and the table was loaded with all kinds of traditional goodies. There were wonderful presents under the tree for each child. Looking at this glorious scene, I knew what sacrifices she'd made to prepare this family celebration.

Then she handed me an envelope. Inside was a dollar bill.

I was so overcome with emotion I had to leave the room. Never before had I been reduced to such poverty that I couldn't buy a sewing machine needle. That dollar meant so much.

We forgot our situation for the rest of the night, and laughter and love filled the house.

On the way home, I kept looking at one bright star and thought of the true meaning of Christmas—it's about family togetherness. That's God's way of surrounding us with love.

My sister's love and a single dollar bill renewed our hope and faith in better things to come. And things did turn better for us with the help of that hope.

Family Greetings Made For "Flashy" Pastime

WE DIDN'T HAVE a hearth in our Iowa farmhouse in the 1940s, but we did have an oil stove that kept us warm and toasty.

Of course, we didn't have TV or videos then either, but Mother kept my sisters and me occupied with a special game. We played "flash cards".

Instead of hanging the Christmas cards we'd received on a door frame or wall, Mother would mix them up in a bowl on her sewing machine.

My sisters and I would take turns being the teacher and ask, "Who sent this card?" The first person to correctly name the sender would get the card. The contestant with the most cards won the game.

Who sent the card with Santa and a bag of toys? Or the one with the red shiny bells?

It was easy at first, but as Christmas drew nearer, more and more cards came in the mail. Did Aunt Jessie send the card with the decorated Christmas tree by the fireplace? Or was it Aunt Lillie?

We spent many happy hours playing this game, thanks to our clever mother and greetings from our wonderful relatives.

—Vera Jennings, Tucson, Arizona

IT'S IN THE CARDS. **The best way to send holiday cheer to family far away is with Christmas cards, of course. These colorful greetings, from Barbara Merritt of Stewartsville, New Jersey, date from the early 1900s. Some were printed in Germany and yes, postage was a penny.**

Going the Extra Mile Made Memories

By Betty Simmons, Brownwood, Texas

"ARE YOU SURE you won't come home with me?" asked my roommate, Beckie. She closed her overnight bag and checked her watch. She didn't want to miss the commuter train home to San Francisco, where her parents readied a Christmas celebration.

"No, but thanks anyway," I said. "I've got to hit the books for my civics test."

The truth was, I didn't want to intrude on her family—and I wouldn't admit out loud how homesick I really was. She waved good-bye and I settled into my chair to study. I couldn't ever remember feeling so alone.

First Christmas Away

On that bleak day before Christmas in 1943, I was 17 and a freshman at Stanford University. This would be my first Christmas away from home.

Born and raised in Great Falls, Montana, I was a country girl who missed the snow, my home, my friends and my parents so far away. World War II raged overseas, and most of the male students at school were Army officers studying the Far East and its languages. They were shipped overseas as soon as they completed their studies.

Regulations about the student soldiers taking leave, wartime gas rationing and the holiday falling in the middle

"You sound so close—like you're next door!"

of finals week meant that many of us would remain on campus. The day after Christmas, finals would resume.

Only those whose homes were fewer than 50 miles away were excused to leave school. The housemother tried hard to cheer those left behind. A decorated tree sparkled in the dining room and Christmas carols played merrily, but nothing lifted my spirits.

Some parents would visit on Christmas Day, but not mine. This was the busiest time of the year at my father's gift store. If he didn't have a profitable season, there wouldn't be enough money for college next year. The store stayed open late on Christmas Eve for last-minute shoppers.

Fragrant Memories Took Hold

On Christmas morning in the dorm, I woke early and thought of home. I could picture a fresh-cut Montana pine decorated with red bows and silver balls. I could almost sniff its sweet fragrance, as well as the aroma of Mother's apple-cinnamon pie bubbling in the oven. I came back to reality and eyed the pile of books on the nightstand.

Later that morning, I took a study break. I was about to phone my folks and wish them a Merry Christmas when the housemother said I had a phone call.

I ran down the hall and picked up the receiver.

"Merry Christmas, sweetheart. It's Mom!"

"You sound so close—like you're next door," I replied, with tears in my eyes.

"Almost that close," she laughed. "Your dad and I are in a hotel in Palo Alto about a half mile away."

My folks had frugally saved their gas rationing coupons, closed the store early and driven all through the night to spend Christmas with me.

When I arrived at their room and saw their dear smiling faces, they looked so tired and bleary-eyed. But they'd managed to put up the prettiest 2-foot Christmas tree I'd even seen. My heart felt so full that my chest hurt as we hugged.

After a turkey dinner in the hotel cafe, we opened our presents and caught up on things. They brought me back to the dorm in time to study, and they returned to the hotel to get some much-needed sleep before heading home.

My parents have been gone many years now, but that Christmas they went the extra mile for me remains one of my warmest memories. ▲

SuperStock

LITTLE BIT OF HOME. The tree Betty Simmons' parents brought her was small, like the one above, but their presence made it best.

MUSICAL GREETINGS. The Gordon Preiser family sang carols around the piano in 1953, as this photo from their Christmas card of that year attests. Gordon, of Lancaster, Pennsylvania, is a retired minister. The boys, Don and Dale, followed in his footsteps—Don (right) is a pastor and Dale's a missionary. These days, the family gets together with an additional seven grandchildren.

Silent Night Came Alive with Love

By Thomas Tinsley, De Soto, Missouri

THE YEAR was 1936, and the country was deep in the Great Depression. My father was a steam locomotive engineer who, by necessity, was away from home a considerable amount of time. We celebrated many holidays without him, so any time he could be home with us was special. This particular year, he was working nearby and was expected home about midnight.

There were 14 children in our family, four of them already grown up and moved away. The 10 who were still home ranged in age from 6 to 16, and Mother decided we could all stay up until Father returned to wish him a Merry Christmas.

I recall how excited I was when Mother woke me and told me to get dressed and come downstairs. She had put blue lights on the tree and they made it all soft and shimmering when they were turned on.

You could hear the wind and snow whistling around the house and trees cracking from the bitter cold. We turned off all the lights and quietly sat waiting in the dark.

Since we had so little money, Father would never take a taxi home. No matter how cold it was, he always walked the mile to our farm. We knew we'd hear him walk up the driveway or at least opening the gate.

Finally, the yard gate creaked and we heard his shoes crunching in the snow as he came down the walk to the front porch. Just as he turned the key in the lock, someone turned on the Christmas tree lights and, in the hushed blue glow, led by the soft, sweet voice of our mother, we started singing *Silent Night*.

We could see Father's silhouette through the front door glass as he stood there, listening to us finish the song. Then he opened the door to the sound of all of us shouting, "Merry Christmas, Daddy!"

That was the first time I saw tears in my father's eyes. ▲

Ken Dequaine

***ALL AGLOW FOR CHRISTMAS.* The glow from the family home at Christmas doesn't come just from the lights. Love and friendship also light up the season.**

Raging Storm Couldn't Stop Christmas Togetherness

FARM LIFE in wintry southeast Iowa was cold, dreary and lonely. We had no electricity, a freezing-cold outhouse and a pump that often froze. But Christmas brought the special warmth of company.

The Christmas I remember best was in 1935, when snow started falling heavily on Christmas Eve. My favorite aunt and uncle always came on that special night and brought a gift for me. This year, though, my folks worried we might spend Christmas alone. They lit the flickering kerosene lamp, put more wood in the heater and brought in an extra bucket of water from the well. No car could make it 18 miles through such deep snow.

I kept watch out the front window and was excited to see headlights finally turn into the drive. The powdery snow sparkled in a way I'll never forget...they'd made it through the storm! Our house was instantly filled with cheer.

My aunt put a nicely wrapped present under the tree for me. But it was my parents' gift to all of us that was really appreciated. It was an Aladdin lamp! Now I could read in bright and steady light way over near the stove!

The next morning, the snow was knee-deep. The wind came up, so our relatives left early, making it home just before a blizzard hit and left us snowbound for weeks.

I'll never forget the joy of company for Christmas when it seemed we'd have none. I'll never forget the sparkle of a million diamonds in deep snow. And I'll never forget the joy of that simple Aladdin lamp near a warm fire.

Funny, but I can't recall what my present was that year.

—Don Johnson, Dardanelle, Arkansas

H. Armstrong Roberts

***NEITHER SNOW NOR WIND* can stop gift-bearing travelers who are heading home for Christmas.**

Peter Burian

MEMORIES IN STORE. Like this old-time general store, Bill Hill's Market sold it all.

Family Market Was Neighborhood's Christmas Hub

By Gary Hill, Fresno, California

AT BILL HILL'S MARKET in Fresno, California, Christmas was just around the corner. I always knew it when the salesmen began putting holiday advertisements over their displays of merchandise, including pork and beans, cleanser, Coca-Cola, Knudsen's dairy products…

I really didn't think Santa had heard of half that stuff. But for me, a young boy working at our family grocery store, Christmastime was *wonderful*.

Dad put a Christmas tree on top of the meat case, complete with lights and ornaments. He also sold Christmas trees, which stood out on the sidewalk. The fragrance of freshly cut evergreens always enhanced my Christmas spirit. A week or so before Christmas, Dad would bring home the tree we'd get to decorate.

"On Christmas Eve, we were so busy it was madness in the store!"

Our family operated the store from 1924 through 1964. Throughout those years, so many of our customers became like family to us. Our store was a place to meet friends and neighbors and to visit and catch up on the latest news. On Christmas Eve, we were so busy that it was absolute madness in there.

The store was always packed with last-minute shoppers, and the phone rang constantly with orders from housewives. I delivered those orders all over Fresno.

Adding to the hubbub was Dad's annual Christmas party for his customers. Dad loved people, and he was at his best when hosting this holiday happening.

My job was to clear out the back of the store and set up cases of canned goods for seats. Dad put together a large selection of cold cuts, smoked oysters, shrimp, cheese and a host of other goodies, including plenty of eggnog and soft drinks.

A Tiring Time

People began showing up at noon, and the party trays were replenished all day long. For my parents, it must have been exhausting trying to run the business and host the party as well, but we also had our own Christmas to enjoy.

After the last customer was sent out the door with a pat on the back and a "Merry Christmas!", the lights were turned off and we hurried home to open our presents. We always opened our gifts then, so Mom and Dad could finally get some rest on Christmas morning. ▲

Christmas Put Song in This Family's Heart

I WAS BORN in 1922, and my childhood Christmases back then were exciting. Though our parents couldn't afford gifts, they made up for it in other ways.

Our mother was a little Dutch lady and a very good cook. Her talents especially shined during the holidays. All her breads, pies and cakes had been baked the day before Christmas, and on Christmas morning, we'd wake to the aroma of the turkey baking in the "Kitchen Comfort" wood-burning range.

At dinner, we gathered around the big table, bowed our heads and folded our hands. Dad gave the blessing and we happily enjoyed Mama's wonderful dinner.

After dinner, one of my older sisters would go to the piano and play Christmas hymns. One by one, we'd go to the living room and join in the singing.

I can still hear my father's beautiful bass voice. My brother sang tenor, a sister took the alto and the rest of us, including Mama, joined in and sang soprano.

***FAMILY CHORUS.* Although her family (above in 1931) gathered around the piano and sang throughout the year, the singing was special at Christmas, says Marjorie Andrasek (first on right). Mama (fourth from left) sang soprano while Dad (fourth from right) added his beautiful bass.**

We gathered to sing often throughout the year, but the Christmas singing was the most special time. I wouldn't trade my memories of these family Christmases of years ago for anything.

—Marjorie Andrasek
Garden City, Kansas

***MUSICAL TREE.* The highlight of Annie Kirr's childhood Christmases was this tree revolving on a Swiss music box. The music box only played two carols, but it was better than any radio or television, she says.**

Music Box Played Sounds of Togetherness

CHRISTMAS was *the* day of the year for my parents, two sisters and me.

On Christmas Eve, our mother told us that Santa had arrived and asked the names of the children. Later, the door to the parlor was opened to a beautiful sight. A Christmas tree was revolving on a music box brought from Switzerland in 1904. We all sat in awe of how Mom and Dad could perform such a miracle.

It played *Silent Night* and *O! Tannenbaum*. We would sit in the candle glow admiring that tree and letting the music play. Then cookies and nuts were put out and we had a cracking good time, topped off with a cup of hot chocolate.

All we had then was the beautiful sound of that music box on Christmas Eve—no TV, no radio. I'll never forget the happy times when we were all together with that wonderful music box playing *Silent Night*.

—Annie Kirr
Stettler, Alberta

Letters to Santa Were Part Of Loving Family Christmas

WHEN my sisters and I grew up during the Depression, we'd begin to write our letters to Santa Claus early each December.

Our masterpieces sometimes took a week to complete, as we'd add, subtract, erase and start again until we had everything we wished for written down. The letters would be sealed and addressed to Santa at the North Pole.

Down the stairs we'd go to the big black furnace that stood in the basement. Mother would put on a heavy glove and open the door. Then she'd take the poker from a nail on the wall and poke at the coals until they spit orange and yellow flame.

Only then would Mother let us close enough to toss our letters into the hungry furnace.

They'd catch fire and burn, taking our messages up into the sky to be carried away to that mysterious place where Santa lived.

Of course, we never got everything we asked for, but we always got many unexpected surprises.

Looking back on the wonder, I realize it wasn't the presents, but our Mother's love, as well as that from the rest of our family when they gathered at Christmas, that made this time of year so very special to me.

—Barbara Patton
Ormond Beach, Florida

Santa Song Unraveled a Mystery

By Catherine Burns, Pittsfield, Maine

THE HOLIDAY SONG *I Saw Mommy Kissing Santa Claus* holds special memories for me.

As Christmas of my sixth year approached, I experienced some profound changes in awareness.

Before then, I had known there were two kinds of people—my size, called "kids", and big size, called "grown-ups". I didn't realize there was anything further to distinguish them, nor did I understand how wide my world was about to become.

As Mom and I visited one department store after another that Christmas season, I noticed a lot of grown-ups smiling. Of course, there were the decorations and lovely songs in the air, but whenever *I Saw Mommy Kissing Santa Claus* was playing, those grown-up faces smiled more broadly. Winks were always exchanged, too, and I knew I was supposed to pretend I hadn't seen them.

Photos: Ewing Galloway

That Was Funny?

Something was going on here—something I wasn't being let in on, and I had to discover what it was. I paid closer attention to the lyrics. Nothing added up. Here's a mommy kissing Santa behind a daddy's back, and people find that funny!

My dad wouldn't be winking about that, no sireee! He'd probably never let Santa come to our house again, and there would go all the fun and presents.

I figured there was probably a lot more to this mystery than my clues were telling me. Then one snowy Saturday morning, when Dad was home and the kitchen was filled with the aroma of holiday baking, that song came over the radio.

I stopped stirring long enough to look across the table at Dad, who was untangling Christmas tree lights. He was humming, and he stopped long enough to look up at Mom...and wink!

Suddenly, Dad stood up with outstretched arms, and Mom dusted the flour from her hands. They waltzed around the kitchen, twirling past the refrigerator, in front of the stove and around me, singing in their off-key voices.

"Dad would probably never let Santa come to our house again!"

I paid special attention to Dad, for I knew the secret lay with him. I stared at his eyes, and suddenly I realized *he* was Santa Claus!

Amazed at the Discovery

I giggled at the amazing discovery that my wonderful, skinny, half-bald father was indeed my hero—Santa, the Tooth Fairy and the Easter Bunny all rolled into one.

When my parents' impromptu dance was done, they rushed over and hugged me, and we all laughed together. But when my giggles didn't subside, they knew it wasn't only their dance I found so funny. They begged me to tell them why I was laughing so heartily, but I couldn't do that to them.

There are some things kids know that grown-ups should never find out.

FAMILY SECRET.* It took some time for Catherine Burns to figure it out, but she finally realized why dads and moms got those silly grins on their faces every time they heard *I Saw Mommy Kissing Santa Claus.

Mom Shared Christmas-Morning Winter Wonderland

AS A TEENAGER, I lived with my parents on a farm in Idaho. Mother loved the holidays, which were filled with love and excitement.

My church youth group always came to our house for a chili supper on Christmas Eve. We'd sing songs and have a great time. One year, Dad came in from feeding the stock and shook the snow from his coat. He announced that a big storm was looming.

Quickly bundling up, all the kids piled into their cars and departed. Our family then went to bed. At 2 a.m., I was awakened by a gentle shake and my mother's voice calling, "Sis, wake up!" The room was unusually bright from the moonlight.

Mother handed me my coat and we walked outside. The storm had passed, leaving a clear sky filled with millions of stars. The snow had drifted and covered everything with a glistening blanket of white. We whispered, for fear of shattering the beauty.

Later, about 5 a.m., my father came down and found us drinking hot chocolate near the stove. "It's Christmas and we can't wait," Mother replied, giving me a big hug. Dad laughed and headed out to the barn.

"I better hurry up and do the chores...since you kids can't wait to open those presents," he said.

—Bettie Bartz, Roseville, California

Older Sister Helped Make Christmas Merry

MY TWIN SISTER, Joan, and I were born in the late 1930s, the youngest of seven siblings.

Before Christmas, Mother spent days preparing cakes and pies, homemade lemonade and many other goodies. Father's job was to make root beer in anticipation of visits from family and friends.

On Christmas Eve, our oldest sister, Cora, and her family drove down from Washington, D.C. to our rural farming and oyster-gathering community. We twins looked forward to seeing them because they always arrived bearing gaily wrapped gifts.

Early on Christmas morning, Joan and I rushed downstairs to see what Santa brought—then we barged into our parents' bedroom to show them. Little did we realize that our poor mother had spent most of the night cooking. Dad had been up assembling toys.

They had just barely made it to bed in time to be "surprised" to see the presents Santa brought. Without fail, he would bring us exactly what we'd asked for.

It was only after Joan and I were adults that Cora finally admitted she'd helped our parents play Santa Claus. She provided many of our toys when they couldn't afford it.

—Naomi Holland Dennis
Churchton, Maryland

Mischievous Prank Caused Glorious Christmas Confusion

I MUST HAVE been about 5 years old on the memorable Christmas when we went to Grandfather and Grandmother's farm.

After supper, we all sat around the fireplace in the parlor. The Christmas tree in the corner gave the room a festive air. The dog, the cat and I were stretched out on the rug in front of the fire, enjoying the lazy warmth. We lay in sort of an arc, with me and the dog at one end, and the cat at the other.

Soon, all the grown-up talk was growing mighty dull. I lifted the dog's floppy ear and eagerly whispered, "Sic 'em!"

The dog took after the cat. The cat ran up the Christmas tree. There ensued a glorious confusion that sure went a long way toward eliminating the boredom.

And I got a spanking...but it was well worth it. *—Walter Langtry*
Metairie, Louisiana

SuperStock

WHITE CHRISTMAS. **Even if you live where snow doesn't commonly fall, the idea of snow at Christmas is enchanting. Bettie Bartz's memory on this page recalls the sparkle of snow on a clear cold Christmas Eve—just the way it should be.**

Would Dad's Christmas Wish Come True?

By Ada Preston, Sacramento, California

"A SNOWBALL in an oven has a better chance than we do of having our family together this Christmas," lamented Dad to my mother.

Dad was nudging 60 that December of 1947, and his health hadn't been good. He and Mom lived in Cleveland, Ohio, but their five children were scattered throughout the United States.

My four brothers had served in four different branches of the armed forces during World War II. Fortunately, all had returned home safely.

The war itself, then postwar economics, had prevented our family from getting together at Christmas for a number of years.

When Mother wrote us about Dad's poor condition and his Christmas wish, we decided that each of us would make every effort to get back home for Christmas and surprise him.

After all, he'd been the best dad we could have had. For 39 years, he worked in a steel mill to support us. He commuted to work from a small town outside Cleveland so he could raise his four sons and me (his youngest child and only daughter) away from big-city problems.

He Kept Family Close

During the Depression when work was slack at the mill, he wired houses, repaired cars and did anything else he could to bring in a few more dollars.

He taught my brothers to hunt and fish so they could supplement our often meatless diet, and he raised a huge vegetable garden so Mother could can the excess to see us through the winter.

Dad kept us together and we'd become a closely knit family. Surely we could make his wish come true.

Letters flew back and forth as we schemed and planned. My brothers and I were either struggling college students, working in new jobs, buying a first home or bearing the costs of newborn children.

"We decided to make every effort to get back home..."

Getting back to Cleveland would be a hardship on everyone, but we decided to do our best to make it home.

Driving was the cheapest way for most of us. My husband and I lived the farthest away, in Stockton, California.

Would our ancient 1929 Erskine (we called her "Becky Sue") survive the arduous trip across the country with her worn-out tires and unreliable engine? And how would we fare on a winter trip in a car with no heater? All we could do was take the southern route and hope for the best.

By Christmas Eve, everyone had made it home (including three newborn grandchildren). Everyone, that is, except my husband and me. Snow had blanketed the states of Ohio, Kentucky and Tennessee, slowing our progress and making it unlikely we'd reach Cleveland by Christmas Eve.

Early that morning, we'd called Dad and explained we probably wouldn't make it in time. He understood but sounded so disappointed.

That afternoon, Dad left the house to make his weekly visits to co-workers who were ill and confined to their homes. He was due back in the early evening.

Not 20 minutes before Dad returned, my husband and I pulled up outside our parents' home. Somehow, Becky Sue got us through!

Though weary and still numb from the cold, we were jubilant. All of us gathered in the front room, where the Christmas tree stood opposite the front door. A ladder was being used to decorate the tree, so my brothers put it behind the tree and had me stand on top.

When my father walked through the front door, one of my brothers asked, "What do you think of the tree, Dad?"

When he looked up at the tree, he saw the gaily decorated branches...and his daughter smiling down at him with tears in her eyes. At last, we were all together again. Dad's Christmas wish had been granted. ▲

Christmas in a Barn Made Holiday Memorable

OUR FAMILY once celebrated Christmas in a barn.

It all started in fall of 1976, when Mom and Dad moved to the country, purchasing 10 acres and a two-bedroom trailer.

The only problem was, where could they hold a family gathering with enough space for 20 of us? We decided to build a barn, working every spare moment whether it rained or there was freezing cold. When the structure was finally completed in mid-December, it had its flaws, yet to us, it was a masterpiece.

Picnic tables, benches and old chairs were placed on the first floor. Dad installed an old wood-burning stove to ward off the cold. The younger kids made paper garlands and ornaments, and the older children went into the woods to look for a tree. Kudzu vines were woven into wreaths for the barn doors.

The whole family gathered in the barn on Christmas Eve. We sang carols, opened gifts and ate until we couldn't eat anymore.

Some people might have questioned our choice of locale for a Christmas celebration. But long ago, God chose a stable as the place for His Son's birth. With all the family present, there was plenty of love...and love made our barn Christmas special.

—*Sandra Sparks*
Forest Park, Georgia

Martin R. Jones/Unicorn Stock Photos

***LOWLY MANGER.* Christmas is special, even when it's in a barn.**

Snowbound Family Enjoyed Christmas Together

By Nancy Soleida, Tucson, Arizona

I SQUINTED up the snow-covered road to see if I could spot any sign of activity. It was Christmas Eve day 1942, and I was at my grandparents' farm in northwestern Pennsylvania. Several feet of snow had already fallen, and it appeared the snow would never stop.

My Uncle Leo had come home on leave from the Marine Corps to be with his wife for the birth of their baby. He was due back at Camp Pendleton, California 2 days after Christmas, but with this weather, there was little hope he'd get back on time. Trains weren't moving, planes were grounded and there wasn't a telephone within miles.

Worse yet, the new baby was on a special diet that required condensed milk and our supply at the farm was dwindling. The nearest store was 6 miles away, and there was no way to reach it.

Through the window, I saw Uncle Leo bring "Bell", Grandpa's horse, out from the barn. The snow was right up under her belly, making every step a struggle.

Made a "Milk Run"

Uncle Leo was going to try and ride to the nearest neighbor's house and see if they had any canned milk for the baby's formula. For me, at age 11, being snowed in just added to the excitement.

All our relatives had made it to Grandpa and Grandma's farm before the storm closed the roads. My cousins, aunts and uncles had come together for the holiday, and the house was exploding with noise, expectation and wonderful scents.

Earlier, two uncles had set off to look for the perfect tree, pulling a sled behind them. Meanwhile, the older grandchildren helped frost the Christmas cookies, and all of us kids eagerly awaited Santa's arrival.

Along toward evening, everyone was becoming anxious about Uncle Leo, who had yet to return. Just as we were sitting down to dinner, someone called out, "There's Leo!"

We ran to the windows and, sure enough, there he was, struggling to get that poor horse up the driveway and into the barn. The men pulled on their gear and headed out to help him.

Barbara Laatsch Hupp/Laatsch-Hupp Photo

SNOWED IN. But at Christmas, who cares? On a snowbound farm like this, Nancy Soleida and her family enjoyed a *very* long holiday.

It turned out the closest farmer had no need for "store-bought" milk, so Uncle Leo had to struggle on another mile to the next farm. But he was finally successful, so now the baby could eat!

Later in the evening, we kids were sent up to bed. But how could anyone sleep on Christmas Eve? There were heat registers in all the upstairs bedrooms, so we lay on the floor, peering downstairs through those registers to see anything we could.

The adults must have suspected what we were doing (they'd probably done the same thing when *they* were children). They moved out of our line of sight—we couldn't see a thing.

> *"The house was exploding with expectation..."*

Suddenly, we heard a sound outside. Bells! Sleigh bells! We looked through a window toward the barn and there it was—a sleigh moving across the snow. It was Santa Claus!

It was really of no consequence to us that the sleigh was being pulled by a horse with bells on her harness. After all, Santa was coming down our road—to our home!

After the sleigh passed beyond our view, we heard Santa stomping his boots on the front porch. We ran downstairs and opened a door just enough to peek into the living room.

There, kneeling by the tree, was Santa, removing toys from a large white canvas bag and placing them under the tree. He was dressed in red velvet, had a beautiful white beard, small glasses, big black boots and the required red hat trimmed with white fur.

Just then, one of the younger children upstairs awoke and began to cry. Before we could run back upstairs, the baby's mother opened the door. We were caught!

Instead of scolding us, she called to the rest of the family to "come see what I found!" Her discovery was greeted with laughs and we were invited into the living room.

We opened our gifts that night and had a great Christmas the next day. As it turned out, we were snowed in for more than 2 weeks!

In consideration of the extenuating circumstances, Uncle Leo was let off with extra KP when he finally returned to California.

That extended Christmas we spent together as a family remains one of the most beautiful and memorable of my life. In fact, the togetherness is such a strong memory that I don't even remember what my presents were! ▲

"Winter Wonderland" Sparks Wonderful Memories

I GREW UP on a farm in the Panhandle of West Texas, and our elderly grandmother lived with us. Since she rarely wanted to go anywhere, my older brother, younger sister or I had to stay home with her.

One Christmas, we pleaded with Grandma to go with us and visit her son and his wife for the holiday. She finally consented.

The night before Christmas, we heated water in the No. 3 tub for Grandma's bath, just hoping nothing would happen to prevent her from going along the next day.

When Christmas morning came, we were delighted to find that a rare snow had fallen during the night. The sun was shining brightly and it looked as if every little weed had been transformed into a thing of beauty. A new song we'd heard on the radio that fall, *Walking in a Winter Wonderland*, seemed to have become reality as we watched the "diamonds" sparkle in the fresh snow.

We gently tucked Grandma in the Model T Ford, wrapped soft blankets around her and then covered ourselves for the 10-mile trip to her son's house.

We had the most wonderful day together as a family, and each time I hear *Winter Wonderland*, the memories come flooding back and my eyes glisten.

Both my parents, my brother and my grandma have gone on to be with the Lord, but I look forward someday to another joyous family reunion. —*Mrs. Bob Morrow*
Midland, Texas

Family Was There For Grandma

By Judy Stibor, Bassett, Nebraska

IT WAS CHRISTMAS EVE 1948. The cold night air rushed into the warm house as my dad and brother came in from outside. The milking chores were done, and they stomped their snowy overshoes and hung up their coveralls, hats and mittens to dry.

Grandma Etta always spent Christmas with us and we eagerly awaited her arrival. To me, her coming was the signal that we'd soon open presents.

Grandma Etta was short and weighty, of solid German stock. She had a thin line of mouth, with corners that drooped a little bit, and there was a waggle of flesh below her chin. Her gray hair was put up in a bun near the top of her head. She wore a belted dress, droopy brown stockings and orthopedic shoes.

Could Depend on Grandma

Her passions were good friends, family, compassion for others, faith in God and a good game of canasta. She was as strong as her lace corset and someone we knew we could depend on in both good times and bad.

This year, we had everything anyone could want. We had a pasture-cut cedar tree with special ornaments saved from year to year, an overabundance of tinsel and a red and white paper chain that was carefully constructed with homemade paste.

Mother always made oyster stew on Christmas Eve. The steamy scent of hot oysters floating in the buttery milk mingled with drying cloves and cedar boughs.

Presents Opened

When mother ceremonially took off her apron after supper, it was the signal to go to the living room to unwrap our gifts. All was well.

We opened our presents and urged Grandma to open hers. She sat quietly, unopened gifts in her lap. She started to cry and said over and over again, "I'm sorry, I'm sorry."

LOVE IS ALL. Judy Stibor's grandmother, like this lady, enjoyed the warmth of home on Christmas.

Ewing Galloway

I couldn't imagine what was happening. I looked to Mother and Dad for some explanation. I thought the worst. She must be dying!

"I'm sorry," she repeated. "This year, I couldn't afford to buy you presents."

For what seemed to be an eternity, we sat silently. Then the four of us spoke as one. "It's okay! We don't care about presents! You are the best present we could ever have," we shouted.

For the first time in her adult life, Grandma Etta needed us to lean on. It felt good to be there for her, just as she'd always been there for us.

Uncle Leo's Homecoming Started 50-Year Tradition

By Rosemary Wickett, St. Marys, Pennsylvania

IT WAS Christmas Eve in 1945, and Uncle Leo was coming home from the war. He had been seriously wounded in the Normandy invasion and spent many months recuperating.

His anticipated arrival stirred a happy glow in our home. My brothers, sisters and I had strung popcorn and helped Mom with other decorations. We wanted this to be the best possible holiday for Uncle Leo.

Dad Put Lights in Order

Dad cut the biggest Scotch pine he could find and set it in the corner, where it took up a quarter of the room. Then he patiently set about putting on the lights in perfect order.

Mom suddenly realized that there weren't enough icicles because this tree was much larger than usual. The stores had all closed early, and the thought of no icicles disappointed Mom, so she made some calls to friends, who were happy to share their icicles for this happy occasion.

I ran to the neighbors, collected the icicles and rushed home. I didn't want to miss the excitement when Uncle Leo walked through the door.

All the other family members arrived and we eagerly waited for our uncle's taxi to appear. He arrived at last and walked into the hallway with everyone there to greet him. There were hugs and kisses, laughter and tears.

Questions Patiently Answered

We visited for a while, and Uncle Leo patiently answered question after question until we finally sat down to dinner. The meal was one of Mom's best, including turkey, homemade pies and lots of fancy Christmas cookies. The grown-ups finally finished their coffee and we gathered in the living room for the tree trimming.

My brothers, cousins and I hung the decorations on the branches along with Uncle Leo. We really enjoyed his company, his teasing and his war stories, and we pretended not to notice his bad limp.

When the last decoration was finally placed, Dad turned on the lights. The icicles danced as they collected colors from

"I didn't want to miss the excitement when Uncle Leo arrived..."

the bright lights, splashing them onto the walls and ceiling. It was magnificent!

Mom had tears in her eyes as she wished everyone a very Merry Christmas. I believe at that moment we felt a unity as a family I shall never forget.

We then heard some quiet sobbing and turned to see Uncle Leo with his face in his hands. Dad put his arm around him and asked what was wrong. He said he was just so happy to be with all of us and finally feel safe.

Of all the Christmases I recall, Uncle Leo's homecoming remains the most memorable. Ever since, our family still feels a wonderful love and unity in spending Christmas Eve together. That joyful Christmas in 1945 started a tradition I hope lasts forever. ▲

Ewing Galloway

HOME AT LAST. When her Uncle Leo made it safely home for Christmas after the war, as this soldier did, Rosemary Wickett's family began a tradition of gathering together on Christmas Eve that continues to this day. That's the way it is with most families. Being together at Christmas helps renew the bonds that hold us together the rest of the year.